Between Self and Society

LITERARY MODERNISM SERIES
THOMAS F. STALEY, EDITOR

Between Self and Society

INNER WORLDS AND OUTER LIMITS IN THE BRITISH PSYCHOLOGICAL NOVEL

John Rodden

University of Texas Press *Austin*

First edition, 2016
First paperback edition, 2016

Requests for permission to reproduce material from this work should be sent to:

Permissions
University of Texas Press
P.O. Box 7819
Austin, TX 78713-7819
http://utpress.utexas.edu/index.php/rp-form

♾ The paper used in this book meets the minimum requirements of ANSI/NISO Z39.48-1992 (R1997) (Permanence of Paper).

LIBRARY OF CONGRESS CATALOGING-IN-PUBLICATION DATA
Rodden, John, author.
Between self and society : inner worlds and outer limits in the British psychological novel / John Rodden. — First edition.
pages cm — (Literary modernism series)
Includes bibliographical references and index.
ISBN 978-0-292-75608-3 (cloth : alk. paper) — ISBN 978-0-292-75609-0 (library e-book) — ISBN 978-0-292-75610-6 (non-library e-book)
1. English fiction—Psychological aspects. 2. English fiction—Social aspects. 3. Social psychology and literature. 4. Psychology in literature. 5. Psychological fiction, English—History and criticism. I. Title. II. Series: Literary modernism series.
PR830.P75R63 2015
823.009′353—dc23
2015007468

doi:10.7560/756083
ISBN 978-1-4773-1223-0, paperback

Vincent Kling

TEACHER, MENTOR, MENSCH

Contents

Acknowledgments ix

Introduction 1

CHAPTER ONE. Smollett's *Roderick Random*:
In Love with Narcissa 9

CHAPTER TWO. Godwin's *Caleb Williams*:
"A Half-Told and Mangled Tale" 23

CHAPTER THREE. Hardy's *The Mayor of Casterbridge*:
The Infernal Triangle 53

CHAPTER FOUR. Ford's *The Good Soldier*:
Movements of the Heart 95

CHAPTER FIVE. Lewis's *Tarr*:
Portraits of the Failed Artist 129

CHAPTER SIX. Lawrence's *Women in Love*:
The Role of Miss "Dawington" 161

Notes 185

Selected Bibliography 221

Index 227

Acknowledgments

THE "RISE OF THE NOVEL," IN THE WELL-KNOWN phrase of Ian Watt per the title of his path-breaking book from the 1950s, has been a topic of frequent discussion in British literary history for more than a half century. *Between Self and Society* probes the phenomenon from a very different perspective than have Watt and most other cultural historians, namely that of modern Western psychology. The book possesses, therefore, a dual focus encompassing both history and social psychology: British fiction since the eighteenth century and the psychoanalytic tradition of Freud and his successors.

It takes a village to gestate and guide a fragile literary brainchild. Thankfully, a fellowship of colleagues, students, teachers, and friends has midwifed this project during these years of research and writing. To Jeffrey Meyers, for his trailblazing study of Lewis, *The Enemy: A Biography of Wyndham Lewis* (1980), which I first read decades ago as a wide-eyed PhD student, I extend my warm thanks. I also profited enormously from my exchanges with Paul Roazen, another distinguished scholar of the psychoanalytic tradition, whose unusual interest in Ernest Becker and Otto Rank, Freud's virtually adopted son and trusted junior associate for twenty years, matched my own and illuminated their work considerably for me. We shared the conviction that Rank properly emphasized the role of human will and the urge for immortality in his psychoanalytic work, adroitly reconceptualized the mother-child relationship, and heralded the humanistic psychology of the 1960s and beyond. Eugene Goodheart, a sharp literary critic and beautiful essayist, read the final chapter on Lawrence with attention and care. I had consulted his pioneering essay on what would be called "Lawrentian psychology," published almost six decades ago. It continues to stand up today, and I cited and learned from it as I developed this book. Strengthening my understanding of the other half of this study, devoted to the British novel, Alan Munton of Exeter University, the former editor of the *Wyndham Lewis Annual*, supported my work both in correspondence and in conversation on both Ford and Lewis. I am grateful to Alan for his reading of the entire manuscript, particularly the chapters on Ford and Lewis that fall within his special expertise.

Special thanks go also to Ashley Nusbaum and Yichun Liu, my editorial assistants in the United States and Taiwan, whose exemplary patience and editorial astuteness saved me from countless errors, both stylistic and substantive. These editorial interns volunteered their energy and enthusiasm in the service of this study, offering their time to check sources and assist with manuscript revisions. Ashley displayed finely honed research skills in the course of catching numerous grammatical mistakes. Yichun showed unflagging tenacity, in a foreign language no less, as she delivered outstanding manuscript detail work. This book would not exist were it not for the selfless dedication of these two young people.

Indeed, this book began long ago in my own personal history, when I myself was a young student. I owe many of my old teachers and mentors from my days as a graduate student in English and German at the University of Virginia and as an undergraduate at La Salle University in Philadelphia—some of whom have become intellectual comrades and even lifelong friends—a debt of gratitude that cannot be repaid, only acknowledged.

In the course of writing this book, therefore, I am beholden in ways that extend far beyond its scholarly terrain and that include a life-wisdom vouchsafed to a young man decades ago that he continues to cherish. For their extraordinarily generous help and guidance as they introduced me to modern British literature, I first thank my Virginia teachers and colleagues. Michael Levenson, then a scholarly prodigy still in his twenties, inspired me to focus my graduate studies on modern European literature and introduced me to the work of Ford Madox Ford and Wyndham Lewis. His dry wit and impassioned devotion to the life of the mind remain indelibly imprinted from our intellectual adventures in his classroom so many years ago, and he represents a guiding spirit of this study. Karen Chase, radiating the same unforgettable youthful vibrancy and enthusiasm, took me on a similar intellectual adventure as we explored the relation of the psychoanalytic tradition to Victorian fiction via the work of Freud and the British psychoanalyst Melanie Klein. Equally important for the contents of this book were courses with Leo Damrosch, another young phenom, just in his mid-thirties yet already a senior professor, whose self-irony, refreshingly self-deprecating humor, and arresting combination of concision and lucidity persuaded this committed modernist that the eighteenth century was a fascinating moment in the history of culture. Thanks to Leo, I read the work of Tobias Smollett and William Godwin, whose novels are addressed in the first two chapters of this study. Last but not least, Paul Cantor, a humanistic polymath also then in his mid-thirties—whose intellectual interests range from classical studies to poststructuralism and postmodernism, and in fact extend far beyond that to fields such as free-market economics and the history of political theory, among other topics—played a decisive role in my early encounters with the work of the French psychoanalytic thinker René Girard, which I discuss at length in Chapter Three.

In addition to these teachers in Virginia's English department, I owe undying thanks to the late Walter Sokel, a cultural historian whose courtly manner and mastery of the European intellectual tradition made him one of a near-extinct species of urbane scholar-intellectuals in an American academy increasingly populated by narrow disciplinary specialists. I came to know Walter in a new and even more enriching way as we developed other aspects of our relationship when I became his junior colleague at Virginia. As we talked over the years, I learned what only the experience of an intellectual father can impart, the blessings of which continued long into his retirement and indeed up to the final weeks before his last days in December 2013. It was Walter, a Viennese who escaped to Paris before the *Anschluss* in 1938, who first introduced me to the psychoanalytic tradition and its legacy. In particular, I thank him for our ongoing discussions about Freud, Otto Rank, René Girard, and many of the other psychological thinkers featured in this study.

My earliest and in some ways deepest obligations fall to my undergraduate teachers and friends in British Studies, not a few of whom have been supportive friends for almost four decades. Especially relevant to this book have been Patricia Haberstroh, whose course on modern British poetry enriched my understanding of the fiction and helped me establish the context for understanding the works that I have discussed. Likewise, I remember the infectious delight that Dick Lautz shared with us in his class in Victorian prose and poetry.

I save my last and deepest thanks for Vincent Kling, professor of English and German at La Salle, my erudite intellectual big brother and bohemian friend, whom I have known for more than thirty-five years. Although I was never formally his student—that is, I never officially enrolled in his courses during my student days in the 1970s—I learned an immense amount from Vince when we met during my senior year as an undergraduate, and even more since then. Still ABD, he had not yet joined the university faculty. Then and later, he honored me with undue respect as an intellectual peer. We soon found that we shared a passion not only for European literature but also, quite specifically, for the German intellectual tradition. Vince's dual focus made him the ideal reader for this book, and I remain forever grateful to him for his wise counsel and good cheer. Vince has taken me on numerous intellectual flights of passage that have been incredible joyrides. It has been a pleasure and privilege to work closely with him on books that I have edited, to which he contributed chapters on topics ranging from the essays of George Orwell to the fiction of the Chilean writer Isabel Allende. Several of the passages in *Between Self and Society* were reconceived due to his prodding; with characteristic tact and generosity of spirit he read every line, pointed out stylistic tics and infelicities, and challenged me to ponder more carefully the "between" between psychology and literature, life and art, and self and society.

Vince, this one's for you.

Introduction

I

Between Self and Society: Inner Worlds and Outer Limits in the British Psychological Novel scrutinizes the rhythms of psyche and demos in six important works of British fiction since the mid-eighteenth century. As the main title suggests, these rhythms are complex, ramified, and multifaceted: the interrelations between "self" and "society" are not either/or, but rather both/and—in fact, almost always "in between."[1] Indeed the emphasis in the book alternates between the individual and the community, the particular and the universal—self and society—but each chapter probes polarities of conflict that configure and generate character in these diverse worlds of prose fiction. Our psychological "case histories" ultimately thus serve as an index of the affective range of the British novel, illuminating its representation of personality and mental life, the textual features of emotional expression, and the reading experiences to which real readers have testified.

"Psychological novel" is a loose term, frequently applied to those first-person novels that reflect narrative techniques such as "stream of consciousness" or explore the individual psychologies and interior conflicts of fictional characters in detail and depth. Fictional prose works such as William Godwin's *Caleb Williams*, Thomas Hardy's *The Mayor of Casterbridge*, and D. H. Lawrence's *Women in Love* are seldom classified as "psychological novels," yet their accent on larger public issues rather than intimate personal matters—*Gemeinschaft* and *Gesellschaft* rather than consciousness and *mentalité*, exterior rather than interior conflicts—reflects a need to broaden our traditional conception of the psychological to include the societal, cultural, intellectual, and even spiritual if we want to embrace the full scope and dynamics of personality. It is important to resist reducing the terms "psychology" and "novel" to the exclusively mental or narrowly aesthetic, letting them instead retain all their suggestiveness and acculturated history of meanings. If we take this stance, we can more fully appreciate their variety and amplitude. Three of the chapters—those on Tobias Smollett's *Roderick Random*, Godwin's *Caleb Williams*, and Ford Madox Ford's *The Good Soldier*—chiefly address narratological questions, especially controversial issues connected with "untrustworthy" narrators, their modes of storytelling, and their dubious claims to truth. In fact, a subtitle for the book might be "Untrustworthy Tellers, Unverifiable Tales," with a nod to Lawrence's famous remark in *Studies in Classic American Literature*: "Trust the tale, not the teller."[2] And, as we shall see, our critical maxim for this trio of chapters will echo that Russian proverb much quoted during the Cold War by wary American leaders negotiating nuclear disarmament with the Soviets: *doverey no proverey,* "trust but verify."

Honoring this maxim—and resisting the lures of reductionism that bestow conceptual tidiness and analytical rigor at the expense of widened apprehension, nuanced understanding, and even occasionally revelatory surprise—is a chief aim of the readings in this book. The prevailing verdict about much of the prose fiction under study here, whether pronounced by formalist or social critics, is too often that novels such as *Caleb Williams, The Good Soldier,* and Wyndham Lewis's *Tarr* represent admirable and valuable, indeed even fascinating or pioneering, literary experiments—yet ultimately prove to be artistic failures. These and other novels discussed in the study are often considered crude, schematic, loaded with structural improbabilities (such as clumsily handled coincidences or ungrounded motivations or fuzzy treatments of time). When looked at either from an aesthetic/formal viewpoint that would illuminate a Henry James novel, or from a social/political stance pertinent to the work of George Eliot, they are typically judged inferior fictions.[3] But if we look at these novels from the standpoint of depth psychology—which attends variously to eros, inner identity, and concealed conflicts in the protagonist and other characters—we can perceive an artistic unity and stylistic consistency often missed by surface readings.

On this view, the book is a critical study in the psychology of character. Or, to phrase it more precisely, a study in character analysis through psychology, especially as it is revealed by a character's unconscious drives or by a narrator's distorted memory and consequently problematic mode of narration. I have sought to take full account of the extant scholarship while expanding it into directions that offer new readings of novels that have been misunderstood, read too restrictively, and therefore devalued. The readings of the novels under discussion draw on psychological approaches and psychoanalytic concepts, which represent the distinctive contribution of the chapters. Some of these novels (e.g., *Caleb Williams, The Good Soldier, Tarr*) are typically denigrated as political treatises, as almost tract-like analyses of social and economic forces. Supposedly heedless of aesthetic form, they suffer from awkward plot development and flat characterization, rendering them little more than sketchbooks illustrating this or that social evil.

By contrast, my own critical premise has been that these ambitious, frequently trailblazing novels are, however flawed, fictional masterpieces which have been unjustly neglected or undervalued, largely because they have violated or defied reigning fictional norms and conventions—and which repay fresh critical reappraisal from sympathetic readers. For instance, I approach several of these fictions via depth psychology to show how a plot that looks random or forced is actually a projection of the narrator's anxieties. Given that approach, the novels under consideration in the first five chapters emerge as complex, challenging works of art when we understand that form and structure correlate with or model the inner life of the characters. This way of reading opens up the novels to possibilities not addressed in the secondary literature so far. In the closing chapter, I shift from a psychoanalytic interpretation to a Lawrentian reading of Lawrence's *Women in Love,* which owes to Lawrence's famous hostility to Freudianism manifested in much of his fiction and made explicit in his anti-Freudian polemics, *Psychoanalysis and the Unconscious* (1921) and *Fantasia of the Unconscious* (1922). From this angle, *Women in Love* presents Loerke and Minette Darrington as exemplars of "mental consciousness," a pathology indicted by Lawrence as the disease of the Northern European mind, allegedly epitomized by Freud, Jung, and their followers.[4] Such Nordic intellectualism, claims Lawrence, heightens and intensifies mental consciousness and thus contributes to neurosis. It reflects an antipathy toward the body and spiritual health that stands opposed to his vitalistic philosophy of "blood consciousness," the cornerstone of Lawrence's racial theory that critics have derided as both misogynistic and anti-Semitic.

Regardless of our judgment of Lawrence's philosophy, however, it undeniably undergirds the *Weltanshauung* of much of his fiction, especially *Women in Love*. Furthermore, it is not just a philosophical viewpoint, but rather represents his own serious, passionately argued attempt to plumb the dynamics of eros and psyche. As such, "Lawrentian psychology" functions as an experience-based metaphysics of the psyche, formulated by a literary artist resolutely antagonistic to Freudian social science and "depth" psychology, indeed to the purportedly "Jewish" psychoanalysis of Freud and his immediate circle.

So I undertake a psychological approach to all six novels in the study. Moreover, all of them are addressed not only from the vantage point of the institutional, "outer" conflicts (family, class, society, status) that they overtly treat, but also from the perspective of the often overlooked psychological, "inner" conflicts that sometimes elevate these works to tragic stature. This dual emphasis is indispensable to a full appreciation of these complex fictions, as the opening phrase of my subtitle, "Inner Worlds and Outer Limits," suggests. While the psychological issues are more crucial than the social analyses to the novels' latent meanings and submerged structures, it is the lawless "black box" space of their reciprocal interaction — the "between" — that above all enjoins our critical vigilance. The unruly passions seething in the inner worlds of many characters inexorably impel them to act out, in unpredictable and frequently destructive ways, in society. Transgressing the furthest boundaries or "outer limits" of the rational and the conventional, the characters find themselves driven to commit antisocial acts that they cannot comprehend, let alone control.

The chaos of this social realm beyond the limits of the rational confronts us readers too as we attempt to understand what the characters do not, which is why I have preferred to draw on depth psychology (*Tiefenpsychologie*) to analyze their social behavior and negotiate their inner worlds. My reading experience has led me to conclude that these worlds within are dominated by forces associated with the psychopathic and the sociopathic. These mercurial, violent drives enmesh, intermesh, and mutually reinforce each other as the narratives churn and swirl along their choppy courses. Hence an exploration of the psyche which addresses these shrouded, often obscure human motives — explored not only through conscious but also unconscious and semi-conscious processes — is advisable. As a result, I have made extensive use of psychological theory in the work of Sigmund Freud, Melanie Klein, Otto Rank, Ernest Becker, René Girard, and other thinkers in the psychoanalytical tradition, rather than turn to more recent, ego-based or behavior-oriented psychologies, such as the rational-emotive behavioral psychotherapy of Albert Ellis, the cognitive psychology of Aaron Beck, or the behaviorism of B. F. Skinner. Despite an often illuminating focus on the social by these approaches, their exclusive focus on surface material, reflecting a disinclination to uncover hidden or repressed motives in the deeper layers of the psyche underlying cognitive and behavioral processes, proves inadequate to a full engagement with the stormy inner and outer realms of the novels under study.

The "between" self and society in these novels knows depths that reason cannot plumb and convention cannot fathom. For that "between" in their narratives is typically a subterranean zone lodged in the near-"unfathomable" inner recesses of the psyche, where the psychodynamics at work are far more complex and contradictory than mere engagement with the surfaces can possibly elucidate. If the danger of depth psychology is reductionism, the peril of rational and behavioral modalities is superficiality.

II

In my investigation of the fictive representations of personality in these selected British novels, I have concerned myself not only with the perplexities of the reading experience, but also with the semiotics of narrative exposition. The psychological novel often seems not just to invite attention to the kinetics of psyche, eros, and demos, but to organize affect into a linguistic construct that stages dramas of the passions. In this regard, theorists of personality development and character structure from Freud through Girard offer valuable insight into the texture of experience prevailing within narrative designs.

Freud and his successors concurred that a basic characteristic of human experience is the limited nature of our freedom. They all agreed that the realm of conscious choice is confined within severe limits. Novelists from Smollett to Lawrence have voiced greater skepticism about these matters, refusing to portray the deeds of human beings as largely the product of material or psychological conditioning—which is to say that modern literary artists strongly resisted becoming social scientists. They acknowledged with Freud that the presumably conscious aspects of human experience might be mere "rationalization" or "repressed desire" or puzzling instances of displacement, projection, and introjection. And yet, in their conception of the inevitable role of "vast impersonal forces" in the conduct of human affairs, novelists have also always insisted on depicting individual choice and conscious mental activity. In a metaphysical and ethical sense, that is, if not in a collective or statistical sense, they have believed that choice-making is personal and that individual choice is free. This is not to say that they deny the significance of the repetitive, irrational, and instinctual in human life, only that they hold that such subterranean drives have their limits—and that the art of the novel consists in exploring the interacting and overlapping relationship between self-determined acts and conditioning forces.

The novels under study both reflect the modern mind and have shaped it. In addition to the thematics of choice-making and psychic freedom, a *leitmotif* of this study is the unfolding, intensifying perception of psychological malaise as the modern novel evolves: a sense of an impending doom, whereby old practices and institutions no longer undergird social reality, a climate of radical uncertainty that pervades novels ranging from Hardy's *The Mayor of Casterbridge* through the modernist fictions of Ford, Lewis, and Lawrence. This sense of the demise of the *ancien régime*, coupled with agonizing doubt as to the forms the brave new worlds might manifest, represents a thematic undercurrent of this book. Our emphasis in these chapters is not only on modes of consciousness, but also on the increasing fact in modern society of "divided" consciousness.

As such, *Between Self and Society* may also be seen as a counterpart, or even an extension, of Ian Watt's *The Rise of the Novel: Studies in Defoe, Richardson and Fielding* (1957). Whereas Watt's pioneering book addressed the origins of the novel in historical and formalist terms, the present work traces the rise of the novel chiefly in psychological terms, showing how a movement exists from the "narcissistic" fictions of the eighteenth century, exemplified by Smollett's *Roderick Random* and Godwin's *Caleb Williams,* to the psychodynamics of character in the novels of the late nineteenth and twentieth centuries, ranging from Hardy to Lawrence and beyond. Watt's conviction about literary interpretation, most fully developed in *The Rise of the Novel,* was that "the whole question of the historical, institutional, and social context of literature is very widely ignored, to the great detriment not only of much scholarly and critical writing, but of the general understanding of literature at every educational level."[5] That was certainly true in the 1950s, given the ascendency of New Criticism and its insistence that texts exist "independently of each other," in Watt's words.[6] But one can also say today that the psychological aspect of the British novel is too widely ignored, to the detriment of scholarship, criticism, and education. This deficiency reflects a deep-seated, long-standing bias in British studies to favor the empirical, including an almost reflexive antipathy toward psychological inquiry,[7] partly in reaction to what was often referred to as the "psycho-autopsies" of sensationalist British biographers and literary critics in the wake of the success of Lytton Strachey's *Eminent Victorians* (1918). Like Watt, who maintains that selective use of biographical, historical, and formalist criticism is indispensable for understanding the rise of the novel, my contention is that psychological interpretation is also invaluable, especially for the novels in this book that deal in complex ways with narratology and the psychology of character.[8]

III

The theorists featured in the present study—Freud, Klein, Rank, Becker, and Girard—were builders of ambitious interdisciplinary systems. We of the postmodernist age have learned to cast a skeptical eye on such grand theorizing and monumental system-building. Yet however limiting the patterns and procedures it imposes, such system-building contrasts fruitfully with the fictional texts on which such theories are often tested or applied. The novels in the present study are loamy, organic particulars that generate fertile insight as they complicate the generalizations and universals of social science. Our primary concern is with the fictions themselves, for these novels represent something far more valuable than opportunities for literary exegesis: they suggest—indeed they imagine—the possibility of new perceptions of character structure and personality development.

Freud and later psychologists came to see the study of society as an immensely more complicated matter than merely fitting observed data into presumably universal constructs of human thought. This growing methodological awareness reflected a heightening of intellectual self-consciousness among social scientists that is a characteristic of twentieth-century psychology, and the narrative issues in the novels under study here portray this new awareness of the problematic character of social observation. But this new self-consciousness slipped all too readily into a radical skepticism: it was a short step from the awareness of the subjective nature of social thought to a denial of the validity of all such thought—or into a form of Lawrentian "think with the blood" or other species of anti-intellectualism.

Imaginative literature—most particularly the novel—has played a serious role in the expression of social values. A major novel manifests and concretizes the often abstract insights of social scientists. It depicts society with a richness and depth that eludes social science categorizations.[9] So my goal in these pages is not simply to see how prose fiction has borrowed from social science, but also to see how it has contributed to social theory: that is, my dual aim is to appreciate the dense interplay of mutual influence between these genres. For a student of human society has much to learn from the literary craftsman, and vice versa: the sensibilities and subject matters of both domains illuminate the art of living.[10]

This image of Tobias Smollett derives from an engraving by John Chester Buttre (1821–1893), a New York portrait painter. Buttre specialized in steel-plate engravings. Among his best-known American portraits were those of President James Buchanan and Martha Washington.

CHAPTER ONE

Smollett's Roderick Random

IN LOVE WITH NARCISSA

[Her] name for the present shall be Narcissa . . . . Her aspect was noble, generous, and humane; and the whole person so ravishingly delightful, that it was impossible for any creature endowed with sensibility, to see without admiring, and admire without loving her to excess.

TOBIAS SMOLLETT, *RODERICK RANDOM*

I was distracted with joy! I could not believe the evidence of my senses, and looked upon all that had happened as the fictions of a dream!

RODERICK RANDOM IN SMOLLETT'S *RODERICK RANDOM*

I

Tobias Smollett's *The Adventures of Roderick Random*[1] has come to be viewed as a novel that does not quite fit the traditional picaresque form[2] and yet is without a clear narrative structure,[3] except for the ubiquitous "I" of Roderick as narrator. The novel's admirers thus find themselves caught, trying to counter an attack on the novel as "amorphous and episodic, with the various adventures disconnected"[4] and yet unable to point to *Roderick Random*'s notable affinities with the picaresque tradition as a defense of its episodic nature. Paul-Gabriel Boucé finds the novel's repetition of abrupt plot turns and coincidental encounters "contrived," like "dramatic strings . . . as nakedly visible as the cables of the *Thunder*. . . ."[5] Robert Alter attributes Roderick's sudden swings from "transports of joy" to "depths of despair" to Smollett's "turgid flood of exclamatory rhetoric," masking his inability to "convey an authentic sense of the experience of love."[6] Damian Grant in effect seals the case against the novel with his claim that in a protagonist such as Roderick

> we are dealing not with a human personality but an excuse, a simple formal stratagem that permits the stringing together of certain episodes . . . causally unrelated . . . . There is no moral centre to Roderick's character at all, nothing on which his experiences can valuably imprint themselves . . . .[7]

It is undeniable that the narrative sequence per se of Smollett's novel is, like the narrator's surname, "random." My contention, however, is that neither the novel's oddly patterned coincidences nor Roderick's extreme mood fluctuations and instant changes of fortune are attributable to Smollett's stylistic faults or to *Roderick Random*'s place in the picaresque tradition. Roderick as narrator and character is not a cardboard "stratagem" or excuse; he is indeed a personality: in the language of psychoanalytic theory, he is a fundamentally narcissistic personality. Within the framework of libidinal development as developed by Sigmund Freud and Melanie Klein, Roderick's narration of "causally unrelated" episodes and his sudden oscillations in mood become understandable as a narcissist's condition. The world of *Roderick Random* is a projection of Roderick's self, and the novel's characters are different aspects of Roderick's fragmented ego. In that light, Roderick's late reflection on his finally possessing Narcissa is unwittingly accurate: "I . . . looked upon all that had happened . . . as the fictions of a dream" (430).

It is highly unlikely that Smollett consciously crafted *Roderick Random* as a narcissistic dream world (though his interest in psychiatry[8] and mirror literature[9] have been persuasively demonstrated), and Roderick himself is certainly unaware of such a prospect. The novel has often been approached autobiographically, however, and Boucé describes Smollett's attitude toward Roderick as "an anguished fascination like that of Narcissus."[10] Of course, it might be argued here that Smollett's treatments of "Narcissa" and the Narcissus myth alone make sufficiently plausible the contention that the world of the novel consists of the "limitless universe of the self"—without requiring the introduction of any psychoanalytic concepts at all. Yet this would leave such an observation at a vague level of generality and fail to elucidate with concreteness and particularity *Roderick Random*'s distinctive psychodynamics and/or explain its widely noted extreme features. By contrast, I am arguing in this chapter that, for both strictly textual and autobiographical reasons, a psychoanalytic approach to Roderick Random as both character and narrator is warranted, for it lends coherence to the novel's "contrived" plot and "turgid flood of rhetoric," its seemingly inexplicable "leaps" of incident and tone.

Let me emphasize that my literary analysis of the novel does not conceive

Roderick Random as a psychoanalytic case study or as an elucidation of any kind of psychological model. Rather, the picaresque genre itself constitutes a narrative mode that allows for the exploration of states of mind that depart from the rationalist paradigms of both the emergent eighteenth-century novel of moral consciousness (e.g., the fiction of Jane Austen) and the anti-rationalist Gothic novel (e.g., Matthew Lewis). Recent work on the picaresque approaches the genre by means of a focus on the "I" of the central character or narrator, a mode of analysis congruent with the psychoanalytic cast of this chapter. Detailed attention to the psychodynamics at work in *Roderick Random* does not serve simply as a textbook illustration of how a picaresque novel shares certain parallels with forms of psychoanalysis. Rather, it facilitates a new and significantly different understanding of the novel's conception of character and mode of narrative consciousness, which thereby invites a more expansive methodological treatment of the picaresque genre and a more nuanced appreciation of *Roderick Random*'s place within it.

Ultimately, the spectacle of Roderick's psychology offers us the opportunity for a flexible and finely tessellated application of psychoanalysis—that is, for a mode of psychological criticism less concerned with proving that characters are suffering Oedipus complexes and more interested in exploring how psychoanalytic insights open up a fictional world, and how its textual energies compel the reader's attention. Quite obviously, Smollett never read Freud, Klein, or other modern depth psychologists—yet the psychological climate of *Roderick Random* demonstrates that he had independently developed his own keen insights into the complexities of interpersonal relations and human psychodynamics. Viewed from the standpoint of twentieth-century psychoanalysis—a historical anachronism that must be fully acknowledged[11]—Smollett's otherwise puzzling eighteenth-century *picaro* possesses,[12] to a surprising and illuminating extent, the clinical profile of a manic-depressive narcissist.[13]

II

"Primary narcissism" in Freud's libidinal theory consists of the unity of narcissistic ego with the external world, in which the infant is unable to distinguish self from others and from the world. The narcissistic ego holds the idea of "limitless extension and oneness with the universe," so that other people—and the world itself—are felt to be an extension of the self. According to Freud, the "need for the father's protection" and the desire "to reinstate limitless narcissism" are the two chief infantile drives.[14] This state of infantile narcissism is also integral to Melanie Klein's theory of the paranoid-schizoid position, which constitutes the earliest "position"[15] of infantile development for her.

This image originally appeared in Smollett's *History of England*, Volume II, published in 1757–1758. It was part of a massive study in four volumes, *A Complete History of England*, to which Smollett added more volumes in the 1760s. The first four volumes sketched England's history to 1748. Smollett is much indebted in the work to historical writings on England by David Hume.

In the center of this illustration from Smollett's *History* is a portrait of George II (1680–1760), who reigned as monarch from 1727 until his death. It was originally an engraving by John Faber, a distinguished artist of mezzotint engraving. The figures depicted below George II represent a scene evoking two soldiers in one of George II's regiments, both of whom suffer serious wounds fighting against the French in Canada but who still insist on remaining on the field of battle. George II himself was a courageous warrior. In 1743, during the War of Austrian Succession (1740–1748), George led British troops into battle against the French at Dettingen. He has the distinction of being the last British king to lead the military into the field.

According to Klein, the infant constructs a complex "inner world" of split-objects, which he or she feels concretely. These objects are felt as both loved and hated by the infant, and they are interrelated both to the self and to one another. The obsessional fear is of losing the good objects (and thereby part of oneself) or that the persecutory objects will overwhelm and annihilate the idealized objects (and the self). This anxiety of psychic disintegration and death is paranoid; the ego's characteristic defense to ward off this fear is "splitting": minimizing the perceived threat, the besieged ego proceeds to fragment the objects populating the inner world, a reaction that is schizoid. Klein describes the projective identification of the ego onto the external world as narcissistic:

> When the ego-ideal is projected into another person, this person becomes predominantly loved and admired because he contains the good parts of the self. Similarly, the relation to another person on the basis of projecting bad parts of the self into him is of a narcissistic nature, because in this case as well the object strongly represents one part of the self. Both these types of narcissistic relation often show strong obsessional features. The impulse to control people is . . . an essential element in neurosis. The need to control others can . . . be explained by a deflected drive to control parts of the self. When these parts have been projected excessively into another person, they can be controlled only by controlling the other person.[16]

Obsessively locked into the paranoid-schizoid position, the narcissistic ego formulates a conception of "extremely bad and extremely perfect objects"[17] and "looks at people mainly from the point of view of whether they are persecutors or not."[18]

Roderick's consuming quest for the "good father" and for Narcissa (the idealization of the orphan's dead mother) forms the main narrative line of the novel's plot.[19] Of course, Roderick remains unaware of this drive. In his role as narrator in control of his own story, however, he is led to control the plot and others as a way of gaining control of himself. Lost narcissistically in himself, Roderick projects a noble, wealthy father—a distinguished "Don"—and a divine Narcissa as his mate "loving her to excess" (219).

In Kleinian terms, Narcissa and Don Rodrigo, along with the other major figures whom Roderick encounters, are split-objects projected from Roderick's ego. Roderick meets either cherished allies or hostile foes, idealized objects of the good and bad aspects of himself. Thus his affect toward them inevitably swings from mesmerized idealization to impassioned contempt, with nary a lukewarm emotion in between. He loves or hates them inordinately not for themselves but simply for whether they burnish or bruise his fragile ego.

Titled simply *Smollett,* this engraving by William Ridley (1764–1838) is based on a portrait painting by Sir Joshua Reynolds (1723–1792), which was completed in 1795. One of the leading London engravers of his era, Ridley engraved many portraits. He was also a printmaker who produced book illustrations and prints from the work of the most famous British artists of his time, including not only Reynolds but also Thomas Gainsborough and Sir Thomas Lawrence. Founder and first president of the Royal Academy of Arts in 1768, Reynolds is arguably the leading artistic figure of the mid-eighteenth century. This portrait of Smollett shows the author with his face turned right, wearing a neck frill, powdered wig, and dark unbuttoned coat over his waistcoat. The inscription that appears under the portrait reads: "Engraved by Ridley, from the original painting in the possession of Rev. D. Smith." At the bottom of the print is a line that originally appeared in the book illustration: "Printed by C. Cooke, 17, Paternoster Row."

III

As we shall see, every major character in *Roderick Random* is a projected aspect of a good or bad feature, or side, of Roderick himself. Roderick desires to "possess Narcissa in that distinguished sphere to which she was entitled by her birth and qualifications" (352). Whether rich or poor, Roderick maintains he is a gentleman; Thomson, Morgan, and Strap all comment on his "birth and talents." Roderick fancies that he has an "intimate connection" with Narcissa and muses, "The idea of my lovely Narcissa always joined itself to every scene of happiness I could imagine" (414). When he reads the signature of her first letter to him, he swoons, "The subscription of *Your Narcissa* yielded me such delight as I had never felt before" (352). "Noble, generous, and humane," Narcissa is the ideal of Roderick's good self (219). She is the perfection of Roderick at his best, such as in his altruistic behavior toward Miss Williams.[20]

Like Narcissa, Don Rodrigo is the "extremely perfect" part-object projected from a good, noble aspect of Roderick's self. As Roderick recalls of his boyhood features, "I strongly resembled my father, who was the darling of the tenants" before Roderick's grandfather exiled him (5). Roderick boasts that he himself was the best scholar in his school and possessed "uncommon genius." He also respects his father's intelligence and understanding, and is "struck with a profound veneration for him at his first coming into the room . . ." (411). Seeing an expression of sorrow on Don Rodrigo's face, seemingly directed toward him, Roderick feels his "heart take part in his [Don Rodrigo's] grief," sensing another intimate connection that fills him with an "irresistible desire of knowing the particulars of his [Don Rodrigo's] fate" (411–412).[21]

Just as Narcissa and Don Rodrigo are the idealized noble aspects of Roderick's self, Strap and Lieutenant Thomas Bowling (Roderick's uncle) are the hero's exaggeratedly innocent, bumbling, foolish aspects. London sharpers, clerics, and noblemen, and even his apparent friends repeatedly deceive Roderick, just as "honest Strap" is bamboozled throughout the novel. Strap worships Roderick as a dog does his master, but Roderick is often as gullible as Strap. (It is interesting that Strap becomes the wealthy M. d'Estrapes once he is away from Roderick's influence.)

Bowling represents a different angle of projective identification. Periodically, Roderick describes the two chief attributes of his own character as "pride and resentment" (200). Bowling is an "honest tar," yet also a man "whose pride and indignation boiled within him" (11). Roderick's uncle is frank, openhearted, and magnanimous, the truly likeable fellow that Roderick becomes on rare occasions.

Finally, Banter exemplifies the roguish, worldly-wise fellow Roderick fancies himself to be. Roderick is "proud of the good opinion of this wit" (278), heeding his advice in the last quarter of the novel as to matrimonial schemes, financial undertakings, and social stratagems. He tries to be a sophisticate like Banter, only to find (as when Banter "disabuses" him for his stupidity in giving Lord Straddle a diamond ring) that he is more an innocent like Strap and Bowling than a cunning tactician like Banter, Strutwell, and Straddle.

Roderick also projects many "extremely bad" objects, from the London sharpers to the *Thunder*'s villains to his romantic rivals.[22] Because the characters of the various adversaries are not described, one must judge from their behavior which aspects of Roderick they reflect. Roderick harbors an immediate, visceral, "mortal aversion" to Sir Timothy Thicket (220), his rival for Narcissa. He is outraged by Thicket's lust, and rescues Narcissa from Thicket's clutches in one of his typically heroic gestures. The proud and haughty Quiverwit challenges Roderick to a duel and apparently wounds the hero fatally, but Roderick finds he is only scratched and proceeds to "vanquish" Quiverwit (247). Arrogant, cowardly Captain Weazel first challenges poor Strap and then Roderick, who pins him in a corner in their duel, and later he relates the story of Weazel's humiliation at being discovered hiding under his wife's petticoats to escape detection by a highwayman.

If Roderick himself often behaves in a lustful, proud, and arrogant manner, it is nonetheless psychodynamically significant that a reactive mechanism springs to play at once. That is, in each gesture Roderick makes at an *amour*, a rival instantly pops up to oppose him and, after some difficulties, Roderick gains control of the situation. A central aspect of the Kleinian model is the narcissistic ego's restless pursuit of secure power through the infant's omnipotent control of his environment. The infant equates effective control with watertight compartmentalization of his split-objects: he feels that he must keep the bad objects as distant as possible from the good objects. Likewise, a perpetually embattled Roderick is driven to gain control of each situation and its inevitable bad characters in order both to gain at least tenuous control of himself and to protect his loved objects.

IV

Along with "control," Klein identifies "triumph" and "contempt" as the triad of feelings the child experiences in his manic relation to objects and which he employs to keep his inner world secure.[23] Roderick's swings from mania to melancholia are most pronounced when his possession of Narcissa is jeopardized, and his manic defenses and susceptibility to severe depression are most evident in those instances. When Roderick unexpectedly sees Narcissa at a large dinner party, his emotions run completely out of control, cascading from mania to melancholia to mania within the span of a few seconds:

> [A] gentleman . . . leading a young lady, whom I immediately discovered to be the adorable Narcissa! Good Heaven! What were the thrillings of my soul at that instant! My reflection was overwhelmed with a torrent of agitation! My heart throbbed with surprising violence! A sudden mist overspread my eyes! My ears were invaded by a dreadful sound! . . . Every thing that was soft, sensible and engaging in the character of that dear creature, recurred to my remembrance, and every favourable circumstance of my own qualifications appeared with all the aggravation of self-conceit to heighten my expectation! Neither was this transport of long duration. The dread of her being already disposed of intervened, and overcast my enchanting reverie! . . . I was stung with the suggestion and believing the person who conducted her to be the husband . . . , already devoted to him my fury, and stood up to mark him for my vengeance; when I recollected, to my unspeakable joy, her brother . . . in the person of her gallant . . . . I gazed in a frenzy of delight . . . . (337)

After being struck on the head and rendered unconscious in his battle against Crampley aboard the *Thunder*, Roderick's grandiosity soars and plummets, and he imagines himself in a "state of annihilation":

> I found myself alone in a desolate place, stripped of my clothes, money, watch, buckles, and everything . . . . *What a discovery must this be to me,* who but an hour before was worth sixty guineas in cash! I cursed the hour of my birth, the parents that gave me being, the sea that did not swallow me up, the poignard of the enemy which could not find its way to my heart, the villainy of those who had left me in that miserable condition; and in the ecstasy of despair, resolved to lie still where I was, and perish. (210, italics mine)

When considering Roderick's flights from a "frenzy of delight" to the "ecstasy of despair," we should recall the fluctuating temporal distance he maintains from events and how his narrative distance repeatedly collapses into the solipsism of his own "I." Roderick is ostensibly narrating events at a point in time two or three years after he first meets Narcissa, for Roderick the narrator is a married man whose passions have been "settled and mellowed" (435). But it is clear, as in the two passages above, that Roderick is often deeply involved in the experiencing (or re-experiencing) of events, rather than detached from them.

As narrator and character, Roderick is repeatedly engulfed in a narcissistic world of his own making. Given his manic-depressive gyrations, it becomes near-impossible to discern when he is a disengaged memoir writer reflecting on a wild bachelor life and when he is the impetuous adventurer.[24] He seldom offers insights or reflections (and, as Grant observes, his reflections are always superficial[25]). Rather, he seems absorbed in events as they are happening. Moreover, because Smollett apparently wants readers (as he writes in the Preface) to "favor" and "sympathize" with Roderick, we too are drawn into the virtual world of Roderick's "I."[26] In this respect, the lack of a "centre" in Roderick, moral or otherwise, is understandable. There can be no defined "centre" to Roderick because he is diffused both temporally and spatially throughout the novel, which consists entirely of the "limitless universe" of his self.

V

We have now arrived at the final, crucial claim in our argument about the psychodynamics of Smollett's *picaro*. If Roderick has indeed created a series of events "as the fictions of a dream" (430), the extraordinary twists of fate and the repetition of utterly fantastic coincidences gain coherence as the processes of a mind in the paranoid-schizoid position. The combined application of psychoanalytic insights from both Kleinian and Freudian theory facilitates this conclusion. In Kleinian theory, the infant has not yet developed the capacity for "linking and abstraction," but can only engage in "disjointed and concrete thinking."[27] In Freudian theory, dreams are "unconscious material from the id (originally unconscious and repressed unconscious alike) which forces its way into the ego."[28] Within the Freudian id there are no conflicts, for contradictions and antitheses exist side by side. The id has no conception of time and knows no values. As a result of the ego's resistance to the id, dreams become distorted, with persons or entities often condensed or displaced unrecognizably. Roderick's dream world exhibits a similar atmosphere and texture. Roderick meets characters whom he does not recognize as aspects of himself. His providential reunions—with Miss Williams in an adjoining sickroom, with Strap and Bowling in France, with Narcissa at the dinner party, with Jackson in jail, with his father in South America, and finally with Thomson—are reconstructed dream material, the "fictions of a dream." They are the shifts of an unconscious mind that recognizes no orderly or sensible progression of events, of a schizoid personality that can engage only in "disjointed" thinking. The transports of joy that these reunions occasion are understandable as the ego's recovery of lost part-objects, the re-introjection of parts of itself that had been split off and seemingly lost. The unbelievable, precipitous calamities that Roderick undergoes—his capture by a press-gang when he is assisting Miss Williams, his kidnapping to Boulogne by smugglers after he has just gained Narcissa's affections—are explainable also as the id completely breaking through the ego's defenses and defying its sense of narrative order.

According to Klein, the manic defenses of control, triumph, and contempt operate to ensure the infant's "omnipotent denial of psychic reality."[29] The clearest exposition of both Roderick's paranoid behavior and his conception of his own omnipotence occurs at the novel's close. At last he succeeds in bringing virtually all his good part-objects together and conquering or controlling his bad part-objects. Through what Klein terms "magic denial,"[30] a fantasy of omnipotence resulting in the total annihilation of his persecutors, Roderick wards off the threats posed by the bad objects both to himself and to his loved objects. He learns that Crab, Mackshane, Oakum, and the wicked schoolmaster are all dead; he rejects Mr. and Mrs. Potion as "low-minded wretches" and one of his female cousins for her inhumane treatment of him in his childhood; he is "pleased" that "Melinda is robbed of all her admirers" by Narcissa as his wife (418). Moreover, he achieves, finally and triumphantly, the august position that his birth and education have naturally qualified him for, at least to his thinking: the status of a gentleman.

In the last four chapters, the novel swirls more than ever with the "hyperactivity" that characterizes the Kleinian condition of manic omnipotence.[31] The plot accelerates into high gear, the improbabilities multiply, and—*mirabile dictu*—loose ends are masterfully tied up and oppositions effortlessly reconciled: Roderick locates his father; Bowling returns; Roderick meets with his old friends Thomson and Morgan; and Roderick leaves Mrs. Sagely with a present of thirty guineas, "resolving to accommodate her with the same sum annually, for . . . the infirmities of old age" (422). Best of all and wonder of wonders, Roderick returns "home" to a great estate in Scotland, where he is "almost devoured by their [his servants'] affection" (426). Likewise, his wife Narcissa is "universally admired" among the town and country folk, and Roderick benevolently provides reparation to faithful Strap for his months of devoted service by furnishing him and his new bride, Miss Williams, with the blessing and largesse of Don Rodrigo. In a declaration of complete victory and seeming omnipotence, Roderick declares, "If there be such a thing as true happiness on earth, I enjoy it" (435). To top it all off, Narcissa is pregnant and Roderick is about to become a father himself. Indeed, what more could one ask for? It is a narcissist's dream.

For Klein, the drive for manic omnipotence is impelled by the desire to "reverse the child-parent relation. . . . A time will come, the child fantasizes, when he will be strong, tall, grown up, rich, powerful and potent."[32] Although Roderick has not vanquished Don Rodrigo (nor expressed any wish to do so),

Edited by David Blewett, the Penguin Classics edition of *Roderick Random* shows on its cover a detail of William Hogarth's *Lord George Graham in His Cabin*. Lord Graham (1715–1747) was the youngest son of the first Duke of Montrose, and he had a distinguished naval career. The original oil painting, which is located in the National Maritime Museum in London, shows Captain Graham in his ship's cabin after a successful attack on French privateers in June 1745.

Hogarth's painting places Graham seated on the right, holding a pipe in his right hand, and apparently waiting for a meal at his table. He is stylishly attired, wearing a red velvet cape draped over his shoulders, a gold brocade waistcoat, a velvet cap, and breeches and slippers. On the left behind the table is a companion in relatively simple dress, sporting a black coat with white collar. Scholars have speculated that he represents a secretary, or even a tutor for Graham, since he is holding a ledger or notes. A black servant boy is located on the far right behind Graham, playing music.

William Hogarth (1697–1764) became known as a celebrated satirist of British and European life, best known for his influential portrait *The Rake's Progress*. That work, like the portrait of Lord George Graham, was part of a series of portrait paintings that Hogarth referred to as "conversation pieces." Although the Graham portrait caused no such sensation as *The Rake's Progress*, it stands today as the most famous example of a cabin scene in British art.

This cover image of The Oxford World's Classics edition of *The Adventures of Roderick Random* depicts a wealthy tycoon feted by fawning courtesans. It thus suitably portrays the eventual success of Smollett's protagonist in the novel. Based on an original watercolor by Robert Dighton, which is entitled *A Rich Privateer Brought Safe into Port, by Two First Rates* (1782), this hand-colored mezzotint print is presently housed in the British Museum. Dighton (1752–1814) was a draughtsman and painter well known for his satirical prints. He belonged to a family of artists: he was the son of an art dealer and the father of three artists. A specialty of their family business in London was the creation of portrait caricatures, ranging from etched plates to watercolors made for engraving. This Oxford edition was originally published in 1979 and edited by the Smollett scholar Paul-Gabriel Boucé, and it remained the authoritative edition for many years.

he has indeed defeated all the bad father-surrogates and become the powerful "gentleman" about whom he has fantasized throughout the novel.

If we read *Roderick Random* as its narrator's projected dream world, the novel ends in blissful wish-fulfillment for Roderick. As a beloved, "universally admired" gentleman blessed with "the adorable Narcissa" and their soon-to-arrive progeny, he has emerged victorious against the "sordid and vicious disposition of the world," the "selfishness, envy, malice and base indifference of mankind" that Smollett railed against in his Preface (xxxv). And indeed Roderick has accomplished these feats by not only regaining but also by *becoming* the father.

Having conquered death, the mightiest foe, he has attained in his omnipotence the psychological security about which the paranoid-schizoid obsesses: the overcoming of psychic disintegration, indeed the vanquishing and/or integration of all split-objects. In doing so he realizes his *sui generis* project: to become the father of himself.[33] Roderick thereby reinstates a secure and limitless narcissism. The omnipotent "I" of the end of *Roderick Random* is a safe inner world in the image and likeness of the hero's "loved" self.

CHAPTER TWO

Godwin's Caleb Williams

"A HALF-TOLD AND MANGLED TALE"

If man were an omnipotent being, and at the same time retained all his present infirmities, it would be difficult to say of what extravagances he would be guilty. It is proverbially affirmed that power has a tendency to corrupt the best dispositions. Then what would not omnipotence effect?

WILLIAM GODWIN, *THOUGHTS ON MAN*

I

In *Things As They Are, or The Adventures of Caleb Williams,* written thirty-seven years before *Thoughts on Man,* Godwin himself presents the fictional answer to his own question. The novel is a terrifying portrayal of omnipotent persecution, corrupted nobility, and deep-ridden guilt. Unfortunately, because of both Godwin's explicit statement of purpose in the Preface and *Caleb Williams*'s publication just one year after his landmark philosophical treatise *Enquiry Concerning Political Justice and its Influence on Morals and Happiness,* critics have traditionally tended to approach the novel's theme of power and powerlessness almost exclusively in sociopolitical terms.[1] According to George Woodcock, the "principal theme" is "the crushing of the individual by the forces of civilized society. . . ."[2] D. H. Monro sees the novel as a study in "the insufficiency of honor."[3] And Godwin himself called *Caleb* a "vehicle" for presenting "the modes of domestic and unrecorded despotism by which man becomes the destroyer of man" (xxiii).[4]

However much these perspectives illuminate certain aspects of the novel and Godwin's philosophical anarchism and utilitarianism, they do not finally account for what readers have invariably testified to as their feverishly intense

Depicting William Godwin in his early fifties, this portrait of the author of *Caleb Williams* was painted by James Northcote in 1802. Godwin was very proud and pleased by the work of Northcote, who was both an artist and a literary contemporary of Godwin. The original oil painting graced a wall in Godwin's home and remained in the Godwin family until the end of the century. It now hangs in the National Portrait Gallery in London.

reading experience of *Caleb*. Godwin himself insists that it was written in "a high state of excitement" and with an eye toward maintaining "interest and passion" in order to create "an epoch in the mind of the reader" (xxvii). Moreover, the focus upon *Caleb* as a gloss on *Political Justice* or as a chronicle of institutional decay has led some critics to castigate Godwin's narrative as "improbable" and "clumsy" even while expressing admiration for his skill in dramatizing political ideas.[5]

It is undeniable that *Caleb Williams* is, as Caleb himself laments in the novel's final line, "a half-told and mangled tale" (378). My contention, however, is that an explanation of *Caleb*'s series of fantastic accidents, abrupt plot turns, and horrifyingly obsessive mood is not traceable to Godwin's oft-bemoaned stylistic faults or to his political philosophy. Rather, this is a story of omnipotence and impotence that can be understood in the language of psychoanalytic theory. Within the framework of libidinal development described by Sigmund Freud and Melanie Klein, Caleb's narration of causally disconnected events and his deep-seated ambivalence toward his master-surrogate father Lord Falkland become understandable when viewed as a fundamentally narcissistic personality unconsciously engaged in a homosexual struggle with his omnipotent father. The world of *Caleb Williams* witnesses the narrator's search for the ideal family of romance, a projection of Caleb's self, with the various characters serving as different aspects of Caleb's fragmented ego. Caleb's immediate reflection on the novel's central incident, "the crisis of my fate" (154)—his breaking into Falkland's trunk—is therefore unwittingly accurate: "It now appeared to me like a dream" (153). In presenting what Caleb himself fears is "an imperfect and mutilated story" (355), Godwin ironically and metaphorically has written the very "mangled tale" that he vowed to avoid when he rested for three months during the third volume's composition: "I endeavored to repose myself in security, and not to inflict a set of crude and incoherent dreams upon my readers" (xxx).

Godwin has indeed created a narcissistic dream world, operating according to the dream mechanisms of secondary revision, disguise, distortion, displacement, and condensation. It is, of course, extremely doubtful that Godwin consciously crafted the novel as dream (though his essay on "Self Love and Benevolence" in *Thoughts on Man* shows he grappled with related issues), and Caleb himself is certainly unaware of his position.[6] P. N. Furbank has approached the novel in autobiographical terms as a "highly dramatized symbolical picture of Godwin himself in the act of writing *Political Justice*."[7] Thus, for both strictly textual and autobiographical reasons, a psychoanalytic treatment of the novel as the enclosed world of a narcissist is warranted,[8] for such an approach can effectively address *Caleb*'s "passion"[9] and lend coherence to its seemingly inexplicable narrative "leaps."

The sociopolitical implications of the theme of power in *Caleb* also need not be limited to that explicit context; the homosexual father-son, master-servant, feudal lord–peasant struggle may also be viewed in the psychosocial, phylogenetic terms of "repressive civilization" as discussed by Freud in *Civilization and Its Discontents*, *Moses and Monotheism*, and his other cultural studies. The price of civilization is the renunciation of our instincts; this is, said Freud fatalistically, "Things As They Are"—alternately the novel's title and subtitle in various editions. Once started, Captain Raymond, Laura, Collins, and Falkland tell Caleb separately that a course of action or belief cannot be altered. "Am I not compelled to go on in Folly, once begun?" grieves Raymond (265).

One might also redirect Raymond's question to the history of scholarship on *Caleb*: we critics are not "compelled to go on" generating readings of the novel in overtly political terms, let alone casting it as a "highly dramatized" expression

The Penguin Classics edition of Godwin's *Caleb Williams* spotlights an embattled, tortured young Caleb. Cast in the image of an agonized Prometheus, he is overburdened yet unbowed, writhing under the horrific consequences of stealing fire from his seemingly omnipotent demigod, Squire Falkland. *Caleb Williams* features a gripping plot and stands both as a brilliant philosophical novel and a discerning portrait of its youthful narrator-protagonist. Indeed it represents an absorbing, dramatic study in psychopolitics and criminal justice, the first great political novel, reflecting the fact that Godwin was an important political philosopher and representative figure of the transition between the Enlightenment and Romanticism. In these respects, *Caleb Williams* anticipates and bears comparison with Dostoyevsky's *Crime and Punishment*.

of "political justice." If we move beyond sociopolitical commentary, we can appreciate how the disordered narrative structure and flow of this "mangled tale" invite a psychoanalytic approach to its "improbable," "clumsy" plot, dreamlike setting, dynamics of characterization, and central themes of omnipotence and paternal domination. Such an argument would reconceptualize the terms in which we approach *Caleb Williams,* with keen attention redirected to its problematic literary issues and oddities—including the role of dreams, the motif of writing and composition, themes of omniscience, narcissism, and father-son conflict—as constituents within a patterned narrative best understood via the psychodynamics of Freudian theory.

Accordingly, this chapter reframes the narrative approach to the novel as it reintegrates the aforementioned topics in the terms of Freudian psychopathology. The argument contends that *Caleb Williams* is a stark exposition of the irreconcilable conflict between the free gratification of man's instinctual needs and the development of civilization, a warring dialectic between the pleasure and reality principles. Caleb and Falkland are shackled and exhausted by their battles and mutual guilt, just as the perpetual inhibitions upon Eros ultimately weaken the life instincts and strengthen and release the very destructive forces against which they struggle. Although Godwin asserted in *Political Justice* both that a theory of the instincts was "absurd" and that "heredity affects nothing"[10] and environment everything, the novel does seem driven toward death: Falkland's physical and Caleb's psychological demise result in a void or Nirvana-like severance, with a defamed Falkland dead and a legally absolved Caleb with "no character . . . to vindicate" (378).

II

Certain distinctive features of Caleb's psychology resemble those of Smollett's Roderick Random. Both characters are the protagonists and narrators of first-person novels—and in a clinical sense, "control freaks." For in his role as narrator in control of his story, Caleb too is obsessively driven to control the plot and other characters in a desperate effort to control himself. Unlike the triumphant eponymous hero of *Roderick Random,* however, Caleb comes to grief in his maniacal, anxious pursuit of (self-)control.

If we approach these psychopathological issues within the framework of Freud's libidinal theory, we can see that, as in the case of Roderick, Caleb too possesses a fragile narcissistic ego. In Chapter One we discussed at length Freud's contention that the infant's narcissistic ego cannot distinguish between the self and other objects. Rather, it conceives reality as an undifferentiated unity, whereby it experiences "oneness with the universe," so that other people and the world itself are felt to be an extension of the self. The "need for the father's protection" and the urge "to reinstate limitless narcissism" form the two chief infantile drives.[11] As we have also previously noted, this condition of infantile narcissism aiso represents the prevailing state of infantile development in Melanie Klein's model of the paranoid-schizoid position, which is characterized by an "inner world" populated by fragmentary, projected love objects and hate objects—that is, persecutory ("paranoia") objects and "split" good/evil ("schizo-") objects.

The relevant passage from Klein's essay on schizoid positions in *Developments in Psychoanalysis* warrants attention again.

> When the ego-ideal is projected into another person, this person becomes predominantly loved and admired because he contains the good parts of the self. Similarly, the relation to another person on the basis of projecting bad parts of the self into him is of a narcissistic nature, because in his case as well the object strongly represents one part of the self. Both these types of narcissistic relation to an object often show strong obsessional features. The impulse to control people is . . . an essential element in obsessional neurosis. The need to control others can to some extent be explained by a deflective drive to control parts of the self. When these parts have been projected excessively onto another person, they can only be controlled by controlling the other person.[12]

Klein concludes that the infantile ego arrested in the paranoid-schizoid positon obsessively projects a world dominated by "extremely bad and extremely perfect objects" and "looks at people mainly from the point of view of whether they are persecutors or not."[13]

Caleb's impassioned drive is to create what Freud called "the neurotic's family romance."[14] According to Freud, the small child's "peculiarly marked imaginative activity" focuses upon his "most intense and most momentous wish": "to be like his parents (that is, the parent of his own sex)."[15] In later childhood, he recognizes his parents' (particularly his father's) fallibility and his imagination becomes engaged in the task of getting free from the parents of whom he now has a low opinion, and of replacing them by others who, as a rule, are of a higher social standing.[16] Freud's observations about the "young phantasy-builder" sound as if they might have been written to annotate *Caleb Williams*:

> He will make use . . . of any opportune coincidences from his actual experiences, such as his becoming acquainted with the Lord of the Manor or some landed proprietor if he lives in the country. . . .[17]
>
> In the replacement of both parents or of the father alone by grander people, we find that these new and aristocratic parents are equipped with attributes that are derived entirely from real recollections of the actual and humble ones; so that in fact the child is not getting rid of his father but exalting him. Indeed the whole effort at replacing the real father by

> a superior one is only an expression of the child's longing for the happy, vanished days when his father seemed to him the noblest and strongest of men and his mother the dearest and loveliest of women. He turns to the father in whom he believed in the earliest years of his childhood.[18]

Caleb relates that he is born of "humble" peasant parents who could leave him little inheritance except for "an honest fame" and an education "free from depravity" (3). Although he makes no mention of his father or his own childhood experiences after the first three pages, his "invincible attachment to books of narrative and romance" suggests his intense longing for the "happy, vanished days" of his real parents' seeming grandeur. Yet, filled with romantic visions, his imaginative childhood mind is seemingly absorbed precisely in "getting free" from his humble parents and yearns to undertake an adventurous aristocratic future: "I panted for the unraveling of an adventure with an anxiety perhaps almost equal to that of the man whose future happiness or misery depended on its issue" (4).

The adventure begins when, during the very moments Caleb's father is lying on his deathbed, Lord Falkland returns to the country from a lengthy trip abroad and "surprisingly" summons Caleb to him immediately after Farmer Williams's funeral. Mrs. Williams had died some years earlier, so that eighteen-year-old Caleb "had not now a relation in the world. . . ." Falkland benevolently agrees to "take [Caleb] into his family," and the boy forms "golden visions of the state I was about to occupy" (5–6).

Nevertheless, narrator Caleb, from a perspective many years after their initial meeting, immediately reflects that this first encounter with Falkland marked the end of his "gaiety and lightness of heart" and the start of days "devoted to misery and alarm." Thus, just as the growing child's awareness of his real father's human weakness incites him to look to a socially superior surrogate, Caleb's heightened understanding of Society and Falkland's vincibility reawakens in him a narcissistic longing for his original godlike parents. His attempt to create a family romance in Falkland's home fails, and his life after his father's death proves unremittingly miserable, with the exception of his brief success in finding a new mother and family, Laura and the Denisons. Caleb "honoured and esteemed the respectable Laura like a mother," judges her children admirable and her husband "shrewd, sensible and rational" (338, 336). Farmer Denison's "obscure retreat" or "remote retirement" in Wales strongly resembles Caleb's father's "remote" cottage. Caleb regresses to childhood, only to be thrust abruptly out of his new family when the spectre of "Falkland" once again intrudes—at the very moment Caleb is about to explain to Laura his past with his master, she informs him disgustedly that she has just learned it all "by a mere accident" (348).

The novel therefore becomes orphan Caleb's romantic quest, as character and narrator, to recover the "good father" and (secondarily) "good mother" whom he lost in childhood. Falkland is the mighty father figure who replaces Caleb's dead father and for whom Caleb feels both reverence and contempt. His master is in a sense the demiurge whom narrator Caleb reacts to ambivalently in place of his good, though infinitely distanced, parents. So all-encompassing is Falkland as a paternal figure that, except for a passing remark of Falkland's footman Thomas about "honest Farmer Williams" (203), neither of Caleb's parents is mentioned beyond the opening paragraphs.

Yet Caleb's narcissism and quest for the good parents extends beyond his unconscious strivings to forge a family romance through Falkland and Laura. In terms of Freud's concept of narcissistic libido, not just Falkland and Laura but *all* the major characters whom Caleb encounters are extensions of the self, grafted libidinally to "the ego itself and finding satisfaction [and distress] in the ego just as satisfaction is usually found only in objects." Caleb indeed also views Forester, Spurrel, and Raymond in a parental light, and he even calls Collins "father." In Kleinian terms, all these characters are split-objects projected from Caleb's inner world, part-objects from whom he feels he cannot be separated without incurring injury or disintegration.

Caleb meets either trusted friends or villainous betrayers. As we shall see, because Caleb's dominant relationship with Falkland is one of ambivalence, several other characters also change from allies to victimizers, just as Falkland does. Each of them is an idealized object representing good and/or bad aspects of Caleb, a projection of a good or bad feature or side of him. Just as Caleb as a character struggles with Falkland for control of this "half-told tale," with Falkland circulating the scurrilous *Wonderful and Surprising History of Caleb Williams* and with Caleb thereupon writing his rejoinder in the form of the novel itself, narrator Caleb often suggests that even his mind did not seem his own but rather a battle for control between the omnipotent Falkland and himself: "I knew his misery so well, I was so fully acquainted with its cause, and so strongly impressed with the idea of its being unmerited, that, while I suffered deeply, I continued to pity rather than hate my persecutor" (262). Or, as Rudolf Storch expressed it in a landmark essay:

> [The characters] are not so much separate persons with their own motivations (or characters in an observed society) as elements within the mind of one person who projects them warring one against the other onto the figures moving. . . .[19]

If each character is a projected aspect of Caleb, Falkland must be viewed as alternately an "extremely perfect" *and* "extremely bad" part-object of the idealized noble and cruel aspects of Caleb's self. Caleb "devours" romances; Falkland lives them. The squire's favorite authors in youth are the Italian heroic poets, and his conduct "assiduously conformed to the model of heroism that his fancy suggested"; as Collins explains, "no Englishman was ever in an equal degree idolised by the inhabitants of Italy" (11). Caleb is also an entertaining conversationalist and "a good and zealous hearer" for Forester; Falkland was the "perpetual delight of the diversified circles" he frequented in his youth and "imparted an inconceivable brilliancy to his company and conversation" (9). The mind of Lord Falkland was "fraught with all the rhapsodies of visionary honor," and Caleb too possesses a "love of praise" (4).

Falkland does therefore appear as Caleb's projected ego-ideal, the perfect paternal object "almost too sublime for human nature" (124). Even after his unspeakable sufferings, Caleb in the closing trial scene affirms Falkland's majesty:

> From the first moment I saw him, I conceived that most ardent admiration. He condescended to encourage me; *I attached myself to him with the fullness of my affection.* (372, italics mine)

Caleb also "attaches" himself to Falkland with the fullness of his antipathy, however, and Falkland stands as the "extremely bad" object whose "insurmountable power" sadistically inflicts infinite torment upon Caleb. Honor becomes Falkland's consuming obsession, and he laughs at Caleb's impotent arguments: "Do you not know, miserable wretch! . . . I have sworn to preserve my reputation whatever be the cost, that I love it more than the whole world and its inhabitants taken together" (177). Yet Falkland's persecution and omnivorous appetite for honor are actually the idealized aspects of Caleb's sadistic, equally obsessive curiosity disguised and displaced onto Falkland. Caleb knows he is torturing Falkland by recalling his master's painful past, but he also views it as an explorer's game in which he means no real harm and cannot be judged guilty. "To be a spy upon Mr. Falkland!" he muses (124).

With each conversation in which Caleb slanders Falkland's heroic Alexander and Clitus as murderers, he drives his master into "convulsive shuddering" and "supernatural barbarity" that "seemed to shake the house" (131). Collins describes Falkland as "a fool of honour and fame" who "in the pursuit of reputation nothing could divert" (116); Caleb's curiosity is an "insatiable desire" stimulated further whenever it is indulged and which "carries its pleasures, as well as its pains, along with it" (141). Thus, "to [Falkland's] story the whole fortune of [Caleb's] life is linked." "My heart," Caleb cries, "bleeds at the recollection of his misfortunes, as if they were my own!" (10).

Messrs. Forester and Spurrel also are both projections of aspects of Caleb's self and father-surrogates toward whom he feels ambivalence. Forester is Falkland's elder half-brother and "in many respects the reverse of Falkland": he has "a violence of manner" and displays a lack of concern with honor. Just as Falkland suddenly returned when Caleb's father was dying, Forester appears on the scene after "a residence of several years upon the continent" and immediately after Caleb's fatal pact with Falkland. "I shall always hate you," Falkland had said, and it is as if Caleb introduces Forester as a superior and rival father figure with whom he has at least a chance for love and affection. The "novelty" of Falkland may be wearing off, as Caleb suggests when he first holds his private discussions with his master, and his second squire may serve as another paternal replacement. Significantly, Caleb draws the comparison and admires Forester with the same filial devotion: "Mr. Forester was the second man I had seen uncommonly worthy of my analysis, and who seemed . . . almost as much deserving to be studied as Mr. Falkland himself" (164). Like Caleb, he is a "man of penetration" (127) and possesses a "severity" similar to Falkland's criticism of Caleb's "harsh" judgments upon Alexander and Clitus. Caleb's "firmness and consistency astonish me," says Forester, "and add something to what I had conceived of human powers" (200). But Forester's relentless pursuit of Caleb through Gines and other instruments across the British Isles is no less superhuman. Caleb prizes above all "the independence of my own mind" (200), and there seems no one in the kingdom more self-confident and of stricter integrity than Forester. As he tells Caleb during the interrogation over Caleb's alleged jewel theft:

> I am indifferent myself about the good opinions of others. It is what the world bestows and retracts with so little thought, that I can make no account of its decision. (187)

On the other hand, Spurrel is, like Falkland, a victim of the world's values: a fool of mammon. He possesses a consuming "love of money" and, in contrast to Falkland's magnanimous spirit and Forester's principled integrity, "a charitable officiousness of demeanour" (311). Yet Caleb identifies strongly with Spurrel, for he "appeared to love me with a parental affection," and Spurrel insists that Caleb's ugly disguise is the "very picture" of his dead son. Spurrel asks Caleb to be his new son and promises to treat him "with the same attention and kindness" as he did his dead son (310). But as with Falkland and Forester, love turns to betrayal. Spurrel turns Caleb over to Gines for money, just as his previous protectors made him the victim of obsessive honor and pitiless integrity. Yet Caleb discusses Spurrel's weakness for mammon in similar terms to Caleb's own irresistible passion for knowledge: he surmises Spurrel was "driven by a sort of implicit impulse" (317). Spurrel's mournful cries when Caleb is captured echo Williams's own plaints following the trunk opening and during the final trial: "I could not help it: I would have helped it if I could!" (316).

Caleb also views Captain Raymond and Mrs. Marney with unreserved filial affection. Both affirm what matters more to Caleb than anything else: belief in his innocence. Raymond declares Caleb "guiltless of what they lay at his charge as that I am so myself," and Mrs. Marney assumes his innocence and "had no desire for any further information than I found expedient to give" (299). He calls Raymond "my protector" and notes that Mrs. Marney "interested herself so unreservedly" in his literary dispatches to the local printer that "she felt either [my] miscarriage or good fortune much more exquisitely than I did" (300). Like Caleb, Raymond possesses a "fervent benevolence," a "candour seldom equaled," and "penetration." He seems to Caleb "eminently superior" to his criminal partners and "out of place" (267), just as Caleb feels himself extraordinary yet painfully cut off from intercourse with mankind. Mrs. Marney too is a "benevolent soul" and "humble," as Caleb's parents were. And like young Caleb who "knew not the world" before he met Falkland, Mrs. Marney is unacquainted with the "cares of wealth and the pressures of misfortune" (298). Most strikingly, she has a "noble" heart and is "sincere" (299), just as Caleb astounds all who hear him speak with the force of his honest spontaneity and heartfelt conviction.

Caleb refers to Laura and Collins as "mother" and "father," yet they repudiate him most severely—as a "monster" and a "machine" (348, 360). They are the final characters he meets before his trial and the only two people with whom he had ever "experienced the purest refinements of friendship" (351). Laura's connections with Caleb as a maternal figure have already been suggested. Like Caleb, she is altogether "extraordinary" (as Collins says of Caleb, 336, 359).

Moreover, Laura's background reaffirms her apparent fitness with Falkland as a choice for Caleb's projected "family romance," for her past and nature are notably similar to Falkland's. Orphan Laura is a highly refined Neapolitan nobleman's daughter who grew continually in "the fund of her accomplishments" (337). Whereas Falkland spends much of his young manhood "idolized" in Italy (and even has a Romance name: "Ferdinando"), Laura grows up in his native England. Both now live in remote English counties because of personal or family scandals. Falkland has withdrawn from society since the Tyrrel and Hawkins murders; Laura's father was banished upon suspicion of political and religious heresy and took her to Wales. According to Caleb, Laura regards "every little relic of her father's with a sort of religious veneration" and reveres Falkland's name because he is discussed "in terms of panegyric" in some of her father's correspondence (341). So even though Laura "treated me as if I had been one of the family," says Caleb, "and I sometimes flattered myself that I might one day become such in reality" (339), he is doubly thwarted: both by a paternal figure from whom he thought himself free and also by one from the distant past whom he never even met. Both Falkland's fabricated *History* and

Laura's father's distorted letters dash Caleb's final hope for a family and wage war against his own "imperfect and mutilated story."

Caleb's chance encounter with Collins in the final pages constitutes his concluding attempt to escape his haunting bad fathers and to find the good father. Collins is the executor of his father's farm and Caleb's "earliest and best beloved friend" who, like Caleb's father, is suddenly "lost" at a critical moment. Just weeks before Caleb's "fatal reverse of fortune" with the trunk, Collins is sent by Falkland to manage his West Indian plantation and remains there ten years. "I always believed that if he had been present [at Forester's interrogation], he would have felt me innocent," bemoans Caleb (356). "Felt," rather than "believed," is the crucial word here, for the narcissist feels the outer world an extension of his self and Freud maintained compassion has a "narcissistic origin." Caleb yearns to have "amiable, incomparable" Collins support him, but his final consideration seems a selfless one: "Might not Mr. Falkland reduce him to a condition as wretched and low as mine? After all, was it not vice in me to desire to involve another man in my sufferings?" (360). Caleb's wild ravings directed toward Collins show his willingness to abase himself before his "father" and his obsessive need to displace his guilt and have others believe his innocence:

> Collins! I now address myself to you. I have consented that you should yield me no assistance in my present terrible situation. I am content to die rather than do anything injurious to your Tranquility. —But remember,—you are my father still! I conjure you, by all the love you ever bore me, by the benefits you have conferred upon me, by the forbearance and kindness towards you that now penetrates my soul, by my innocence—for, if these be the last words I shall ever write, I die protesting my innocence! (365)

To injure Collins would be to injure a part of himself; to control him is to begin to gain control of himself. In fact, so strongly does Caleb identify with Collins that the novel's first volume is actually Collins's story filtered through Caleb (with the Tyrrel trial scene in Collins's own words).[20]

Repeatedly Caleb as narrator attributes or surmises thoughts and behavior that he could not have learned even at a narrative distance of several years. This too suggests that the novel's "accidents" may not be merely unexpected events which narrator Caleb later reports but are instead part of his unconscious manipulation of his world. The next two sections will illuminate how, if *Caleb Williams* is examined in light of the dream mechanisms at work in the novel, both Caleb's repressed homosexuality and the psychic reasons for Collins as narrator in Volume One and Caleb as narrator thereafter become clear.

III

Caleb Williams's texture is that of the superficial rationality of dreams, in which threatening unconscious thoughts undergo preconscious censorship to make them less ominous to the ego. Extremely sensitive material is subjected to a "far-reaching," "tendentious" second censorship, which Freud calls "secondary revision." This second process "fills up the gaps in the dream structure with shreds and patches," so that the dream "approximates to the world of intelligible experience."[21] Fully successful secondary revisions result in dreams which seem "logical and reasonable," arrive at conclusions "caus[ing] no surprise," and possess an "appearance of rationality" which betrays a meaning "as far removed as possible from their true significance." The dream-work produces "absurd dreams and dreams containing absurd elements if it is faced with representing any criticism" in the dream thoughts.[22]

On close reading, *Caleb Williams* proceeds like a dream, full of "irresistible forces" and "mysterious" impulses (188) causing sudden shifts in action and setting. The dreamlike irrationality of *Caleb* is manifested by narrator Caleb's mysterious descriptions of time and place, by the extraordinary number of unexplained "miraculous accidents," and by narrator Caleb's seeming omniscience about others' behavior when he could have no knowledge of their thoughts and actions.

First, although Caleb prays fervently to an absent Collins to preserve his record of events, Caleb is inexplicably ambiguous as to the details for the novel's settings. Why should he be so secretive if he wants his record preserved? Caleb refuses to tell us in what year his contact with Falkland began (4) or how much time elapses between his father's death and his meeting Laura. He vaguely calls it an "intervening period" and says his Welsh respite was followed by "several years" of "dreadful vicissitude and pain" (354). Only his memoir writing served as a "source of avocation" for "some years" (352). He quotes Collins as reporting only that "some years" passed between the time of Falkland's murders and Collins's storytelling. Furthermore, while Caleb does mention his stays in London and Wales, he absurdly conceals the location of the prison, where he and the Hawkinses were kept (253).

The wildly improbable plot leaps and sudden character appearances, most of them connected with Falkland's seeming "omnipresence," reinforce a sense of *Caleb*'s dreamlike quality. Caleb often uses the words "miraculous accident" in relating plot shifts; the number of coincidences is legion: Falkland appears when Caleb's father is on his deathbed (4); he arrives suddenly to save Emily Melville from the burning house (48); his accidental presence in the forest preserves Emily from Grimes's clutches (74); "mere accident had enabled him to return home earlier than expected . . . at a critical moment" to humiliate Tyrell at the county assembly (108); two rustics "accidentally on the spot" identify the Hawkinses as near the murder scene (19); Caleb finds "by some accident" Hawkins's letter to Falkland behind a drawer (131); Falkland enters the blazing manor house room at the moment Caleb pries open the trunk (152); Caleb loses his way to an errand and "by accident" arrives at Forester's (170); "as if he had dropped from the clouds," Falkland materializes at Forester's (172); Caleb wakes at the instant the thieves' old woman is about to knife him (268); she makes an "extraordinary" "disappearance" (270); by a "miraculous accident" Mrs. Marney observes Gines following her and warns Caleb (307); Laura's father writes glowingly about Falkland and Laura prizes the letters (341); as Caleb is about to explain his past to her, Laura repudiates him because she was "informed of it by a mere accident" (348); Collins appears on the road after Caleb has spent several paragraphs musing about him (358).

Caleb describes Falkland as "the eye of omniscience" (354), but narrator Caleb makes many observations that even from a perspective of "some years" later could only be inferred or reconstructed. Gines is the instrument of Falkland's "omniscience," but Caleb seems to know every piece of minutiae about Gines's whereabouts and even thoughts:

> Upon my arrival in town he for a moment lost all trace of me. . . . He went from inn to inn (reasonably supposing that there was no private house to which I could immediately repair) till he found, by a description he gave and the recollections he excited, that I had slept for one night in the borough of Southwark. But he could get no further information. . . .
>
> Having traced me to my second inn, he was here furnished with more copious information. . . . An old woman, of most curious and loquacious disposition . . . who rose early . . . espied me. . . . She thought there was something Jewish about my appearance. . . .
>
> The information thus afforded to Gines appeared exceedingly material. But . . . he could not encounter every private house into which lodgers were ever admitted. . . . He walked the streets, and examined with a curious eye the countenance of every Jew about my stature; but in vain. . . . He was more than once upon the point of giving up pursuit. (304–305)

If Caleb's life, as he muses in Wales, has indeed been a "distempered and tormenting dream" (342), these ambiguities in setting, extraordinary twists of fate and fantastic coincidences, and peculiar narrative omissions and suppositions become understandable as unconscious material arising from the id and forcing their way into the ego. In the id there are no conflicts; contradictions and antitheses exist side by side. The id has no conception of time and knows no values. As a result of the ego's resistance to the id, dreams become distorted, with persons or entities condensed or displaced unrecognizably. Thus Caleb meets characters whom he does not recognize as aspects of himself. In Kleinian terms, the narrative gains coherence when viewed as the processes of a mind in the paranoid-schizoid position, at which point the infant has not yet developed the capacity for "linking and abstraction" and can only engage in "disjointed and concrete thinking."[23] Falkland's providential or calamitous materializations in Caleb's narrative are the shifts of an unconscious mind that recognizes no orderly or sensible progression of events, of a paranoid personality that can engage only in "disjointed" thinking.

Narrator Caleb's oddly eclectic omniscience is a desperate preconscious (or ego) attempt to impose narrative order, which the id overpowers by puncturing the patchwork with manifest improbabilities. Klein explains in *The Psychoanalysis of Children* that one mode of the ego's attempt to master anxiety is to "get the better of the unconscious" by "overemphasizing all that is tangible, visible and perceptible to consciousness."[24] Caleb's occasional "omniscience" (as in the Gines passages), therefore, may be understood as the ego's frenzied overcompensation for narrative gaps.

Klein identifies this anxiety defense as the "homosexual" mode; narrator Caleb's repressed homosexual guilt is evidenced by his displacement of criticisms about his veracity. His characters insistently voice criticisms that he unconsciously knows are true. Forester admires his verbal "dexterity" but ridicules his guarded request for asylum as "a disjointed story with no common sense"; Falkland is stunned by his speechmaking but declares he will be an "imposter" in the world's eyes no matter how "plausible" his tale; Laura admires his "abilities" but cannot "tolerate" his "character" and condemns him though he pleads she has "heard only one side of the story" (347).[25] For although he claims at the trial and elsewhere that he has merely "told a plain and unadulterated tale" (375), Caleb knows unconsciously that he has manipulated content if not form. He must have Collins report and accept full responsibility for Volume One because it contains his most deeply repressed homosexual guilt feelings. But it indeed is the volume most disguised and distorted by secondary revision. Caleb takes Collins's telling of events and in his composition constructs a series of remarkable unconscious identifications which confirm his latent homosexuality and link Volume One with Volumes Two and Three.

At least four individual instances of character identifications between the volumes supposedly written by Collins and Caleb are notable: (1) Emily-Caleb; (2) Hawkins-Caleb; (3) Grimes-Gines; and (4) Tyrrel-Spurrel.[26]

The most significant and revealing link as to Caleb's feelings toward Falkland is his tie to Emily. Both Caleb and Emily are teenage orphans when Falkland enters their lives. Like Caleb, Emily experiences her most intense encounter with Falkland during a fire, in which he saves her from death. While Emily lay in Falkland's arms, Caleb writes, "she lived an age in love" (50). On the other hand, after the Caleb-Falkland trunk confrontation, Falkland rages that he will "always hate" Caleb. Moreover, several of Emily's phrases re-echo from Caleb's lips. "You may imprison my body, but you cannot conquer my mind!" Emily announces to Tyrrel (65). Caleb later rails against Falkland: "I say, he may cut off my existence, but he cannot disturb my serenity" (216). Even Emily's final hallucinations are not of the Falkland she has ever seen, but of the "haggard, ghost-like" Falkland whom Caleb sees at the trial: Emily sees a "mangled corpse" whom she longs to embrace; Caleb beholds "the appearance of a corpse" who "to my infinite astonishment, threw himself into my arms!" (376).

Caleb's identification with the Hawkinses springs from his fascination with their innocence. "Never was a story more affecting!" than the fall of Hawkins and his son, thinks Caleb (124). Just as the Hawkinses have been victimized by Tyrrel and Falkland, Caleb believes he has been wronged by Falkland: "I consulted my own heart, that had nothing to whisper but innocence" (210). At the close of the previous chapter, he had made his emotional link to the Hawkinses explicit: "I was conducted to the same prison which had so lately enclosed the wretched and innocent Hawkinses. They too had been the victims of Mr. Falkland" (204).

Ego resistance can distort not only persons but also words, and given the other identifications within the dream structure, and their roles in Volume One, "Grimes" and "Tyrrel" appear to resonate as "Gines" and "Spurrel." Just as Grimes serves as Tyrrel's loathsome tool to oppress Emily, Gines is Falkland's unyielding instrument for Caleb's persecution. Tyrrel betrays Emily though she regards him as a father; Spurrel hands over Caleb to Gines after asking Caleb to serve as a substitute for his dead son.

Because Collins's raw reportage (with the exception of the Tyrrel trial) is reconstructed through Caleb's mind in the act of writing his mangled tale, these character links may be viewed as unconscious identifications which reveal Caleb's psychic propensity toward homosexuality. He views himself as a victim like Emily and the Hawkinses and as betrayed by Falkland and Spurrel. Caleb unconsciously represses his violent hatred of Falkland, metamorphosing it into Falkland's omnipotence, much as Freud described five-year-old Little Hans as doing because of castration anxiety:

> The instinctual impulse . . . was a hostile one against the father. One might say that impulse had been repressed by the process of being transformed into its opposite. Instead of aggressiveness on the part of the subject towards the father, there appeared aggressiveness (in the shape of revenge) on the part of the father towards the subject.[27]

This cover image for the 1977 Norton paperback edition of *Caleb Williams* was designed by Tim Gaydos. A contemporary American artist residing in New Jersey, Gaydos is a distinguished pastelist and watercolorist who seeks maximum emotional impact by emphasizing simple shapes, bare detail, and strong composition in his paintings. In this image of the young Caleb, Gaydos imagines him hiding in the woods or in a forest. Caleb is covered by leaves, with his eyes darting rightward and head tilted, as if to listen intently for what the posse of pursuers are saying. Only the right side of his face is fully visible before the sunlight, as the vigilantes, rifles in hand, confer as to what direction their manhunt should follow.

Caleb's constant fear of being "crushed" or annihilated by Falkland corresponds to Little Hans's fear of being "devoured" by his father, which "gives expression, in a form that has undergone regressive degradation, to a passive, tender impulse to be loved by him in a genital-erotic sense."[28]

Falkland's sentence of everlasting hatred upon Caleb merely gives rise to more loving feelings by Caleb and his fantasizing of an even more invincible Falkland. Caleb identifies with Emily because, despite Collins's avowals that

Falkland acted from chivalry rather than passion in saving her, Caleb knows she loved him and can rationalize from events that he loved her. As Alex Gold puts it simply, "Caleb wants to be loved the way Emily is loved"—the way that he can romanticize she was loved.[29]

Caleb's alternate "hostile aggressiveness" and "passive tenderness" toward Falkland and his other father figures constitutes the emotional "ambivalence" which Freud considered a defining characteristic of latent homosexuality, in which "in the course of their development from auto-erotism to object choice" persons remain "at a point of fixation between the two."[30] It is therefore inaccurate to consider *Caleb Williams* a laboratory model world of primary narcissism. More precisely, Caleb displays narcissistic object-choice, in which the subject's own ego "is replaced by another one that is as similar as possible."[31] Because this "narcissistic type" prefers homosexual object-choice, it is very close developmentally to primary narcissism:

> Homosexual object-choice originally lies closer to narcissism than does the heterosexual kind. When it is a question, therefore, of repelling an undesirably strong homosexual impulse, the path back to narcissism is made particularly easy.[32]

Thus, Caleb's introjection of part-objects remarkably similar to his own ego marks him as narcissistic, while his homosexuality indicates that he is tending toward object-choice. Caleb is indeed at a "point of fixation between the two." Even the conception of an omniscient Falkland and a relentless Gines corresponds to Freud's observations in "Libido Theory and Narcissism" (1917) that the narcissist's suspicions of constant surveillance are an effort to reinstate primary narcissism:

> The patient is betraying a truth to us which is not yet sufficiently appreciated when he complains that he is spied upon and observed at every step he takes and that every one of his thoughts is reported and criticized. His only mistake is in regarding this uncomfortable power as something alien to him and placing it outside himself. He senses an agency holding sway in his ego which measures his actual ego and each of its activities by an *ideal ego* that he has created . . . with the intention of re-establishing . . . primary infantile narcissism. . . .[33]

As if he were an anguished Narcissus staring into the stream, a dejected Caleb cries out at the novel's close, "Why must my reflections perpetually center upon myself?" (377). The answer is that Caleb is trapped, enclosed in a narcissistic world that is without security, an orphan wanting to hate and to love his fathers—and wanting to be a father. In "Dostoevsky and Parricide," Freud expresses the consequences of repressed hatred toward the father in the Oedipus complex in the formulation: "'You wanted to kill your father in order to be your father yourself. Now you *are* your father, but a dead father'"—and further . . . "'Now your father is killing *you*.'"[34] Caleb's attempt to create a family romance has turned into almost a classic case of *paranoia persecutoria*, which redoubles upon him with Falkland's death:

> The person of the same sex whom the patient loved most had . . . been turned into his persecutor. This made a further development possible: namely the replacement of the beloved person, along the line of familiar resemblances, by someone else—for instance, a father by a schoolmaster or by some superior. Experiences of this kind lead us to conclude that *paranoia persecutoria* is that in which a person is defending himself against a homosexual impulse which has become too powerful.[35]

By the novel's final lines, Caleb is the father, though he is little more than physically alive. As narrator and character, he has triumphed in his Oedipal struggle with Falkland by reducing him to a mere corpse and letting his own shame extinguish the remaining flicker of life. Although he has lost his "mother" Laura to the Falkland she adored, Caleb with his mighty phallic pen finally "stabs Falkland in the very point he was most solicitous to defend!" (365). Caleb "wins" the trial. It is, of course, a Pyrrhic victory.

IV

> This is the empire that man exercises over man! Thus is a being, formed to expatiate [to roam freely], to act, to smile, to enjoy, restricted and benumbed. How great must be his depravity or heedlessness who vindicates this scheme for changing gaiety . . . into the deep furrows of agony and despair! (209)

Domination. Renunciation. Suffering. Caleb's outcries in jail echo the Enlightenment conviction that civilization corrupts pristine human nature. But his anguished protest inevitably raises questions that extend beyond political systems into the realm of psychology and man's instinctual nature. In *Civilization and Its Discontents*, Freud argues that history demonstrates that mankind's struggles center upon "the single task of finding some expedient (i.e., satisfying) solution between individual claims and those of the civilized community."[36] Because community life necessitates the partial renunciation of instinctual gratification, and therefore incites rebellion, "every individual is virtually the enemy of society"[37]—and vice versa. Born to roam freely, to smile, to enjoy, to seek pleasure, we are fettered by the realities of institution and law.

Thus, a psychoanalytic approach to the themes of omnipotence and impotence in *Caleb Williams* is not limited to the conflict of father versus son but also includes the social struggle of master versus servant, squire versus peasant, and society versus individual. For Caleb must contend not only with Lord Falkland but also with a social system of privilege and an unjust Law. The underlying thrust of all Freud's social studies was the "similarity between the process of cultural development and that of the libidinal development in an individual."[38] *Caleb Williams* is doubly structured: just as it enacts narrator/dreamer Caleb's internal psychic battle of id against ego, so it is also a bitter war of pleasure principle against reality principle, in which Caleb's only moments of contentment occur within Laura's family, his brief source of narcissistic satisfaction.

At first glance *Caleb* seems not only a political allegory of *ancien régime* versus new order but also a theological parable. Caleb's thirst for knowledge, the forbidden trunk, Caleb's "soul-ravishing" epiphany in a garden, and Falkland's open claim to possess more might than the "omnipresent God" all fit a transparent archetypal mythopoeia of concupiscence, Garden, apple, Original Sin, Fall, and punishment. Yet this overworked religious symbolism also furnishes the clear basis for a psychosocial treatment of *Caleb* beginning with Freud's phylogenetic explanation of "repressive civilization."

In *Moses and Monotheism* and *Future of an Illusion*, Freud argues that religion springs from "a longing for the father" and "a need for protection" and the beginnings of civilization spring from the murder of the "primal father." This parricide is provoked by the oppression of the father, who achieves total gratification by imposing his iron will on others. In *Caleb Williams* the murderers' conspiracy gives rise to a "primal horde," which negotiates a kind of social contract that inevitably necessitates instinctual renunciation and does not efface the murderers' guilt. The horde is civilization's first cell. It signals both the onset of an irreversible evolution toward security from Nature's domination and the chaos of anarchy and lessening "happiness" from reduced gratification: "recognition of mutual obligations, institutions declared sacred, which could not be broken—in short, the beginnings of morality and law."[39] Religion, in the form of monotheistic rituals of human sacrifice and eating of the fathers, evolves out of the original parricide, with Christianity displacing the parricide by sacrificing the son instead.[40] In social terms, the ambivalence toward the father which fomented rebellion and subsequent guilt remains and grows. Parricide becomes possible when a strong man is confronted by his superior, but community life presupposes "a number of men united together in strength superior to any single individual [and] remain[ing] united against all single individuals."[41] The

The cover illustration of the Oxford World's Classics edition of *Caleb Williams* is a detail from *Self-Portrait* (1794), by Jacques-Louis David (1748–1825). First published as an Oxford World's Classics paperback in 2009, this reprint is edited by Pamela Clemit.

Painted in his jail cell by David shortly following his arrest and imprisonment after Thermidor (2 August 1794) and the fall of Robespierre, the self-portrait depicts a resolute David who looks directly at the viewer. It expresses the middle-aged David's resolve, poise, and calm in the face of adversity. The picture projects David's powerful resilience, as if to predict that he would survive and prevail. Which he did: the artist was released from prison and lived until the ripe old age of seventy-seven.

united body's strength is then proclaimed "Right" and any opposition is "brute force." Revolution therefore entails even greater guilt than for the first assassins because it includes both the overthrow of "Right" and the "archaic heritage" of parricide. Mankind's "memory-traces" of repeatedly reenacted rebellions and parricides resemble the individual's repressed unconscious thoughts. The implications for evaluating civilization are momentous:

> If we assume the survival of these memory-traces in the archaic heritage, we have bridged the gulf between individual and group psychology: we can deal with peoples as we do with an individual neurotic. . . . After this discussion I have no hesitation in declaring that men have always known (in this special way) that they once possessed a primal father and killed him.[42]

The sense of Kafkaesque guilt pervading *Caleb Williams*—a guilt for something one did not do, so much so that it devours even innocents like Emily Melville and the Hawkinses—is deeper than the characters themselves, inherent in the fabric of their civilization. "Things As They Are" is not merely a system of judicial graft or aristocratic depravity; community life oppresses aristocrats like Falkland and Tyrrel just as surely as peasants like Emily, the Hawkinses, and Caleb. The overt difference is merely physical and ultimately a matter of degree rather than kind. Of course, the physical and mental torment for the peasants is effected in the name of "Right" through a perverted legal system: Tyrrel ridicules Hawkins for "gentlemanly" pretensions and persecutes him for not wishing to raise his son as a servant; Falkland rages at his "insolent domestic" Caleb, who is jailed without due process; innocent Brightwel dies in prison without a trial; noble Raymond is compelled to turn to thievery; Caleb is indicted as an Irish robber even though he has no brogue; his efforts to bring Falkland's crimes to light are dismissed contemptuously by magistrates. Yet Caleb's almost saintly private pledge to preserve his integrity and not ruin his respected master by betraying his secret is wrapped in a crippling guilt. Godwin captures Caleb's convulsive trauma in his essay "Of Self-Love and Benevolence":

> The disciple of the theory of self-love, if of a liberal disposition, will perpetually whip himself forward "with loose reins" upon a spiritless Pegasus, and say, "I will do generous things; I will not bring into contempt the master I serve—though I am conscious all the while that this is but a delusion, and that, however I brag of generosity, I do not set a step forward, but singly for my own ends, and my own gratification." (223)

Even before Falkland's trial, Caleb "knows" too he has already murdered him, as in Freud's formulation: "You wanted to kill your father in order to be your father yourself."

Yet even Tyrrel and Falkland are victimized by Society. After Tyrrel's cruel jailing of Emily results in her death, Society brands him "the most diabolical wretch that ever dishonoured human form" (102). Falkland rails against a world that could vilify, as Caleb does, a heroic Alexander: "Detested be the universe, and the laws that govern it. . . . If it were in my power I would instantly crush the whole system into nothing!" (135).

Tyrrel's and Falkland's angst is not explainable simply by the murders they commit; for there is an insidious fatalism in *Caleb Williams* which renders the crimes not only a cause for the aristocrats' suffering but equally a manifestation of the neurotic civilization of "Things As They Are." Over and over again, Falkland and Tyrrel express the thought: "Man's nature is what it is—it cannot be changed." Falkland warns Count Malvesi that had the Italian's affront been public, "it would not have been in my power" to decline the challenge (17). Tyrrel justifies his plan to marry Emily to Grimes with the words "what must be must be" (58), Falkland speaks with Calvinistic omniscience to Caleb: "I know what I am, and what I can be. I know what you are, and what fate is reserved for you!" (330). And Tyrrel rebukes Falkland's effort at reconciliation with quintessential fatalism: "I am neither a philosopher nor poet, to set out on a wild goose chase of making myself a different man from what you find me. As for consequences, what must be must be" (33). Such fatalism directly evokes Freud's conclusion in *Civilization and Its Discontents* that the central problem of man's existence as a social being lies in the "claim to individual freedom against the will of the multitude" and "whether a solution can be arrived at in some particular form of culture or whether the conflict will prove irreconcilable."[43] This is the ultimate question in Freud's cultural works, a level to which Blake alone among Enlightenment thinkers penetrated; Voltaire, Rousseau, and Godwin, with their focus upon institutional vice, never seriously asked whether guilt and evil were not rooted in man's own psyche. As in Blake, the implication of Freud's work is that human improvement is possible only by transforming human nature, not by change in political form. Freud, like Godwin's Tyrrel, was less than optimistic.

Although Godwin's moralism never enabled him to see so deeply as to raise Freud's questions overtly, it is remarkable the extent to which *Caleb Williams* as an anarchist's and utilitarian's "vehicle" does implicitly address Freud's psychosocial preoccupations. Freud's fundamental individual and cultural conclusions sprang from his investigations into how "energy"—instinctual energy—was "applied": to bind into ever-greater unities (Eros, the life instinct) or to loosen and to destroy (Thanatos, the destructive instinct). Caleb too ponders energy "applied" and "misapplied," albeit in a sociopolitical context. He reflects upon the vigor of Captain Raymond's thieves:

> Uninvolved in the debilitating routine of human affairs, they frequently displayed an energy which, from every partial observer, would have extorted veneration. Energy is perhaps of all qualities the most valuable; and a just political system would possess the means of extracting from it . . . its beneficial qualities, instead of consigning it, as now, to indiscrimi-

> nate destruction . . . the energy of these men . . . was in the highest degree misapplied . . . directed only to the most narrow and contemptible purposes. (254)

Of course, the thieves are a small, self-contained community; they consider themselves employed in the "profession of justice" and expel Caleb as a "disgrace to our society" (251). Freud holds that modern civilization cannot do this on a massive scale, and so, like individuals gripped by instinctual tension and deep guilt, civilization writhes as the struggle between Eros and Thanatos mounts:

> It is not really a decisive matter whether one has killed one's father or abstained from the deed; one must feel guilty in either case, for guilt is the expression of the ambivalence, the eternal struggle between Eros and the . . . death instinct. This conflict is engendered as soon as man is confronted with the task of living with his fellows. . . . Since culture obeys an inner erotic impulse which bids it bind mankind in a closely knit mass, it can achieve this aim only by means of its vigilance in fomenting an ever-increasing sense of guilt. That which began in relation to the father ends in relation to the community.[44]

In *Caleb Williams* one may therefore witness a schematized (and admittedly reductive) psychic duel played out between the id's instinctual impulses and the ego's reality principle until the destructive end. The novel's mediating reality principle is the poet Clare. Once he dies, the onslaught between Eros and Thanatos rockets out of control. Volume One pits honor against pride. Whereas Falkland's obsessive honor (his "love of fame") is an "attraction" force that seeks to draw others to him, Tyrrel's manic pride is largely concerned with "unknotting" and destroying opposing wills: in these respects they broadly correlate to the pleasure principle and the death instinct of pre-Freudian faculty psychology. Volumes Two and Three pit curiosity against vengeance (the drama of Forester's pitiless justice and Falkland's offended honor turning vindictive). Inasmuch as Caleb's insatiable curiosity, his "thirst for knowledge," is a pleasure-seeking principle, he is Eros; because Forester's iron impartiality and Falkland's vindictiveness seek to reduce Caleb (to "crush" him) and they gain no real pleasure from it, they are Thanatos.

Clare is described by Collins as "the great operative check" upon "the excesses of Mr. Tyrrel": "This rustic tyrant had been held in involuntary restraint by the intellectual ascendancy of his celebrated neighbor" (41). Clare "dispose[s] [Tyrrel] to submission" and "the conduct of Mr. Tyrrel had even shown tokens of improvement since Mr. Clare's residence in his neighborhood" (42). The poet also warns Falkland about his "impetuosity" and "imagined dishonour," concluding, "I would have you governed by justice and reason." Falkland replies, "I will behave better" (39).

Clare's death unleashes an escalating cycle of vengeance that leads from Volume One to the novel's close. As Caleb mourns: "And because they regarded each other with a deadly hatred, I have become an object of misery and abhorrence" (21). Clare had been the one person "who could have most effectively moderated the animosities of the contending parties" (41). With the ego gone (and the novel is without a superego force), the id's demolition duel commences. Falkland's honor is a cancer that feeds on itself, and Tyrrel's pride is unconquerable. Falkland's years abroad bring regularly "some fresh accession to the estimation in which he was held, as well as his own impatience of stain or dishonour" (18). By the end of Volume One, he is the "fool of honor":

> a man whom, in the pursuit of reputation, nothing could divert; who would have purchased the character of a true, gallant, undaunted hero at the expense of worlds. . . . (117–118)

Spoiled by his mother since infancy, Tyrrel believes "everything must give way to his accommodation and advantage; every one must pay the most servile obedience to his commands" (19). He sets out to "destroy the prospects of a man . . . eminently qualified to enjoy and communicate happiness" (21). And from the "moment" that Hawkins tells his master that he would prefer his son not become a servant, "Mr. Tyrrel was bent upon Hawkins's destruction" (83).

The impulses in the succeeding volumes are equally unquenchable. Caleb notes that his curiosity is a "restless propensity," which "does but hurry [one] forward the more irresistibly the greater is the danger that attends its indulgence" (130). By Volume Two, Falkland's obsession has turned psychotic: "Miserable wretch! . . . I love [my reputation] more than the whole world and its inhabitants taken together!" (178–179). And Forester in his severe justice "overlooks the sensibility of the sufferer and the pains he inflicts" (161).

In a deeper sense, of course, Falkland and Caleb are not destroyed by Tyrrel or Forester, or even by each other. Their false gods, knowledge and fame, contain the seeds of their own destruction. Freud in this respect reached a similar conclusion with the Nirvana principle in *Beyond the Pleasure Principle*, in which he considered Eros and Thanatos alike in their mutual tendency toward relaxation of tension:

> The dominating tendency of mental life, and perhaps nervous life in general, is the effort to reduce, to keep constant or to remove internal tension due to stimuli (the "Nirvana Principle" . . .)—a tendency which finds expression in the pleasure principle; and our recognition of that

fact is one of our strongest reasons for believing in the existence of the death instincts.[45]

In *Beyond the Pleasure Principle* Freud therefore postulates that the pleasure principle is actually serving the destructive instincts, with Eros and Thanatos both existing as forms of the more fundamental Nirvana principle. Freud here shifts his focus from "applied" versus "misapplied" energy, or binding versus loosening, and suggests instead that one energy principle is basic to mental functioning in opposition to the reality principle. In that they are explicitly described as driven toward the elimination of excitation, Caleb's curiosity and Tyrrel's pride—identified with Eros and Thanatos respectively—may likewise be subsumed under the concept of the Nirvana principle. Caleb's description of the nature of curiosity and his passion for it are expressed in language that virtually echoes Freud's *Beyond the Pleasure Principle*:

> Curiosity is a principle that carries its pleasures, as well as its pains, along with it. The mind is urged by a perpetual stimulus; it seems as if it were continually approaching to the end of its race; and as the insatiable desire of satisfaction is its principle of conduct, so it promises itself in that satisfaction an unknown gratification, which seems as if it were capable of fully compensating any injuries that may be suffered in the career. (142)

> I panted for the unraveling of an adventure, with an anxiety perhaps almost equal to that of the man whose future happiness or misery depended on the issue. I read, I devoured compositions of this sort . . . my imagination must be excited; and, when that was done, my curiosity was dormant. (4)

Similarly, Tyrrel has an almost sadistic "compulsion to repeat" persecution:

> When he had once formed a determination, however slight, in favour of any measure, he was never afterwards known to give it up . . . the only effect of opposition was to make him eager and inflexible, in pursuit of that to which he had before been nearly indifferent. (79)

> It has been my character, when I had once conceived a scheme of vengeance, never to forego it; and I will not change that character. (88)

In the final analysis, does a psychoanalytic approach to *Caleb Williams* mean that "what must be" must be, that things are as they are? Herbert Marcuse in

Eros and Civilization argues that twentieth-century Western civilization has advanced to the stage at which technology can eliminate *Anake* (scarcity), which "provide[s] the rationale for the repressive reality principle" (137).[16] Technology has the potential to abolish the social demand for domination based on economic scarcity and therefore the need for repressive labor. Energy devoted to maintaining domination is then freed, permitting the development of a nonrepressive libido.

Of course, whether or not Marcuse's vision is well grounded theoretically, eighteenth-century England had not progressed industrially even to the point of satisfying its citizens' minimal needs. The characters in *Caleb Williams* voice their hope for ultimate human happiness via three different paths. Clare and Brightwel present the first possibility. On his deathbed Clare speaks of the "prospect of human improvement" (38), and Brightwel in jail delights in the thought that "the time would come when the possibility of such intolerable oppression would be extirpated" (221). Clare admits that the last half of his days have been lived in a "perfect" "serenity" (38); Brightwel believes he has "discharged his duty" and, although he dies with disappointments, "never was despair more calm, more full of resignation and serenity" (21). Clare and Brightwel typify Freud's classic example of "aim-inhibited" love, Francis of Assisi, for they too "direct their love, not to single objects, but to all men alike":

> These people make themselves independent of their object's acquiescence by displacing what they mainly value from being loved on to loving; they protect themselves against the loss of the object . . . and avoid the uncertainties and disappointments of genital love by turning away from its sexual aims and transforming the instinct into an impulse with an *inhibited aim*. What they bring about in themselves is a state of evenly suspended, steadfast, affectionate feeling.[47]

A second solution in the novel, also a form of aim-inhibited love, is faith in the perfectibility of the next world. Raymond's words imply his trust in religious salvation and belief in heaven. After Caleb forcefully convinces him of the injustice of his thievery, Raymond laments:

> Alas! Williams . . . it would have been fortunate for me, if these views had been presented to me previously. . . . It is now too late. Those very laws which, by a perception of their iniquity, drove me to what I am, now preclude my return. God, we are told, judges all men by what they are at the period of arraignment, and whatever their crimes, if they have seen and abjured the folly of those crimes, receives them to favour. But the institutions of countries that profess to worship this God admit

> no such distinctions. They leave no room for amendment, and seem to have a brutal delight in confounding the merits of offenders. . . . How changed, how spotless, how useful avails him nothing. . . . Am I not compelled to go on in folly, having once begun? (264–265)

Freud noted that religion was often used as a substitute fulfillment for the gratifications of the pleasure principle. Religion was an "illusion"; in fact, aim-inhibited love itself was deficient: "A love that does not discriminate seems to me to forfeit a part of its own value, by doing an injustice to its object."[48]

Caleb, if not Godwin, seems to reject both solutions as unworkable for him. He chooses upon Brightwel's death to pursue a life of "benevolence in a narrow circle" (222), presumably within the small community. Indeed his only period of brief happiness (in adulthood) is in the Denison family, where he was treated "as if I had been one of the family, and I sometimes flattered myself that I might one day become such in reality" (339). Caleb's unconsciously incestuous desires toward maternal Laura notwithstanding, he develops with the Denisons a deep intimacy, a "growing friendship" that is more than a "suspended, steadfast, affectionate feeling." Freud called family life "modified aim-inhibited affection" and thought it preserved (even without sexual intercourse) a measure of sensual love.[49] He also considered it possible that larger communities could live happily together based on the concept of a "narcissism of minor differences." People can "bind together" "in love" in fairly large numbers "so long as there are other people left over to receive the manifestations of their aggressiveness": the differences can be national, ethnic, religious, gender, occupational, or otherwise.[50] National differences seem to mollify the peasantry in *Caleb*'s England, who think like Caleb that Britain has nothing resembling the Bastille (209) and believe, like the servant Thomas, that prisoners chained and without beds "never happen but in France, and other countries the like of that" (233).

Sigmund Freud in his cultural treatises and William Godwin in *Caleb Williams* seem to hold faint hope that human civilization can exist on a worldwide scale without victims to oppress. Nor do they anticipate that neighbors can be both fully human and live peaceably together as social beings. Marcuse's revisionist theoretical project of a nonrepressive civilization may indeed lie within sight, but for Godwin—and for us today—the great challenge remains Freud's in the final paragraph of *Civilization and Its Discontents*:

> The fateful question for the human species seems to me to be whether and to what extent their cultural development will succeed in mastering the disturbance of their communal life by the human instinct of aggression and self destruction.[51]

And although Godwin never penetrated to the question's core with Freud's incisiveness and brilliance, it would be denying the philosopher his due to overlook that exactly a century earlier he directly addressed the subject's moral correlative:

> It is a thing deeply to be regretted that . . . man will frequently be compelled to devote himself to pursuits comparatively vulgar and inglorious because he must live. . . . The life of such a man is divided between the things which his internal monitor strongly prompts him to do, and those which external power of nature and circumstances compel him to submit to.[52]

This photograph of the author of *The Mayor of Casterbridge* was taken during his forties around the time that he was working on the novel. It is undated, but it was published widely, including in the U.S., and is presently part of the Bain Collection at the Library of Congress in Washington.

CHAPTER THREE

Hardy's The Mayor of Casterbridge

THE INFERNAL TRIANGLE

It seems that he had also set to work on the Agamemnon *and the* Oedipus. . . . *He had secretly wished that [his Casterbridge friend Horace] Moule would advise him to go on with the Greek plays, in spite of the severe damage it might do [to his planned architectural career]. . . . He did take up one or two of the dramatists years later, but in a fragmentary way only.*

FLORENCE HARDY, *THE EARLY LIFE OF THOMAS HARDY*

I

Young Thomas's "secret wish" to "go on" with Greek drama was never truly abandoned. Its ultimate fulfillment constituted much more than a fragmentary avocation, for unlike hapless Jude Tillotson in *Jude the Obscure* (1895), Hardy's reluctant boyhood renunciation of his Greek studies did not prevent him from achieving rich creative expression of his classical and dramatic interests. One critic has in fact argued that Hardy utterly mastered classical versions of Aeschylean, Sophoclean, and Euripidean tragedy,[1] so that he fully justified Swinburne's praise as "the most tragic of authors."[2] Hardy's most powerful tragic novel, written a quarter century after "forsaking" his classical pursuits, is usually considered to be *The Mayor of Casterbridge*, called by critics "a modern *Oedipus*,"[3] "unmistakably similar to *Oedipus Rex*."[4] The novel has also received detailed comparison with other Greek and Shakespearean tragedies.[5]

The Mayor opens in an apparently archetypal setting on "a road neither straight nor crooked, neither level nor hilly," within a "scene [that] might have been matched in almost any spot in any county in England at that time of year"

(11).[6] The scene depicts a lonely, silent trio of laborer, wife, and baby trudging along through Upper Wessex toward the large village of Weydon-Priors. This gripping image of the trio's weary march has provoked readers to view the scene in religious terms as the exhausted plodding of the Holy Family; in anthropological terms as the mute, ritualized procession of the primal horde toward civilization; and in Marxist or sociological terms as the incarnate transition from oppressed feudal laborers to exploited capitalist victims. The figure of the triangle frames this archetypal scene. The family trio's "stable" triangle of Michael Henchard, wife Susan, and baby quickly collapses when a new "triangle of confrontation" intervenes: Henchard, Susan, and Newson. But the crisis of collision and breakdown is momentary and clearly resolved. A new family triangle of Newson, Susan, and baby emerges. This progress of family triangles developing swiftly into acute crises of triangular conflict and then suddenly dissolving altogether, only to be immediately restructured into new family triangles, forms the fundamental structural patterning of the novel. As we shall see, *The Mayor of Casterbridge* is a series of interlocking, potentially explosive and self-destructive triangles involving Henchard, Susan, baby Elizabeth-Jane, Newson, mature Elizabeth-Jane, Lucetta Templeman, and Donald Farfrae.

The original triangle of desire is, of course, the Oedipal triangle, and the oft-discussed characterization of *The Mayor* as "a modern Oedipus"—not to mention the suggestive references to Hardy's "repressed" boyhood "wishes" about Greek drama—obviously invite an examination of *The Mayor* as a series of Oedipal triangles. Such a reading would serve as a contribution to the excellent scholarship devoted to the psychology of Hardy's life and art, especially the growing tendency to approach the author in autobiographical and/or Freudian terms, with the complex, multifaceted characters populating his rich fictional works probed to uncover the dearth of information about his very private life.[7] For example, critics have used *Jude the Obscure,* along with both Hardy's love poetry and novels such as *A Pair of Blue Eyes,* to "reconstruct," as J. Hillis Miller phrases it, "[the major] hidden episode of Hardy's life," his alleged love affair with his cousin Tryphena Sparks. The exact nature of his relationship with his wife Emma Gifford has also been widely considered.[8] Following Miller's classic statements that "love is Hardy's urgent theme"[9] and that "he was recurrently driven to enact in his own life a drama like that in his fiction and poetry,"[10] an interpretation of *The Mayor* as the agonized baring of Hardy's guarded personal life is plausible. On this reading, the relationships among Henchard, Farfrae, and their women can be understood as a veiled portrait of Hardy's own tormented inner selves struggling to find expression. More explicitly, they can be read as the story of his real-life triangle with Emma and Tryphena, a plot driven by a divided nature that alternately led him to shifting, Oedipally grounded, divided loves.

Such an oedipal reading of *The Mayor* overlooks at least one fundamental paradox: this sublime novel by Hardy, the preeminent tragedian of romantic love, is not a love story at all. *The Mayor* is "unique," as F. B. Pinion observes, "in its town setting, the long-drawn conflict between two men, the subordination of the love element and its presentation of a hero of dynamic and explosive personality."[11]

No, the novel is not a "love story," but rather a "war story." It is ultimately far more a chronicle of rivalry than romance, and its featured pairing involves not male-female intimacy but rather male-male bonding. Of course, "love" triangles often possess bellicose sides or a martial axis; what is so distinctive and compelling about *The Mayor* is how Hardy interweaves and reconfigures romance (and women) as he spotlights male competitiveness and combativeness.

The uniqueness of *The Mayor* points us back to its opening triangular scene and forward to its closing triangular scene of Newson, Farfrae, and Elizabeth-Jane, for whom a dead Henchard shortly thereafter only reaffirms the "teach[ing] that happiness was but the occasional episode in a general drama of pain" (327). These opening and closing scenes represent, as it were, the rising and falling curtains on Hardy's tragedy, a tragedy of happiness and pain, of triangulated families and strangers, and of the ever-recurring Hardyean battle between Nature and Civilization. The novel's dynamic energy and absorbing readability are fueled by its spasmodic, erupting alternations between the individual and the social, the personal and the communal, which derive less from the male-female relationships than from the rising tensions between Henchard and Farfrae, Lucetta and Elizabeth-Jane, and (obliquely) Henchard and Newson.

These narrative attributes represent the guiding force behind this chapter's central claim: the novel's pervasive triangular patterning finds the women (or men, or material possessions) not as objects desired for themselves, but rather as objects of contention in a power struggle between the men (or women). As we shall see, *The Mayor*'s dramatic action proceeds by what Hardy once termed (in an explicit reference to *Tess of the D'Urbervilles*) a "ritual of succession," with characters participating in "a shifting of positions" that "often began in sentiment—and such sentiment begins . . . a novel."[12] I contend that Hardy's magnificent "Oedipal" novel enacts a similar design, advancing by seemingly inexorable succession rituals as the seeds of "sentiment" lead abruptly to position shifting and thereupon to impetuous rivalries, precipitous supplantings, and renewed battles for dominance. But the arresting fact is that the "desired" objects of the power struggles are *not* really desired by the rivals—that is, not for themselves, but rather only for what they represent.

Envy, not desire per se, governs the rivalry patterns. Each rival's ever-heightening desire as Self is to imitate what the Other possesses, finally leading to fatal conflict, which represents the psychosocial pattern of "mimetic desire" and "conflictual imitation" in René Girard's provocative reformulation of Sigmund Freud's theory of the Oedipus complex.[13] Indeed, with this pattern of mimetic conflict in mind, I might have alternately entitled this chapter: "That Obscure Imitation of Desire." Moreover, because Hardy explicitly structures the plot of *The Mayor* in terms of successive shifts of role and status, Girard's ritual-based, ethnological-anthropological theories about the relations among violence, the sacred, and mimetic or "substitutive" desire prove revealing. They illuminate the fundamental psychodynamics of *The Mayor,* showing how Hardy's ritualized narrative functions: how its "musical chairs" plot[14] structures and de-structures the novel's advance.[15]

These distinctions recast Hardy's great tragic novel as a truly "modern" *Oedipus.* For *The Mayor of Casterbridge* is a series of conflictual triangles, not Oedipal triangles. Rather than display object desire as described in the traditional, fully developed Freudian model of the incest-patricide triangle, *The Mayor*'s characters exhibit imitative desire. To have or not to have: that is the question for them. According to Girard, human beings hold one darkest and best-concealed wish: we want what we want because others possess it. And when our wishes converge on the same object, as they inevitably do when we create "models," our loved exemplars turn to hated rivals.

II

The forms of rivalry in which Hardy's characters in *The Mayor* engage are a series of "infernal triangles," whereby desire repeatedly explodes and metastasizes, spreading like wildfire though invariably manifesting itself in patterns of triangular conflict that recur in and shape the action of *The Mayor.* This psychosocial interpretation of *The Mayor*'s unfolding entails a close textual rereading that attends to its architectonics.[16] My intent is not, therefore, to draw parallels between Hardy's biography and fiction or to investigate *The Mayor* as a projection of the author's Oedipal fantasies. My view is that the novel is not chiefly a tragedy of Thomas Hardy or of the social destruction of the English corn merchant. Rather, as has so often been stated—yet only casually accepted, not thoroughly explored—*The Mayor* is indeed "a modern *Oedipus.*" Despite the repeated comparisons of *The Mayor* to *Oedipus Rex, Hamlet, Lear,* and other tragedies with triangular patterning—and notwithstanding Miller's perceptive remark that the novel is "remarkably well-structured"[17]—no sustained attempt has yet been made to describe that structure in detail and explain its shifting nature.[18] I contend that the triangles are the key to *The Mayor* both as a modern *Oedipus* and to its intricately patterned structure.

My aim is thus to demonstrate just how apt are the casual comparisons of

The Mayor to classical tragedy: it is indeed a five-act tragedy in the form of a novel. Each act's ending climaxes in a conflictual triangle, which immediately demolishes the existing triangle and resolves itself into a new "marriage" or family triangle. The bulk of the novel is therefore "a general drama of pain"—with the family or legal triangles associated with boredom, drudgery, and suffering. The moments of "happiness" in the drama consist of fragile, often terrifying romantic triangles, each of which promises excitement and hope, and yet which—because they threaten to obliterate the mundane and familiar—also provokes anxiety and dread.[19] Not only the love triangles but also the legal triangles, however, are at base conflictual and inherently unstable—the family triangles are not simply destroyed from without by apocalyptic confrontational triangles. They also contain within themselves the seeds of their own destruction.

Was such a careful triangular structure a matter of conscious design by the erstwhile architectural apprentice? Biographical critics might profitably investigate this possibility, which lies outside the scope of this chapter. It warrants notice, however, that *The Mayor*'s self-consuming triangular structure is drawn with the precision of a skilled craftsman. It is almost geometrically symmetrical, with the first and last "acts" and the middle three "acts" each containing the same number of chapters, respectively.[20] Each confrontational triangle is provoked by the appearance of an intruder from the outside or a character's disappearance (or death). These intrusions and withdrawals therefore constitute the triggers for the collapse and reshaping of the legal and love triangles, the latter of which may be said to punctuate the former, much as a wave finally breaks after continued undulation, only to begin fluttering and cresting immediately again. The central scene in each act also concerns the keeping or revelation of a secret and changes its setting in a fitting chronicle of Henchard's progressive degeneration.

Let us briefly summarize the flow of Hardy's tragic novel in terms of its dramatic structure. Act I (chapters i–ii) opens with the Henchard-Susan-baby triangle and climaxes with Newson's entrance, creating the Newson-Henchard confrontation over Susan. Act II (chapters iii–xv) begins with the broken triangle of Susan, mature Elizabeth-Jane, and the presumed-dead Newson—although Susan is already coming to realize that her actual husband and proper third in the triangle is Henchard. Confrontations about love and work follow, with the veiled triangle of Susan-Henchard-Lucetta never quite surfacing to bring the two female rivals together; but the Henchard-Farfrae friendship turns to rivalry for respect and authority, exploding at the close (chapter xv) with the Abel Whittle incident.

Act III (chapters xvi–xxx) opens with the family triangle of Henchard, Susan, and Elizabeth-Jane. With Susan's death, both Henchard and Elizabeth-Jane become linked to new triangles, with Henchard vying with Farfrae for Lucetta and Elizabeth-Jane competing with Lucetta for Farfrae. Meanwhile the Henchard-Farfrae work rivalry escalates, with property and community reputation becoming the triangle's third. The act culminates in Henchard's rescue of Elizabeth-Jane and Lucetta from the charging bull, after which the Henchard-Lucetta confrontation unveils Lucetta's secret marriage and the Lucetta–Elizabeth-Jane confrontation ends with a broken Farfrae family triangle.

Act IV (chapters xxxi–xliii) begins with the Farfraes, Elizabeth-Jane, and Henchard all living apart. With Lucetta's death, Elizabeth-Jane and Henchard establish a "filial" couple and the Henchard-Farfrae–Elizabeth-Jane triangle reforms, this time with heightened intensity because of Henchard's desperate dependence upon his "daughter." With Newson's second reentrance in Act IV, the Henchard–Elizabeth-Jane coupling is severed, with Henchard fleeing to avoid a direct confrontation. The final family triangle of Newson-Farfrae–Elizabeth-Jane is now on the horizon.

In Act V (chapters xliv-xlv) this triangle is cemented legally in the marriage of Donald and Elizabeth-Jane. And just as the wedding links the remaining protagonists in a final family trio, Henchard's death prevents the attempted formation of a new and reconciled family triangle with Elizabeth-Jane and Farfrae—Henchard dies just thirty minutes before the newlyweds arrive at the Egdon Heath cottage. But Henchard had been lovingly cared for by Abel Whittle, who takes pains to explain to the Farfraes that he nursed the old mayor. So Henchard is ultimately joined in affectionate familial bonds with a former antagonist—and within an intimate triangle—after all.

Scholars have criticized *The Mayor* as overpowering yet artistically and stylistically inept, with Hardy's prose jagged and wooden, with its "unbalanced" plot containing more than twice the number of incidents in its second half than its first half, and with the scenes of its closing chapters hastily concluded and too loosely connected.[21] *The Mayor*'s style, narrative development, and plot movement gain coherence, however, if we grant their *psycho*-logical verisimilitude, that is, if we grant that they ricochet across the wildfire of rising compulsions that periodically sweep through the novel. Or to phrase it more pointedly: if we view the cascading pattern of progressions, regressions, and (apparent) digressions as motored by the pyrotechnics of Girard's imitative desire, then Hardy's alleged clumsiness instead emerges as a writer's deeper, intuitive understanding of narrative psychodynamics and social reality.

Just as the novel's dramatic structure is geometrically proportionate to chapter length, its narrative line escalates geometrically, stoked by the bursting conflagration of imitative desire and conflict. *The Mayor*'s leaps in plot and tone and its unforeseen reversals are products of a "mimetic crisis" that characteristically advances (in Girard's description) "with increasing speed," engendering a feeling of "vertigo" in which plot reversals "keep shifting around at a constantly accelerating tempo."[22] Simply put, two geometric figures direct *The Mayor's* development and lead to a symmetrical dramatic structure (with a confrontational triangle climaxing each "act"): the shifting triangle mirrors the characters' ambivalent relationships; the accelerating vertical line represents the quickening plot movement. Both figures operate in tandem to chart Henchard's hastening decline and Farfrae's meteoric rise. The accelerating plot line is located within the structure of triangular desire and is itself the explosive catalyst for each triangle's collapse and reshaping, and thus also for the narrative's relentless onward death march.

Yet before chronicling this "war story" as the five-act tragedy of a "modern Oedipus" caught in triangular desire, Girard's stimulating revisionist view of *Oedipus Rex* and of Freud's theory of the Oedipus complex requires explanation. Girard's approach is a bold and comprehensive one. For our purposes in this chapter, Girard's concepts of mimetic desire and rivalry, generative violence, and unanimous victimage are central. Such an examination of Girard's mimetic insights casts light not only on *The Mayor's* structure, development, and tempo. It also illumines the nature of Hardy's novels as classical tragedies and his inveterate preoccupation with the conflict between religion and society, whose tensions permeate the ubiquitous Hardyean motifs of "Nature" and "Civilization" in what Ian Gregor has termed "The Great Web" of Hardy's fiction.[23]

III

> The instinct of imitation is implanted in man from childhood, one difference between him and other animals being that he is the most imitative of living creatures, and through imitation he learns his earliest lessons . . .
>
> ARISTOTLE, *THE POETICS*

The work of René Girard posits a concept of imitation that takes literature as its point of departure yet crisscrosses numerous disciplines. Girardian criticism is wide-ranging, integrative, and often eclectic, making extended forays into psychoanalysis (Freud, Lacan), anthropology (Lévi-Strauss, Victor Turner, Lévy-Bruhl, Frazer, Malinowski), sociology (Weber, Durkheim), classical philosophy (Plato, Aristotle), history, and literary theory. From his early, chiefly literary studies (*Deceit, Desire, and the Novel*)[24] to his subsequent ethnologically oriented works (*Violence and the Sacred*[25] and *To Double Business Bound*[26]) to his later, prolific period of writings (on topics including ritual killing,[27] the psychopolitics of envy,[28] and the "laws" of rivalry and desire[29]),

Girard has challenged several major contemporary thinkers and appropriated their ideas into his own theoretical project. That project is the systematic exploration of the dynamics of imitative or "mimetic" desire—a quest that he refuses to limit conveniently to any single discipline because the dynamics of mimetic desire, maintains Girard, govern all cultural phenomena. As we shall see, Girard views "the scapegoat ritual" as the generative principle of ritual, primitive religion, and "even culture as a whole." For Girard, "the immolation of victims" represents "the fundamental ritual action," whose investigation "cannot fail to be interdisciplinary." Girard adds: "I am not a specialist of ritual. I was not trained as an anthropologist, but as a historian." Yet he insists that the burden of proof rests with the specialists, whose academic fields limit their vision and imagination: "The attitude that needs justifying" is any sort that opposes his purportedly "excessive" interdisciplinary approach.[30]

Girard aims to shatter "the dearest of all our illusions, the intimate conviction that our desires are really our own, that they are original and spontaneous."[31] We are unaware of mimetic desire in our own striving. Girard claims this blindness explains the traditional incapacity of theorists of imitation—in classics ranging from Aristotle's *Poetics* to Auerbach's *Mimesis*—to show how *mimesis* functions as secondhand, destructive desire. The classics of literary theory have described only one side of *mimesis*: its aesthetic, edifying facet. They have seen it as exclusively positive, as the imitation of ancient masterpieces or as "true-to-life" social reality, failing thereby to perceive its divisive, negative dimension: its pathological dynamic of scarcity, appropriation, and conflict. As Girard writes: "When any gesture of appropriation is imitated, it simply means that two hands will reach for the same object simultaneously: conflict cannot fail to result."[32]

Our collective hallucination that *mimesis* possesses exclusively a noble, constructive, "true" nature arises, according to Girard, not only from our need to cling to the illusion of autonomous desire, but also from our misreadings of the lessons of the literary masterworks. The historical emphasis upon *mimesis* has been correct; literary historians and theorists, however, have taken a Bloomian swerve or *askesis*. Or, as Girard describes it:

> The enormous emphasis on mimesis throughout the entire history of Western literature cannot be a mere mistake; there must be some deep-seated reason for it that has never been explained. I personally believe that the great masterpieces . . . , primarily the dramas and the novels, really are 'more mimetic' in . . . that they portray human relations and desire as mimetic, and . . . reintroduce into their so-called fictions that conflictual dimension always eliminated from the theoretical definitions of this "faculty."[33]

Girard therefore advocates that "instead of interpreting the great masterpieces in the light of modern theories," thinkers should "criticize modern theories in light of these masterpieces"[34]—works such as the major Greek tragedies, the *Divine Comedy*, Shakespeare's great tragedies and comedies, some prose fiction by Flaubert, Stendhal, Dostoyevsky, and a few select others.[35]

What "laws" of *mimesis* do the masterworks reveal? That *mimesis* possesses two "sides," "one that disrupts the community and another one that holds it together." Mimetic desire is triangular. It moves from the Self's acts of admiration and desire—exemplified by its assumption of a "model" or "mediator" for its "goal" or "object of desire"—to conflict when the Other as model forbids possession of the same object. The Other then quickly turns from model to "rival," and antagonism grows. As the rivals become more and more alike in their desires, possessions, and even selves, conflictual, destructive mimetic rivalry escalates. They approach, though never fully achieve, complete "undifferentiation." Destructive *mimesis* soon infects more than just the rival pair, extending into their community and finally exploding from mere reciprocal violence into "generative violence"—e.g., Paris's competition for Helen becomes the Trojan-Greek war. Finally, as so many trial myths and rituals effectively attest, generative violence can only be ended by the process of "unanimous victimage," in which the community arbitrarily selects a scapegoat or "surrogate victim." This victim "dies so that the entire community, threatened by the same rate, can be reborn in a new or renewed cultural order. . . . In so doing he bestows a new life on men."[36] This is the violence at the heart of the sacred.

The victim's *arbitrary* selection is a key Girardian point. For Girard's mimetic investigations, unlike those of Plato and Hegel, do not begin with the human species but at "the more primitive level of appropriation common to all primates." Conflictual *mimesis* prevails throughout the animal kingdom, but the "braking mechanisms" of animals are instinctive, a form of species programming "installed," as it were, within each individual creature. Animals of the same species never fight to the death. But because humankind lacks this protective biological mechanism, we substitute the "collective, cultural mechanism of the surrogate victim."[37] The scapegoat's arbitrary selection by lottery or enshrined ritual enables the community to avoid guilt and the certainty of continued retribution. Whether king or young warrior or virginal maiden, says Girard, the victim is really an arbitrary choice, the result of fickle Fate that rules the ritualistic mind.

I dwell at length on the surrogate victim's impersonal status not only because it is the hidden, root fact underlying Girard's mimetic and unanimous victimage theories, but also because it undergirds Girard's trenchant critique of Freud's theories of the "primal horde" and Oedipus complex.

Freud advances the "primal horde" theory, despite its heuristic weakness and even obtrusiveness, claims Girard, because the idea focuses the collective murder on the father figure and preserves the "precious axioms of psychoanalysis": the incest-patricide model of the Oedipus complex. Girard's examination of Freud's early and late work on the Oedipus complex reveals a subtle, decisive, yet unacknowledged shift away from *mimesis* toward object desire—in the very same way that Freud went on to privilege the primal horde hypothesis over the collective murder theory in his later works. In *Group Psychology and the Analysis of the Ego* (1921), Freud locates the boy's *identification* with the father as anterior to his sexual cathexis toward the mother. But in *The Ego and the Id* (1923), he inverts this order and, while not explicitly repudiating the earlier view, stresses the boy's maternal attraction and his father as *rival* only, not model. Girard judges that Freud ultimately dropped both identification and the mimetic theory from his later work because he sensed their incompatibility with a theory of object desire.[38] Girard speculates that Freud chose cathectic desire to preserve the force of both his patricide-incest drive and Oedipal insights, reserving the mimetic drive for the sphere of the superego.

Pace Freud, Girard insists his own mimetic reformulation of the Oedipus complex is superior in economy and precision to the cumbersome cathectic Freudian model. According to Girard, the father turns from venerated model to hated rival, with the desired mother an object of contention and the dispute leading to reciprocal violence and death. Girard's explanation claims at least three advantages over Freud's: it eliminates any subsequent necessity to repress desire; it banishes the unconscious as it resolves Freud's awkward "ambivalence" or "double-bind" concept through the mimetic mechanism; and it unites, in cooperation with the mimetic mechanism, the model-rival Freudian split, which Freud separates and divides into two distinct psychic structures, the superego and the differentiated id.[39]

Ironically, although Girard "rivals" Freud in the near-megalomania of his rhetoric, I find his concepts of the arbitrary victimage mechanism and mimetic desire compelling and his overall revision of Freud's genetic hypotheses of culture and the Oedipus complex persuasive. Girard proceeds in these critiques first by explicating select literary masterworks, and our presentation of his work now equips us to appreciate the direct relevance of insights he gleaned from them for our argument about *The Mayor.*

Girard's major examples are taken from Greek tragedy, particularly Sophocles's *Oedipus Rex*. Tragedy for Girard is the "least tendentious" of mythic forms because it "partially deciphers" the mythological disguises. It "desymbolizes" myth and ritual, yet in gaining historical and social verisimilitude, tragedy necessarily also enters the field of progressive differentiation—thereby obscuring patterns of emblematic import. Whereas myth trafficks in monsters and twins, tragedy is populated by villains and enemy brothers. The latter's gain in social reality entails a corresponding loss of symbolic value. In the dynamics of mimetic desire and rivalry, this means an increase (as in substituting brothers for twins) in surface differences — and a departure from the mimetic mechanism's process of continued undifferentiation.

Oedipus Rex participates in the differentiating by foregrounding three male characters who appear strikingly "individualized." We admire Oedipus for his "noble serenity"[40] yet also witness his angry outbursts against Tiresias and Creon. But then, Girard notes, we observe the same alternation of calm and anger in Tiresias and Creon themselves. Soon all three characters see themselves above the rising conflict, want to assume the roles of judge and arbiter, and rage when their prestige is challenged. The mounting violence is symmetrical and reciprocal, and as each character is unwittingly drawn into the violent matrix, their differences grow dimmer and dimmer. The murder of Laius and the incest are transformed into a series of mutual recriminations, with Oedipus and Tiresias each attempting to blame the city's plague on the other. The reciprocal violence merely reflects how the generative violence (the plague) has infected the community. To purge themselves of the violence, Girard argues, the community accepts Tiresias and Creon's joint version of the story: "Oedipus' imminent fall has nothing to do with any heinous sin; rather it should be regarded as the outcome of a tragic encounter."[41] The search for a scapegoat is the easiest of all hunting expeditions — and Tiresias and Creon have successfully fixed the blame on Oedipus. He is the arbitrary surrogate victim.

Having elaborated those aspects of Girardian metaphysics pertinent to a reinterpretation of *The Mayor,* we are positioned to sketch the main "acts" of Hardy's tragic novel. Let me emphasize that my particular interest has not been to defend Girard's Freudian revisionism or his reinterpretation of *Oedipus Rex,* but rather to present Hardy's own "modern Oedipus" in a new and profitable light. Like Girard's select masterpieces, *The Mayor* does possess an intersubjective, interlocking triangular form that mutates in accordance with the dynamics of *mimesis,* or what Girard terms the "law of desire": a recurring cycle from modeling and rivalry to victimage.[42]

IV

> The ruin of good men by bad wives, and, more particularly, the frustration of many a promising youth's high aims and hopes and the extinction of his energies by an early imprudent marriage, was the theme. (16)

The Mayor's very first sentence limns the figure of the triangle: "a young man and woman, the latter carrying a child." The young couple walks so as "to suggest afar off the low, easy, confidential chat of people full of reciprocity" but "on closer view" the man trudges "in ignoring silence" (11-12). This alternation of narrative perspective is accompanied by the sudden shift in the staging of the setting and of the reader's perception. When the woman's face is caught "by the rays of the strongly coloured sun," she looks pretty, and a warmth that "sets fire to her lips" radiates down upon her little daughter. But when the woman "plods on" in the hedge's shade, "silently thinking," she bears "the hard, half-apathetic expression of one who dreams anything possible at the hands of Time and Chance except, perhaps, fair play" (12). The "chief" and "almost the only" attraction of the young mother's face is also the cardinal characteristic of the novel's triangular structure: its mobility. The narrator summarizes the cause of her alternating facial appearance simply: "The first phase was the work of Nature, the second probably of Civilization" (12).

This overarching Hardyean dualism of Nature and Civilization epitomizes these aforementioned alternations between sun and shade, distance and closeness, and confidential chat and ignoring silence. It also serves to introduce and encapsulate the reciprocations that reverberate throughout the novel's succeeding chapters: between disorder and order, *Gemeinschaft* and *Gesellschaft*, fascination and boredom, county and city, passion and convention, strangeness and familiarity, secret and revelation, custom and law, mutuality and alienation, Self and Other, ancient and modern, personal and communal—and Henchard and Farfrae. As in most of Hardy's work wherein Time and Chance hold sway, however, these alternating concepts constitute neither homologous relational sets nor simple polarities easily equated to each other. Rather, they are interwoven "strands" embedded together in the dense thematic complex of Hardy's "Great Web." The world of Casterbridge is one in transition between country and city, *Gemeinschaft* and *Gesellschaft*, but the former is often visible only in traces and the latter almost always prevails. It is the world of Farfrae, not Henchard, "a general drama of pain," with only "occasional episodes" of happiness.

Although Farfrae and Henchard, Elizabeth-Jane and Lucetta do at times seem virtual incarnations of one or more of these sets of opposing Hardyean ideas, the characters in *The Mayor* are never mere allegorical figures. Hardy's major alternating concepts and his characters' own portraits are presented ambivalently—and the ideas move dialectically, forever interpenetrating and disengaging. As Ian Gregor notes, "The ambivalence present in the idea of Nature could be said to extend into . . . neighboring concepts such as law, society, justice."[43] That the characters too are therefore "threads" embodying many concepts that finally "interlace" into a complex "web" in the form of triangles—consisting of family or strangers, whether harmonious or alienating—fits well the ongoing alternation patterns. For as Jean-Paul Sartre argues in *Search for a Method*, the family is the single unit that "mediates" dialectically the individual and social, the existential and Marxist, Nature and Civilization.[44] Girard's psychosocial theories are superior to Freud's in *The Mayor*'s case because they explain functionally why the mediated triangles keep exploding: a "model" mediates desired objects and turns into a perceived rival:[45]

> The main difference between the mediation principle and psychoanalysis is that, in Freud, the desire for the mother is intrinsic. . . . All relationships remain fundamentally independent of each other. In the love-hate relationship with the father, the love and the hate are juxtaposed rather than truly united. Only the mimetic process can make the three characters within the triangle truly dependent on each other; only that same process can show that the same drive makes the mediator venerable as a model and hateful as an obstacle.

> The truth is . . . one does not really know why the Oedipal triangle should go on generating substitute triangles. . . . The mimetic triangles must be perpetually repeated. . . . It is a search for a successful subject's desire; ultimately it is this interference itself that will be actively sought.[46]

Freud deals with the model-rival transformation by ascribing excessive paternal (or maternal) affection to "bisexuality," elevating the word "ambivalence" to the level of a mechanism in its own right. He therefore constructs a second "abnormal" Oedipal complex version: the homosexual mode. Freud's five-year-old Little Hans has "a passive, tender impulse to be loved by [his father] in the genital-erotic sense."[47] But Freud has no functional way to explain this abnormality: "As long as the fascination for the rival remains moderate," Girard notes, "the 'normal' version of the complex remains adequate."[48] Freud's "explanation" is descriptive and regressive. He sees "love" and "hate," calls them "ambivalence," and lets that serve as his basis for two separate models of desire.[49] Girard does not finally deny the possible existence of biological homosexuality. But he insists that Freud carries it as a "dead weight" and finally submerges it in "biological opacity," failing to integrate it into the dynamic of desire or to give it any structural *raison d'être*.[50]

I mention Girard's explanation of homosexuality through "mediated" desire not only because it will bear directly on *The Mayor*'s central male relationship. It also offers a unified explanatory dynamic for the novel's continued alternations. The central characters and ideas are not merely "ambivalently" related but exist in what might be called "a universe of radical opposition," "working to destroy what it creates, crushing into death what it coaxes into life."[51] Susan, Lucetta, and Henchard are not done in by an easily fingered malignant star, whether in the form of a vengeful Chance or a cruel Society. Rather, they serve as sacrifices to all of these—and the cosmic choice of them as victims is arbitrary. Girard judges such victimage as the climax not just of the mimetic dynamic but of tragedy itself. Like Hardy's Casterbridge, the world of Greek tragedy was a transitional period, with the "opposition of symmetrical elements" representing the tragic form's "most characteristic" trait.[52]

Although *The Mayor* is a "universe of radical opposition" in constant flux and transformation, it is clear from the outset that the primary associations with the "family" triangles are boredom, convention, law, and alienation. Before we even know the solitary trio's relationship or their names, the narrator concludes: "There could be little doubt. No other than such a relationship would have accounted for the atmosphere of stale familiarity which the trio carried along with them like a nimbus" (12).

As the family approaches the "large village" of Weydon-Priors, however, they discover quite unexpectedly that it is Fair Day—and the exotic and passionate, complete with hag and rum, immediately intrude. A drunken Henchard launches forth on an apostrophe to the first act's "theme"—"the ruin of good men by bad wives" (16)—and makes his fateful, defiant offer to sell Susan for five guineas.

Is it descriptive happenchance—or deliberate architectural design[53]—that Newson's thundering "Yes!" to Henchard's proposal is delivered "standing in the triangular opening which framed the door of the tent"? (19). The confrontation lasts but an instant and appears "like some grand feat of stagery in a darkened auditorium" (21). The entrance of the mysterious "stranger" culminates the Fair Day's excitement. With Newson's payment to Henchard, a new family triangle is formed: Newson, Susan, and baby Elizabeth-Jane. The tragedy's first "act" closes with Henchard unable to locate Susan largely because he keeps secret the circumstances of their parting.

A vague yet persistent sense reigns that Henchard thereafter pursues Susan for months and vows his abstainer's oath not so much because he loves her as because another man has taken her. Although the fair's rum obviously clouded his judgment, the circumstances surrounding the wife-selling bear the imprint of mimetic desire. When a former coachman offers "unexpected praise" of Susan, Henchard is jolted, "half in doubt of the wisdom of his own attitude toward the possessor of such qualities" (17). And when Susan actually "calls his bluff" and goes off with Newson, Henchard exhibits a "stolid look of concern, as if he had not quite expected this ending" (20). Two more sharp declarations of Susan's virtues follow, yet an inebriated Henchard obstinately keeps his seat, falls asleep, and waits until the following day to begin his search. He never really gives up that search. Rather he ends it only when he receives word that Susan and Newson have probably emigrated, and this seems to him to resemble his object's and rival's deaths rather than their mere departure. It is as if only the vast Atlantic Ocean could douse the raging mimetic fires.

This view is consonant with Girardian theory and with Henchard's behavior throughout *The Mayor*: we want not what we possess but what others possess—and yet, when "it" is infinitely distanced beyond recovery (and a proximate rival ceases to exist or becomes an ethereal, unimaginable idea), we lose our desire. Distance is the spring of desire, as Miller argues, and Henchard's desperate search for Susan is the first of his many failed efforts to fill the "emotional void" within, "a distance of oneself from oneself" (148). Thus the final and anguished opposition in the novel's triangular intersubjective structure of Self and Other is between "presence" and "absence."[54] "To possess the beloved would be to replace separation by presence," Miller observes, "emptiness by a substantial self."[55] Henchard begins in "ignoring silence" and ends "a self-alienated man" (322), disavowing by means of his crumpled sheet of paper finally even the solace of memory as desire.

V

> Friendship between man and man; what a rugged strength there was in it, as evinced by these two. And yet the seed that was to lift the foundation of this friendship was at that moment taking root in a chink of its structure.
>
> ELIZABETH-JANE, MUSING ON HENCHARD AND FARFRAE TOGETHER (100)

Act II opens eighteen years later at the same furmity tent in Weydon-Priors, the scene "changed only in details." The Newson family triangle is broken (as we later learn) by Susan taking leave with Elizabeth-Jane (Newson) from Canada upon Newson's circulated false report of his drowning at sea. This scene is indeed a testament to "Nature's powers of continuity" (27), for even the same old hag is present—and it sets the course throughout the entire "act" for Hardy's multiplying alternating oppositions: the familiar versus the exotic, the "respectable" versus the spontaneous, Elizabeth-Jane versus Susan. Elizabeth-Jane summarily rebukes her mother as not "respectable" (29) for talking with the furmity tent mistress; Elizabeth-Jane desires to become a woman of "higher repute" (34); she counsels her mother to follow "respectable" young Farfrae to the Three Mariners Inn for night lodging (50). And when Susan fears that even the Three Mariners Inn is too expensive, Elizabeth-Jane replies: "But we must be respectable." "We must pay our way even before we must be respectable," responds Susan (50). Yet Elizabeth-Jane, too, in turn, swallows her pride, just as Susan had in setting out to look for Henchard: Elizabeth-Jane volunteers without any suggestion to defray their accommodations by assisting the hotel management. The narrator's remark on Elizabeth-Jane's decision accents the mother-daughter distinction: "If there was one thing . . . that characterized this simple-hearted girl, it was a willingness to sacrifice her personal comfort and dignity to the common weal" (51). Elizabeth-Jane's standard of respectability is grounded in a sense of social welfare; Susan's spontaneity derives from her simplicity, disturbed only by the encroachment of moral necessity. Even Elizabeth-Jane's volunteering reflects in its circumstances the mediation between the communal and personal—it occurs in the town's "middle-quality" inn (between the King's Arms and the Mixen Lane) in "old-fashioned" Casterbridge, itself neither rural nor urban.

Indeed Casterbridge is a "rare old market town" (68) that "announced old Rome in every street, alley and precinct" (75). As Act II shifts scenes, it moves from the grimy furmity tent to the stately classical King's Arms Hotel, in which Henchard as Mayor is chairing the Town Council meeting. As did the Fair Day setting of the furmity tent in Act I, this setting suggests the path of Henchard's fortunes since Susan's departure: consistently upward. The mayor presides over town affairs like a king. The narrator's repeated use of qualifying conjunctions to describe Henchard, of course, is meant to distinguish him sharply from another man just then entering the King's Arms: Donald Farfrae.

Like the play of sun and shade in Act I, the imagery of light and dark in Act II illustrates the reciprocal interplay between the forces of Nature and Civilization. But the relationships within Hardy's web in "urban" Casterbridge are precisely inverted from their configuration in the Upper Wessex countryside. Henchard muses on these differences as the formal business meeting gives way to a casual social hour. The contemporary style of the Three Mariners Inn likewise reflects the fact that old Casterbridge is entering the harsh light of modern England.

The differences between Susan and Elizabeth-Jane, Henchard and Farfrae, and Elizabeth-Jane and Lucetta seem obvious when we meet these characters, just as in *Oedipus Rex*. Henchard himself intuits from Farfrae's build and manner their extreme differences. Physically and temperamentally, the two men appear poles apart: Henchard is six foot one, robust, and coarse; Farfrae is five foot nine, slight, and gentle. Henchard perceives their talents as fully complementary. Their differences are also finely balanced and symmetrical, and turn on a peculiar sense of identity. To Elizabeth-Jane, the men seem more like two halves of a divided self. Henchard feels himself "drawn" (63) to Farfrae and senses an almost fraternal bond: "Your forehead, Farfrae, is something like my poor brother's—now dead and gone; and the nose too isn't unlike his" (55). Henchard's business is corn and hay, and he finally persuades Farfrae to become his corn manager while the former hay trusser maintains direct supervision over the hay branch.

These initial stages of the Henchard-Farfrae relationship correspond to what Girard identifies as the period of "external mediation": "When the distance is sufficient to eliminate any contact between two spheres of *possibilities* of which the mediator and the subject occupy the respective centers."[56] His status as the town mayor and the younger man's employer notwithstanding, Henchard here has taken on Farfrae as his model. But Farfrae's strengths are within a domain from which Henchard does not feel threatened. This distance between subject Henchard and model Farfrae, of course, is not physical but spiritual. Henchard does not desire what Farfrae desires; the distance between them precludes conflict. Yet Farfrae's superiority is intellectual only; Henchard's is physical, material, social.

So Henchard is also Farfrae's model: by virtue of his gregarious, expansive nature, Henchard in effect imposes himself upon Farfrae as a model. Elizabeth-Jane notices that Henchard's "tigerish affection" for Farfrae, his "tendency to domineer," and his demand to have the Scotsman always near him occasionally provoke "real offence" from the mild-mannered young manager. The narrator does not relate Farfrae's perception of their relationship at this stage in the novel, but Elizabeth-Jane's repeated observations from her "omniscient" view in her room high above the granaries suggest that the external mediation is reciprocal.

Neither Farfrae nor Henchard is conscious of being modeled by the other, and Farfrae remains unaware of it throughout much of the novel. But whereas the process of single external mediation of disciple to model (Don Quixote to the unattainable Amadis; or Sancho for his master) preserves harmony because their distance seems insuperable to both, reciprocal or "double" mediation marks the narrowing of difference and onset of rivalry. The distance between mediator and subject in the triangle's "sides" shortens and ultimately closes, giving way to a relation of "internal" mediation. In "double" mediation the "metamorphosis of the object is common to both partners." In "internal" mediation, the subjects' spheres close to the point where they "penetrate each other more or less profoundly" and a collision takes place.[57]

The first disputed "object" of contention between Henchard and Farfrae is authority. The mayor's domineering manner is not directed to Farfrae alone. As his threats to Abel Whittle suggest, Henchard at times appears like an imperious monarch to his workmen. Abel, chronically late to work, cries. Abel is a member of the hay-weighing crew, and so is within Henchard's sphere by the terms of division of labor with Farfrae. But when Henchard humiliates the slumbering Whittle by marching him out of bed minus his breeches, Farfrae sees it as "tyrannical" of Henchard and orders Whittle home.

This event marks the first decisive turn from mimetic modeling to rivalry: it is the opening salvo of the unfolding "war story." That moment is the "seed" that "lifts the foundation of their friendship." Henchard himself intuits that the Whittle incident is the tipping point that will shift his relationship with Farfrae from friendship to rivalry. Although Farfrae's "antagonism" quickly subsides, especially when he learns of Henchard's kindness to Whittle's poor mother, Henchard's bitterness seethes and intensifies, stoked by his perception that his workers regard Farfrae as the business's real master: "Ask Mr. Farfrae. He's master here," Henchard growls later that day (103). "Here" underlines the narrowing of distance: in overriding Henchard's command, Farfrae has literally entered Henchard's domain of authority. Farfrae thereafter becomes the real master: "Morally Farfrae was the master: there could be no doubt of it. Henchard, who had hitherto been the most admired man in the circle, was the most admired no longer" (103). The cornfactor's conversation with a little boy, who represents a virtual Casterbridge Chorus, heightens by unflattering comparison Henchard's perception of his rivalry:

> "Why Mr. Farfrae?" said Henchard. . . . "Why do people always want Mr. Farfrae?"
>
> "I suppose because they like him so—that's what they say."
>
> "Oh—I see—that's what they say—hey? They like him because he's cleverer than Mr. Henchard, and because he knows more; and in short, Mr. Henchard can't hold a candle to him—hey?"
>
> "Yes—that just it, sir—some of it."
>
> "Oh, there's more? . . ."
>
> "And he's better-tempered, and Henchard's a fool to him, they say. And when some of the women are a-walking home they said, 'He's a diment—he's a chap o'wax—he's the best—he's the horse for my money' . . . And they said, 'He's the most understanding man o' them two by long chalks. I wish he was the master instead of Henchard,' they said." (103–104)

Even after the Whittle incident, Henchard had supposed his inferiority to Farfrae was largely intellectual. He now finds it extends to his reputation throughout the community.

But though the Whittle incident is the "seed" that disturbs the men's "foundation" of friendship, the narrator notes that the seed "took root in a chink of its structure" (100). This "chink" is the "double bind" embedded in the core of the triangular structure of desire. The subject supposes his model is "already endowed with superior being," and therefore concludes that his objects of desire "must surely be capable of conferring an even greater plenitude of being."[58] The subject's desire is always for greater being, in which he feels lacking and surmises his model possesses in abundance. The object's desirability is invariably conveyed by example, not words. Thus Henchard and Farfrae give each other "contradictory double imperatives." Henchard's message is "Be strong!" Farfrae's message is "Be intelligent!" The dualities of these messages climax and collide in the Whittle incident, which exposes, reconfigures, and inverts the Henchard-Farfrae relationship as it pivots on the issues of authority and efficiency. Farfrae has viewed Henchard as a successful mayor and cornfactor exercising power and always dominant. Henchard witnesses his "crude *viva voce* system" (94) of memory and oral bargains give way to a much more profitable system of record-keeping and new technology. Whittle's chronic lateness might have been overlooked or more excusable under Henchard's old system. But now it poses a threat not only to Henchard's authority but also to Farfrae's efficiency. The "double bind" "chink" existed in the Henchard-Farfrae friendship from the start; the Whittle incident widens and deepens it.

The negative command of the double bind incites Henchard's antagonism and fear: he fears Farfrae has appropriated his being with his counter-order to Whittle. Henchard suspects that Farfrae embarrasses him publicly because he told the Scotsman "the secret o' my life": his early marriage to and selling of Susan and his illicit liaison with Lucetta. Henchard shudders that Farfrae can use the knowledge as blackmail or as leverage. As Act II closes, Henchard and Farfrae part "in renewed friendship." Henchard feels "repose." And yet the mimetic sparks have been only doused, not quenched: "Whenever he thought of Farfrae, it was with a dim dread; and he often regretted that he had told the young man his whole heart, and confided to him the secrets of his life" (105).

As the Henchard-Farfrae rivalry progresses in the foreground, the Susan-Lucetta rivalry for Henchard takes shape but never materializes. Lucetta does not even appear in Act II; indeed the two women never meet, so that Henchard is never a conscious object of their rivalry. Yet the tragedy's symmetrical, reciprocal oppositions—here between secret and revelation, family and business—also structure their "rivalry." Henchard regards himself as a potential object of rivalry as he explains his predicament to Farfrae. Although the cornfactor thinks it "odd" that he should be confiding "a family matter" after he and Farfrae have just met on a "purely business ground," Henchard nonetheless bares his soul to the young man at the end of their very first day of acquaintanceship. Henchard fears that "by doing right with Susan I wrong another innocent woman" (83). Although Farfrae advises a simple and frank disclosure of his past to Lucetta and Elizabeth-Jane, Henchard insists he must recompense Lucetta and keep Elizabeth-Jane ignorant.

The painting that graces the cover of the Signet Classics edition of *The Mayor of Casterbridge* is George Stubbs's Sir John Nelthorpe (1776). Stubbs (1724–1806) is best remembered for his paintings of animals, especially horses and dogs. He received many commissions for single portraits of the latter. The cover image for *The Mayor* applies well to Henchard at the height of his career in Casterbridge, before Donald Farfrae's ascendancy, when Henchard stood tall as a popular mayor, leading townsman, and prosperous merchant. As in the case of Squire Falkland in *Caleb Williams,* Henchard establishes himself as a respected and prosperous pillar of his community, but just beneath the story of his success lurks a shameful secret in his past and a self-destructive pride and barely controlled rage. Subtitled "The Story of a Man of Character," the narrative possesses a rare psychological depth and a deep understanding of social conflict. Set in the fictional Wessex of Hardy's literary imagination, the novel is one of the great works of prose fiction in world literature. Published in 1984, this Signet edition is edited and introduced by Elliot Perlman.

With Henchard's marriage to Susan, the family triangle of Henchard-Susan-Elizabeth-Jane is established. A romantic, confrontational triangle thereby seems avoided. But the "secret o' my life" on which Act II closes places this family triangle too merely in "repose," not stable tranquility. Henchard's deceit fans the simmering flames of mimetic desire.

VI

> Buying over a rival had nothing to recommend it to the Mayor's headstrong faculties. (116)

> The time of the riding world was over; the pedestrian world held sway. (169)

Henchard's momentary loss of authority to Farfrae in the Whittle incident is the first public sign of his approaching business downfall. The mayor's remarriage to Susan, which exposes him to general ridicule and after which he "feels the lowering of his dignity" (87), is the first outward sign of the family tragedy to come.

Act III marks the clear beginning of both falls, inextricably tied together by his now-transparent rivalry with Farfrae. The act opens with Henchard's manner toward Farfrae "insensibly more reserved" (106), which Farfrae merely sees as evidence of Henchard's improved self-control and "good breeding," if attended with a loss of warmth. Henchard's animosity burns just beneath the narrative surface, needing only tinder to set it ablaze. That tinder enters in the form of a few old rick-cloths which Farfrae borrows to stage a small Casterbridge gala celebrating a recent English national event. Although Henchard had given no thought to organizing such a festival himself, he is immediately "fired with emulation" upon seeing Farfrae's preparations.

So Act III turns on structural repetitions. It is set on another Fair Day from which unexpected, tragic consequences will follow. Likewise, the rick-cloths, which are stacks of hay thatched for rain protection, become symbolically important as a second instance of Farfrae closing his social distance from Henchard and as the key to the fair's success. As Farfrae borrows Henchard's hay, the mayor glimpses a potential "exploit" (107), an opportunity to win the town's admiration and outdo Farfrae.

When Henchard sees Farfrae's makeshift West Walk exterior of rick-cloths in assorted colors and sizes, Henchard is "easy in his mind," for "his own preparations far transcended these" (108). His perceived competition is no figment. Farfrae is apparently the only townsman oblivious to it, for when Henchard's extensive efforts are foiled by rain, a neighbor immediately remarks to him: "He beat you." Others too taunt Henchard about the rivalry: Farfrae is an "opposition randy," "Jack's as good as his master," "Take a leaf out of his book," "He'll be top-sawyer soon of you two," and other mocking jibes (111). Even his own daughter, dancing with Farfrae, seems a betrayer. Impetuously Henchard fires his manager, and this time Farfrae takes him at his word.

With this business break and Henchard's terse instruction for the Scotsman and Elizabeth-Jane to "be as strangers," Henchard and Farfrae appear to stand at two points of maximum divergence. The narrator judges Farfrae "just the reverse of Henchard" (117), and Henchard declares him "an enemy to our house!" (116).

But Henchard's hostility is actually another sign of the triangle's shrinkage. Internal mediation now manifests itself in Farfrae's choices: rather than leave Casterbridge, he stays and sets himself up in the corn trade—as an explicit, if unintended, competitor. Farfrae first declines to vie with Henchard for his customers. But though he tries to "avoid collision" with Henchard, a time soon arises when "in sheer self-defence" Farfrae is forced "to close with Henchard in mortal commercial combat" (117). Here on the business front, where they seem most divergent as characters, the archetypal process of progressive undifferentiation characteristic of the primitive mind—and classical tragedy—is under way. Already Henchard and Farfrae are beginning to resemble the enemy brothers of tragedy.

Oedipus and Creon, of course, are brothers-in-law. Even though *The Mayor,* a late nineteenth-century tragic novel, desymbolizes the Henchard-Farfrae fratricide into a relationship of merely metaphorical brothers, Girard's classic pattern of reciprocal violence remains. Double mediation quickly metastasizes into multiple reciprocal mediation as more and more people are drawn unawares into the rivals' vortex. Elizabeth-Jane makes every effort to avoid even mentioning Farfrae's name in Henchard's presence; and when Susan makes that very error, Henchard glares, "What—are you, too, my enemy?" (118).

The expansion from commercial rivalry to romantic competition now unfolds with geometric precision, as if it were the manifest destiny of the novel. Just as the Whittle incident seems linked (at least in Henchard's mind) to his impulsive disclosure about Susan, and Farfrae's gala success is connected to Elizabeth-Jane's dancing with him, the men's corn business combat soon turns into a contest for the same woman: Lucetta Templeman.

With Susan's death, Henchard first discovers why she had preferred Elizabeth-Jane not be renamed "Henchard": the girl is Newson's daughter after all. Susan's scrupulosity in this particular in the face of her complete secrecy about Elizabeth-Jane's true identity—a secret withheld from both Henchard and Elizabeth-Jane herself—is ironically fitting. It is a characteristic example of

This Penguin Classics cover of *The Mayor of Casterbridge* features a photograph of the Scotsman Hugh Miller, which the Scottish painter-photographer team of David Hill and Robert Adamson produced. The pair created photographic sketches rather than traditional portraits, and therefore were among the first artists to master the techniques of paper photography. Hill worked out the overall design, including the positioning of his sitters and suggestions about the kinds of expressions they might adopt, whereas Adamson operated the camera and handled all technical procedures pertaining to the optics and chemical formulae. Like numerous other photographs of theirs produced during the mid-1840s, their portrait photography represented a major artistic breakthrough in photography specifically, and in portraiture more generally.

simple Susan's "honesty in dishonesty" (128), another inversion in the novel's universe of radical opposition. Henchard's bitter realization that his daughter is not really his own poisons their relationship and sets Elizabeth-Jane looking outward for a new living situation. As accidentally as Henchard met Farfrae, she soon encounters Lucetta, whom she regards wondrously as a model in much the way Henchard first viewed Farfrae, yet again not without ambivalent overtones.

Like Newson and Farfrae, Lucetta is a "stranger." And just as the furmity tent and King's Arms so accurately reflected Henchard's fortunes as the settings for

Act I and II's central scenes, High Place Hall bares Lucetta's past and points toward her future: the door is studded; the arch's keystone is a mask displaying a comic leer, which looks as if it has been "eaten away by disease" because of boys hurling rocks at the mask's open mouth. The mask suggests "one thing above all others as appertaining to the mansion's past history—intrigue" (142). The building evokes the same sensation of the exotic amid the pedestrian as does Lucetta herself, while its exposed present condition tragically prefigures the approaching fall of the gentlewoman and mayor's wife from her high place.

The contours of the incipient Elizabeth-Jane–Lucetta rivalry are identifiable when Farfrae pays a call to Elizabeth-Jane, now living with Lucetta at High Place Hall, only to find that Lucetta is the woman of the house and Elizabeth-Jane absent. The scene marks the increasing loss of difference among all the protagonists. As Henchard had sought Farfrae's judgment on his personal life secrets, Lucetta, remaining behind her "mask," uses Elizabeth-Jane as a sounding board for her fictionalized version of her past. Like Henchard with Farfrae, Lucetta has habitually "leant on Elizabeth-Jane's judgment." Like Farfrae, Elizabeth-Jane speaks "judicially" and acts the part of the "experienced sage" (172). Even her sudden move to High Place Hall, which seemed to Henchard like "taking time by the forelock" (145), resembles Farfrae's alacrity in seizing the moment for his celebration plans, at least from Henchard's perspective: "Farfrae had been so cursed quick in his movements as to give old-fashioned people in authority no chance of the initiative" (106). And Lucetta's interest in tradesman Farfrae, which she would never have entertained as a younger woman, springs from an emptiness that mirrors Henchard's cavernous "emotional void" (148): "Her heart longed for some ark into which it could fly and be at rest. Rough or smooth, she did not care so long as it was warm" (163).

Yet despite their obvious mutual needs, Lucetta's interest in Farfrae leads her to sidestep Henchard's marriage proposal, thereby escalating the men's commercial competition into a romantic rivalry. Already Lucetta's heightened desirability in the world's eyes as the result of her inheritance has "sublimed her into a lady of means" for Henchard and "lent a charm to her image which it might not otherwise have acquired" (148). Although Henchard judges Farfrae not "a conscious rival," just the suspicion that Lucetta is desired by another stiffens Henchard's resolve to see her a second time at High Place, a visit interrupted by Farfrae's accidentally calling in the middle of it. Henchard's parting "sense of occult rivalry in suitorship" adds "an inflaming soul" to the men's "palpable rivalry" in commerce (180).

This "vitalized antagonism" draws in another character, one who dislikes Farfrae "as the man who once usurped his place" (181): Jopp. The pace of the violence and undifferentiation accelerates. Henchard and Jopp plot to "snuff out" Farfrae's corn trade by all legal means. But when Henchard relies on the weather-prophet's predictions of disaster and overstocks his granaries, Chance intervenes in the form of sunny weather and a bumper harvest—and prices plummet, causing a tremendous loss for Henchard. Prices skyrocket as high winds and sunless days follow, forcing Henchard into bankruptcy only months later. Meanwhile, Farfrae prospers by the market fluctuations.

The cancer of sick desire metastasizes further. More and more townsmen are sucked into the commercial competition as "the rivalry of the masters [is] taken up by the men" (189). Voicing the mushrooming rivalry aloud and more explicitly than did the young boy whom Henchard met in Act II, one of Henchard's hands explains after a conflict with a Farfrae worker witnessed by Lucetta and Elizabeth-Jane, "Why, you see, sir, all the women side with Farfrae—" (190). Even Lucetta and Elizabeth-Jane momentarily lose their identities here; Henchard must remind his hand that he is Lucetta's suitor. Reciprocal violence is turning to generative violence. The town is gradually assuming "sides" as differences are increasingly effaced by the rivals' heightening antagonism.[59]

When Henchard overhears Farfrae's marriage proposal to Lucetta, he immediately threatens her with a public airing of their illicit past—yet not out of passionate rage at his loss of her so much as a way to frustrate Farfrae's plans. For if "Lucetta's heart had been given to any other man in the world than Farfrae," Henchard would have probably "pitied" Lucetta (194). But Farfrae as "supplanter" is an "upstart" in Henchard's view, "who has mounted into prominence upon his shoulders, and he could bring himself to show no mercy" (195). Lucetta submits to Henchard's threat to destroy her reputation and agrees to marry him.

Yet now another intruder reappears to expose Henchard's own past and the grave marital secret concerning Susan: the furmity woman. In traditional psychoanalytic terms, her reappearance would signify "the return of the repressed." In Girardian terms, whereby the novel is structured by radical oppositions—Act III features "revelation" versus "secrecy"—the furmity woman's entrance marks another oscillation typical of the triangular pendulum of *mimesis*. As Susan's revelation had catastrophic consequences for Henchard's personal happiness, so the furmity woman's report shatters his public reputation.

Act III closes on two more sets of confrontational triangles and two additional revelations. First, Henchard saves Lucetta and Elizabeth-Jane from a charging bull, only to discover in a cruel irony that he has actually saved not Miss Templeman but Mrs. Farfrae. Second, Lucetta discloses to Elizabeth-Jane the news of her marriage, pleading with the girl to join a new family triangle. But Elizabeth-Jane rejects the offer, for her own still-kept secret is that she too loves Donald Farfrae.

VII

So much for man's rivalry, he thought.

HENCHARD (282)

News of the police-court report of Henchard's wife-selling opens Act IV and forms the "turn in the incline of Henchard's fortunes." For "almost at that minute he passed the ridge of prosperity and honour, and began to descend rapidly on the other side" (215). As if operating by the laws of physics, the vertical plot line and Henchard's fortunes now begin their downward spiral, moving with ever-increasing velocity as his social and business declines interact. Girard explains that such an acceleration is characteristic of tragedy, especially in dialogue exchanges (*stichomythia*) and plot reversals, both of which are commonly framed by alternating *kudos* (glory) and *thymes* (sublime rage) in alternation.

Soon Henchard hits financial rock bottom: bankruptcy. All Casterbridge abandons him, except Elizabeth-Jane: "She believed in him still, though nobody else did" (217). Yet Henchard ignores her letters and visits. Meanwhile Farfrae's resemblance to Henchard grows after he marries Henchard's former lover. Next Farfrae purchases Henchard's former business, then also his residence and furniture. Personal appropriation follows commercial appropriation, and back again. Henchard as defeated rival is still Farfrae's model, and even after bankruptcy Henchard continues to relinquish his objects and being to Farfrae. A reduced Henchard greets the news from Jopp of Farfrae's family plans with some of his old fury.

In the town's eyes, Farfrae's commercial triumph has been as complete and decisive as his matchmaking masterstroke. Elizabeth-Jane's innocent inversion of Henchard's cynical declarative twenty chapters earlier now possesses a savagely ironic accuracy: "Mr. Farfrae is master here?" (215). Early in Act IV, Henchard sinks to his level upon entering Casterbridge twenty years earlier, this time as journeyman day laborer for his former manager—also fulfilling the angry prophecy he delivered earlier to Jopp: "My furniture too! Surely he'll buy my body and soul likewise!" (222).

And for a few shillings per week, Farfrae does. Henchard's former hatred of Farfrae returns and the rivalry becomes a single-minded obsession, with every workday at his old granaries reminding him incessantly of his "triumphant rival who rode roughshod over him" (226).

As Farfrae's selection as Mayor becomes inevitable, Henchard undergoes a "moral change" and grows preoccupied with the approaching end of his abstainer's oath. "He has taken everything from me," a drunken Henchard moans in The Three Mariners Inn on the day his pledge has expired, "and by heavens if I meet him I won't answer for my deeds!" (232). Even though Elizabeth-Jane and the townsmen inform Farfrae of Henchard's extreme animosity, the corn merchant fails to recognize it and remains "incredulous" (239).

The Scotsman's elevation to mayor in Act IV marks the widest social disparity between Farfrae and Henchard in the novel. Now Farfrae is not only "master here" but also "mayor here": he has usurped the title role of the novel and relegated Henchard to the shadows. In Act IV, their rivalry reaches a heightened pitch: first in the public arena with the Royal Personage's visit; then immediately in private hand-to-hand combat. Henchard has a "passing fancy" to participate in the reception of royalty, which Farfrae's and the Town Council's united "opposition crystallise [into] a determination" (260). But when Henchard sets out to greet the royal guest as his vehicle passes, Farfrae, "with Mayoral authority" (263), seizes Henchard and drags him back. Henchard "by an unaccountable impulse gives way and retires" (263), as if realizing that in the modern world the authority of office invests Farfrae with superhuman power.

In Girardian terms, even as the processes of undifferentiation among the characters accelerate, this interlude exemplifies the main function of ritual: to restore differences and channel violence.[60] The Royal Personage's visit presents the mayor and Council in full array. And for the first time we see a glimpse of the town's envy of Lucetta and Farfrae. Lucetta accurately perceives that many townsfolk are bent on "snubbing her at this triumphant time" (263). And Farfrae's rise has not been attained without some loss of affection in Casterbridge. But ritual's restoration of difference is only apparent; it is truly a stage of consolidation in the ongoing undifferentiation process.

Of course, Henchard and Farfrae's hand-to-hand combat is also a ritual. It is a ritual that does restore differences, a ritual based on strength rather than efficiency or vested authority, as in ancient Rome. It is, as Henchard says, literally a continuation of their morning wrestle, and fittingly occurs high aloft in the corn-stores—the elderly hay trusser attacks the Scotsman in his own sphere: a matched reversal of Farfrae's intrusion into Henchard's corn domain during the Whittle incident and the Fair celebration. With one hand tied behind his back, Henchard wrestles Farfrae down against the loft's edge. But he cannot bring himself to kill the Scotsman. Instead he cries out, "God is my witness that no man ever loved another as I did thee at one time!" (269). But Farfrae's violence, the retribution of communal authority, is cast as the "good"; Henchard's self-appointed role as vigilante, even in a fair fight on the field of combat, is "bad," given the values of the modern age.

For Henchard is an epic hero trapped in a small and pedestrian world. He is a Coriolanus whose "oppressive generosity," "tigerish affection," and bouts of rage seem extreme for a modern Casterbridge, as if instead part of the grandeur and stature of Rome itself. He is a warrior "with the education of an Achilles," unfit for "grubbing subtleties" like bookkeeping or noticing Lucetta's coquettish glances at Farfrae. Even in bankruptcy, he refuses Lucetta's financial assistance and displays the warrior's "haughty indifference of the society of womankind" (87). And yet Henchard is the man of *Gemeinschaft*, of personal relations, whom one would expect to function so well in a small world. This paradox, illustrated by Henchard's fortunes in his public and private combats with Farfrae, recalls the paradoxes at the core of the novel's "universe of radical opposition." For Henchard is the man of Nature, Farfrae the man of Civilization; yet Henchard's desperate need is to fill his "emotional void," a need *for* society. He feels desperately lonely and isolated; he craves Farfrae's objects in order to fill his "absence" with presence. Thus he turns from Farfrae to Susan to Elizabeth-Jane (*neé* Henchard) to Lucetta and back to Elizabeth-Jane (Newson), seeking to restore his loss of being.

Henchard is a classical hero displaced into a modern and shrunken Rome of lesser mortals. So his "spirit" longs for Nature, the contented isolation and self-sufficiency of the jungle lion and tiger to which he is compared. But his "desire" craves Civilization, an overpowering yearning itself created by the culture into which he has been accidentally thrust.

The mimetic mechanism governing Casterbridge creates and promotes dependent relationships as the price for efficiency. Technological advance, based upon specialization—the "letters and Ledgers" (94) and "scales and steelyards" (219) replacing the *viva voce* system and guesswork—stresses social efficiency over individual strength. The slightly built, intellectual Farfrae is at home in the modern world, with no spiritual craving at all. He is first loved by Casterbridge for his melodious voice, "giving strong expression to a song of his dear native country that he loved so well as never to have revisited it" (317). For Henchard, on the other hand, music possesses a visceral force, a "regal power" (290). Henchard succeeds in Casterbridge only so long as he can dominate and run his business like a war machine: he accurately tells Farfrae that "strength and bustle build up a firm. But judgment and knowledge are what keep it established" (55). Henchard can build up, yet when reduced to the everyday necessities of organization and administration—and the subterfuges of domestic politics—he is frustrated and stymied, reduced to "a netted lion" (296). Even the constant association of Henchard to jungle beasts indicates in the mimetic process the extreme disparity between modernity's "superhuman" Farfrae and the "animalistic" Henchard. Farfrae has indeed bought Henchard's "body and soul" for wages and appropriated even his would-be wife.

As the "pedestrian world" rather than the "riding world," Civilization rather than Nature, prevails in modern Casterbridge, it is perhaps not surprising that the three major characters who suffer death are identifiable with Nature and its linked oppositions: Susan, Lucetta, and Henchard. Yet the fact and certainly the order of their deaths is indeed "arbitrary," inasmuch as it is not their particular *identities* but their places within the novel's structured oppositions that unleash the verdict wrought by the unanimous victim mechanism to fall upon each one in his or her turn.

Susan's death is traceable to her submerged rivalry with Lucetta for Henchard and to Henchard's already developing commercial-family rivalry with Farfrae. Just as Susan rallies after her illness, Henchard receives Lucetta's letter and, pitying her, vows to marry her "if ever I should be left in a position to carry [it] out." A few sentences later, Susan "weakens visibly" and dies during Elizabeth-Jane's vigil. Susan is the novel's first instance of the surrogate victim mechanism operating in this "universe of radical opposition" between Nature and Civilization, working to crush what it has coaxed into life. Elizabeth-Jane's pained musings during her mother's vigil bear particularly on the arbitrariness of Susan's death: Elizabeth-Jane wonders "why things around her had taken the shape they wore in preference to every other possible shape" (121).

Why did Susan die? For Lucetta too is associated with Nature. Act I's "theme" was "the ruin of good husbands by bad wives" (16). As the Henchard-Farfrae rivalry reaches its first crisis point, "violence must be deflected to some individual."[61] Susan is the least well defined and "can be easily disposed of,"[62] in Girard's phrase about victimage. As if they were Tiresias and Creon, Lucetta and Henchard, who represent Roman strangers in modern Casterbridge, manage to "shift blame"[63] for the unbalanced alternations onto Susan—and she becomes the town's first scapegoat. She is the first sacrifice of Nature to Civilization. Her sacrifice temporarily quells the mounting crisis, as Act II ends with the men "in renewed friendship" (105) and Henchard committed in his mind to marrying Lucetta.

But the crisis of undifferentiation has merely paused and will advance inexorably. Lucetta's victimage is a sacrifice to the spreading plague of multiple reciprocal mediations engulfing the entire town in the male protagonists' rivalry. Suddenly, Jopp re-intrudes into the novel's foreground, and his reading aloud of the Henchard-Lucetta love letters provokes the town skimmity ride that kills her. Of course, Henchard too is implicated by the letters. But Lucetta has much farther to fall; the forces of Society and Fate typically unite to punish the woman for sexual infidelities. Lucetta is thus the second victim claimed by Civilization, as Henchard reflects: "So much for man's rivalry, he thought. Death was to have the oyster, and Farfrae and himself the shells" (282).

As in the case of Susan, Lucetta's victimage only temporarily quells the rising violence spread by the mimetic plague. With Lucetta's death, a new double triangle forms, as Farfrae and Newson vie with Henchard for Elizabeth-Jane's affections. Henchard turns to Elizabeth-Jane after Lucetta's death and "develops the dream of a future lit by her filial presence" (285). With Newson's return,

Introduced by Phillip Lopate, a distinguished literary critic and essayist-novelist, the cover of the Barnes & Noble Classics edition of Hardy's *The Mayor of Casterbridge* portrays Michael Henchard, the main protagonist of the novel and its first longtime mayor. Published in 1883, *The Mayor* is set in a fictionalized version of Dorchester, where Hardy lived during its composition, and in which he resided soon after its completion in a home that he designed and constructed called Max Gate until his death in 1928. Although Hardy's ashes were interred in the Poets' Corner of Westminster Abbey in London, his heart was buried on the outskirts of Dorchester.

The cover art for the Barnes & Noble Classics edition of *The Mayor of Casterbridge* is Paul Cezanne's *Self-Portrait*. Unlike *Self-Portrait* by Jacques-Louis David, which adorns the Oxford World's Classics edition of *Caleb Williams*, Cezanne's post-impressionist *Self-Portrait* features the artist looking at the viewer from the corner of his eyes, turned halfway in a sidelong glance. The image is well chosen to portray the mature Henchard, who is always at least half-enveloped (and imprisoned) by his shadowy past, and always driven to gaze backward in tortured ambivalence and anguished regret.

the ambiguous sense of Henchard's latent rivalry with the sailor takes firmer hold: "Stimulated by the unexpected coming of Newson to a greedy exclusivessness" (289) towards Elizabeth-Jane, Henchard impulsively tells Newson a lie — that she is dead. Newson departs, and Henchard clings to Elizabeth-Jane even more desperately. Reduced now to the level of a "fangless lion" (300), Henchard accepts the inevitability of Elizabeth-Jane's approaching marriage to Farfrae, hoping like Pere Goriot "only for the privilege of being in the house she occupied" (303). Yet this acquiescence is not without deep remorse, for he cleaves to Elizabeth-Jane not for herself but from his mimetic rivalry with Farfrae still. Henchard desperately holds onto Elizabeth-Jane because Farfrae does; to lose Farfrae, his obstacle-model and double, would be to lose his guide for desiring — and therefore doom himself to his unfilled void alone.

Act IV ends on a revelation and a broken confrontational triangle as Henchard evades a showdown with Newson. Elizabeth-Jane discovers her true father and her original identity. Meanwhile a new and final family triangle of Farfrae-Newson–Elizabeth-Jane looms.

VIII

> His attempts to replace ambition by love had been as fully foiled as his ambition itself.
>
> HENCHARD (312)

During Lucetta's dying hours, Henchard's life "seemed centering on the personality of the stepdaughter whose presence he but recently could not endure" (284). Even after his voluntary exile from the town on Newson's approach, Elizabeth-Jane remains Henchard's personal center; likewise he wanders unintentionally but surely in a geographical circle "of which Casterbridge formed the center" (312).

Act V foregrounds the oppositions of convention and passion, and Henchard's circular maunderings reflect the mimetic mechanism's obstacle-model cycle of contempt and veneration: for "the centrifugal tendency imparted by weariness of the world was counteracted by the centripetal influence of love for his daughter" (312). That centripetal desire also includes "rivalry for Farfrae" — and it and Henchard's need for presence finally prove overpowering. He is drawn back to Casterbridge for Elizabeth-Jane's wedding to Farfrae, for "to endeavor strenuously to hold his own in her love . . . was worth the risk of repulse, aye, of life itself" (314).

The Penguin Classics edition of Hardy's *The Mayor of Casterbridge* portrays an aging Michael Henchard on its cover. Formerly the town mayor and a prosperous merchant, Henchard suffers a terrible fall both in his professional fortunes and personal life. By the novel's last chapters, as this cover image portrays, he is a towering wreck worthy of classical tragedy. This image reflects Henchard's star-crossed fate as if to adumbrate his exclamation of despair (which is bannered on the back cover of the Penguin edition): "I have not always been what I am now!" Edited by Keith Wilson, the Penguin *Mayor* includes an introduction, a chronology of Hardy's life and works, detailed explanatory notes, and Hardy's prefaces to both the 1895 and 1912 editions of the novel.

On yet another symbolic Fair Day, Henchard himself now stands as the intruder before the Newson-Farfrae–Elizabeth-Jane family triangle. But this triangle does not collapse and metamorphose in the face of Henchard's weak confrontation. Exhausted by an enervating rivalry and starved by an unrequited, ambivalent love for the wedding couple, the alienated, already fully domesticated Henchard soon dies after receiving a sharp rebuke by Elizabeth-Jane, who is surprised that Henchard appears at the wedding. The fate of love-starved Henchard resembles the famished condition of the caged goldfinch, "the poor little songster" (322) that he buys the nuptial pair as a wedding gift. Henchard has risked both repudiation and even life itself on Elizabeth-Jane, and he has lost on both. As on Fair Day at the tragedy's outset in Act I, he has lost a fateful wager.

With Farfrae's attainment of Elizabeth-Jane, the object over which he and Henchard have battled longest and hardest, the structural displacement of the older by the younger "mayor" is complete: Farfrae has appropriated the erstwhile social identity of Henchard. Just as Elizabeth-Jane's experience of renunciation has been "less a series of pure disappointments than a series of substitutions" (177), Farfrae's triumph over Henchard has been more a round of displacements than pure victories. The pattern of substitution, metamorphosis, displacement, appropriation, and identity extends directly to Newson too, as it reaches the whirlwind force of a vertiginous tornado during the wedding dance, effacing all differences. Newson as Elizabeth-Jane's partner seems to "out-Farfrae Farfrae" and substitutes for Henchard too: "That happy face—Henchard's complete discomfiture lay in it. It was Newson's; who had indeed come and supplanted him" (319). The narrator has also called Farfrae a "supplanter." Even Henchard touches on the mimetic patterning in his cry to Elizabeth-Jane about Newson: "O my maid—I see you have another—a real father in my place. But don't give all your thought to him. Do ye save a little room for me!" (318).

Although the characters are now well-nigh indistinguishable and undifferentiated, the substitution is exact—and the verdict of unanimous victimage is set to fall upon Henchard. The three men—Farfrae, Newson, and Henchard—match the protagonists of *Oedipus Rex* as doubles of one another, and it only remains for a scapegoat to be chosen. Girard explains that this structural development follows tragedy's own mimetic sequence:

> The characters in tragedy are ultimately indistinguishable. The words to describe any one of them . . . are all equally applicable and equally adequate. If the commentators have failed to remark that these traits are the common property of all the characters in the play, it is because they are not all affected by them at the same time.
>
> If violence is a great leveler of men and everybody becomes the double or "twin" of his antagonist, . . . all the doubles are identical. . . . Any one can at any given moment become the double of all the others, that is, the sole object of universal obsession and hatred. A single victim can be substituted for all the potential victims . . . for each and every member of the community. . . . The slightest hint, the most groundless

accusation, can circulate with vertiginous speed and is transformed into irrefutable proof.[64]

The wedding is the central scene in Act V. Its events illumine ritual's function in modernity: to consolidate and erase differences even while seeming to restore them. During the royal visit, Farfrae and Lucetta on the platform are the only prominently identifiable townsmen—all the other faces (except for Henchard) are opaque or obscure. Yet *after* the ritual of the Town Council meeting in the King's Arms, the men are also faceless, with all the social differences of the daytime blackened out.

Of course, the distinction between the two events is the *type* of difference effaced, though both sorts stream into the ongoing undifferentiation process. A wedding, the ritual *par excellence* of *Gesellschaft*, restores formal differences as it eliminates all personal difference; the King's Arms social hour, a less structured ritual, restores a degree of personal difference as it effaces formal differences. Of course, by the time of Elizabeth-Jane's wedding at *The Mayor*'s end, the novel has reached such a dizzying pace of mimetic alternations that all differences are effectively erased.

The "series of substitutions" that began with Newson taking Susan and Farfrae entering the corn trade finally reveals the transparent truth that all three men represent the tragedy's desymbolized enemy brothers. As Girard explains, "the antagonists never occupy the same space at the same time . . . but they occupy these positions in succession. There is never anything on one side of the system that cannot be found on the other side provided we wait long enough."[65] Farfrae advances inexorably from small corn trader to large merchant to Lucetta's husband to the owner of Henchard's business, home, furniture, and Self—and finally becomes mayor. Henchard's panic-stricken anxiety with every allusion to Farfrae's mayoral prospects is not mere envy, nor is it simply accident that Farfrae's election coincides with Henchard's "moral change" and their "official" and hand-to-hand confrontations. Farfrae's elevation contrasts with Henchard's diminished being, and it is as if Farfrae's status as the new mayor of Casterbridge represents the ultimate "rape" of Henchard, the appropriation of his last possession: the title hero's role.[66]

To view the novel within the mimetic pattern of metamorphosis, identity, and substitution is to enrich the title's significance, for though Farfrae is mayor for the final two acts, the novel is not titled in the plural. The mimetic mechanism also reveals the final irony of Farfrae seizing what was never really Henchard's to begin with: Elizabeth-Jane.

Of course, as Girard notes, characters' differences never vanish entirely but are "constantly inverted" until all cardinal distinctions disappear. Farfrae "becomes" a corn merchant, Lucetta's lover, and the mayor. Newson "becomes"

Susan's husband and Elizabeth-Jane's father. The men's real difference with Henchard, as in the case of Creon and Tiresias from Oedipus, lies in the distinct points in time in which they enter the tragic action; once introduced, they stalk one another like the doubles whom they finally resemble. As Girard explains:

> The only distinction between Oedipus and his adversaries is that Oedipus initiates the contest, triggering the tragic plot. He thus has a certain head start on the others. But though the action does not occur simultaneously, its symmetry is absolute. Each protagonist in turn occupies the same position in regard to the same object. . . . All are drawn unwittingly into the structure of violent reciprocity.[67]

That Farfrae fails to notice Henchard's hatred for so long is remarkable,[68] but Henchard likewise fails to distinguish its mimetic nature. Even at his bitterest moments as Farfrae's workman, he does not realize that the reason he "never wished to claim [Lucetta] as his own so desperately as he regretted her loss" (226) is that he desires her because Farfrae possesses her—and possesses everything else that Henchard once had. Henchard's fury and depression stem less from the fact of Elizabeth-Jane's romantic yearnings, his dwindling number of customers, a disastrous harvest, Lucetta's rejection, bankruptcy, his loss of possessions, and his decline to hay trusser than from his inconsolable feeling that the beneficiary in every instance is Donald Farfrae. Farfrae had misinterpreted Henchard's generous and garrulous behavior as "domineering" and "tyrannical"; instead, with his characteristic mildness, Farfrae tolerated yet resented it. Likewise, Henchard misinterprets Farfrae's gentleness as callousness, and sees in the Scotsman's every movement a foe's designs. Both men fail to understand the mimetic, fluctuating dynamics of their relationship because they see each other only from the "inside," without the temporal perspective of the future.[69]

Farfrae and Henchard not only misinterpret each other but also see the hand of Fate in almost every event. To Farfrae, it is "the way of the waarrld." To superstitious Henchard it is a "power" "roasting a waxen image" of him or "stirring an unholy brew" (188). Yet a welter of bad "accidents" befalls Henchard, starting from the novel's opening scenes: he miscalculates his defiant selling offer; Susan encounters the same hag eighteen years later, who directs her to Casterbridge; Henchard meets Farfrae ahead of his hired manager Jopp; Henchard's celebration plans are rained out; he opens Susan's letter just after telling Elizabeth-Jane that she is his daughter; Elizabeth-Jane happens to meet Lucetta and decides to live with her, as Henchard's request for her to stay comes "ten minutes" too late; Farfrae meets with Lucetta when she sends Elizabeth-Jane out so that Henchard will not be deterred from visiting; Henchard happens to preside over the hag's case and she reveals his past; Henchard hears wrongly that Farfrae tries to prevent rather than help him open a little shop; Henchard wrestles with Farfrae hours before he begs the now completely distrusting Scotsman to return to a sick wife; and the Farfraes arrive just a half hour after Henchard's death. These accidents and others not surprisingly give Henchard a "persecution complex" toward Farfrae and Casterbridge, typified by Henchard's belief that he alone has been singled out for humiliation when, as a citizen without official standing, he is not permitted to greet the royal visitor.

Traditional Freudian psychoanalysis would interpret both Henchard's rivalry with Farfrae and his "persecution complex" as a father complex, with the textual motifs of "enemy brother" and "threatened king" as unconscious identifications that reveal both men's psychic propensity toward homosexuality. On this reading, Henchard "suffers" willfully before Farfrae and confesses his great secret to him, masochistically pays the little boy for painful news of Farfrae's superiority, and finally returns as a Farfrae laborer in order to be reminded daily of his failures. Henchard's self-admission to Farfrae of "being by nature something of a woman-hater" and finding "no hardship to keep mostly at a distance from the sex" suggests the depths of his repression and the extent of his paranoia (83).

By contrast, a mimetic interpretation of the protagonists' relationship would not deny the links to "brothers" and "king" or "tyrant," Henchard's misogyny, or Henchard's (and Farfrae's) latent homosexuality, but rather focus upon the nature of their desire. Are their desires motivated by substitute fathers—or related to each other as the novel's patterned oppositions suggest? Do their desires for the same women spring from a "spontaneous and independent" desire for the mother? Why do the two men seem to move in a "series of substitutions," desiring the same objects in successive order? According to Girard, Freud answers these questions by way of his unwieldy, "abnormal" Oedipus complex, which postulates a "bisexual component" in addition to the child's natural paternal "affection." This component's feminine element drives the child, confronted by the terror of castration, to invert fear into love and present himself as a paternal love object.

My view is that Girard's unified, dynamic mimetic mechanism explains more straightforwardly and precisely not only the protagonists' latent homosexuality but also their successively identical desires—and it does so not by postulating a distant childhood past not explicitly presented in *The Mayor*, but rather by scrutinizing the developmental conflict embedded in the circumstances of the narrative events and relationship patterns. It also offers a view of its dramatic structure and an integrated approach to the novel as tragedy, as a "modern *Oedipus*" whose very title shows the mimetic mechanism at work. Girard explains how a condition of latent homosexuality can be fully compatible with a mimetic model.[70]

As with Girard's earlier reformulations of Freud's primal horde and collective murder theories, the real key is not the father's *identity* but rather his function. Just as the father's victimage unified the community, a mimetic interpretation of *The Mayor's* events provides an integrated, coherent explanation of its relationships and plot structures.

Act V closes with Henchard's victimage, occurring just thirty minutes before the Farfraes arrive in search of him and thereby foreclosing the possibility of their forming a reconciled family triangle. Yet Henchard's death is not a complete turning of the unanimous victimage mechanism against him, for he does die in a family triangle of sorts: Abel Whittle nurses him in his last hours because Henchard "were kind-like to mother if he were rough to me" (325). Henchard's surrogate death is not so much forced upon him, however, as self-willed. He in effect gives up on this world and embraces the next, as his words on Newson's approach prefigure: "'I—Cain—go alone as I deserve—an outcast and a vagabond. But my punishment is *not* greater than I can bear!'"(307).[71]

According to Girard, surrogate victims are typically "on the fringes" of society. So Henchard is the "perfect" "arbitrary" choice as both "king" and *pharmakos*.[72] Yet Henchard is not a complete "outsider" to Casterbridge, as are Newson and the furmity woman. Nor of course is he an "insider" like Christopher Coney, Solomon Longways, or Mother Cuxsom. Rather, like victims Susan and Lucetta (and also Farfrae and Elizabeth-Jane), Henchard is both "outsider" and "insider," as is characteristic of ritualistic victims. Henchard as mayor and Henchard as wife-seller reflect his double status, showing him as king and *pharmakos*. Even Whittle's appearance as a "poor fond fool" (325) to Henchard's King and as Abel to Henchard's Cain follow Girard's idea of victimage's patterning: the fool shares his master's status as an outsider and is "eminently 'sacrificeable'"[73]—the arbitrary verdict could fall on either person. But it is Henchard who can perform the communal function that Girard identifies in the sacrificial rituals of African tribal kings: "He is the catalyst who converts sterile, infectious violence into positive cultural values."[74]

Thus the victimage mechanism ultimately performs a social function: "To restore harmony to the community, to reinforce the social fabric," and "to prevent conflicts from erupting."[75] Yet for Girard it has much greater significance than even this. For since violence permeates all forms of myth and ritual, the surrogate victim mechanism is "simply another aspect of the symbolic process. . . . There can be nothing in the whole range of human culture that is not rooted in violent unanimity—nothing that does not find its source in the surrogate victim."[76] The arbitrary nature of the mechanism's operation masks its status as the basis for all violence and therefore all religion "in its broadest sense," whereby religious ritual serves as another term for man's efforts to defend himself against his own violence."[77] And so while our judicial systems and penal codes appear founded on a national consensus or an implied social contract, our unanimous acquiescence to them is actually "an institutionalized and legalized form of mob violence."[78] Accordingly, societal norms define Mayor Farfrae's dragging away Henchard as public duty, whereas Henchard's wrestling Farfrae with an arm behind his back is a public crime.

Girard's mimetic and surrogate victim theories finally represent a more comprehensive articulation of Durkheim's basic view that culture begins with religion. For Girard, religion is "simply another term for the surrogate victim, who reconciles mimetic oppositions and assigns a sacrificial goal to the mimetic impulse."[79] Fully developed in *Violence and the Sacred,* Girard's work amounts to a theory of evolution "rivaling" Darwin and Lamarck: culture is rooted in religion, which is but the social expression of violent unanimity, whose source is the surrogate victim guarding man through violence against his own violence.[80] And so violence is "venerated" in primitive religion because "it offers men what little peace they can ever expect. Nonviolence appears as the gratuitous gift of violence."[81]

Although Girard makes no reference to Hardy or his fiction anywhere in his work, the degree to which they share the same traditions and concerns is striking. Hardy the non-academic "philosopher of experience"[82] and Girard the scientific "apologist of Reaction"[83] both defend the ageless truths of ritual against the supposed advances of Enlightenment humanism and science. Both ultimately accept the limitations of reason in the face of larger social and mystical forces. This acceptance places the two thinkers in an empirico-mystical, chiefly French romantic-positivist tradition stretching from Saint-Simon and Comte through Taine, Durkheim, and Bergson. Hardy was deeply influenced by Comte and Darwin, and the resonance of the Hardyean ideas of "Immanent Will" and "unsympathetic First Cause" with Schopenhauer's Will, Spencer's Unknowable, and Bergson's *élan vital* are undeniable and have often been noted.[84] Moreover, Hayden White identifies Girard's affinities as a sophisticated, unsentimental modern prophet of apocalypse with the thought of Maistre, Bonald, and Durkheim, all of whom set out to defend religion "by a theory . . . more scientific than the scientists."[85] This project, implicit in Hardy's fiction and explicit in Girard's *Violence and the Sacred,* accounts for both men's ceaseless, almost obsessive inquiry into how the primitive and superstitious intrude suddenly upon the scientific and modern.

Thus, Hardy's oft-criticized, purportedly "artless penchant" for "lazy" plot devices such as accident, coincidence, and reversal may in fact be viewed as fitting artistic and narrative choices for dramatizing how culture originates in the religious. Such *deus ex machina* plot devices abound throughout Hardy's oeuvre, which might itself be conceptualized as a "universe of radical opposition" between Nature and Civilization. Given this characteristic Hardyean world and his already-noted similarities in tradition and outlook with Girard, it would be useful to examine beyond *The Mayor* the degree to which the surrogate victim mechanism lies at the basis of all Hardy's work.[86]

IX

Let me close this chapter with a brief observation that might contribute toward such a project. I do not think it would be unreasonable to view all five of Hardy's great "tragic" novels as structured by triangular desire, with *The Mayor*'s total of ten principal love and legal triangles as his most ambitious geometric (or architectural) experiment. Hardy's other novels do not offer as many possible triangular relationships because there is usually no child (as with baby and mature Elizabeth-Jane) to "trade" places. Therefore Hardy's other fictions highlight romantic triangles. These novels are indeed love stories, not war stories; yet mimetic rivalry is always present, if not typically foregrounded, and it surfaces repeatedly and with tragic consequence.

Far from the Madding Crowd (1874) is shaped by four romantic triangles: Gabriel Oak-Bathsheba Everdene-Sergeant Troy; Gabriel-Bathsheba-William Boldwood; Fanny Robin-Troy-Bathsheba; and William-Bathsheba-Troy. The novel turns on a series of coincidences: the initial loss of Oak's sheep, his squelching a fire on the farm which Bathsheba inherits; the storm that ruins Troy's flowers laid on Fanny's grave and precipitates his disappearance and presumed death; the loss of Boldwood's hayricks in a second storm; and many others. Fanny's and her baby's (by Troy) drowning precludes the imminent formation of the family triangle of Fanny-Troy-baby. And as the novel ends with Boldwood in a mental institution and Troy shot dead by Boldwood, violence and the victimage mechanism have claimed four lives.

In *The Return of the Native* (1878), Hardy creates three major love triangles: Clym Yeobright-Eustacia Vye-Damon Wildeve; Eustacia-Damon-Thomasin Yeobright; and Diggory Venn-Thomasin-Damon. The brutal reality of Egdon Heath, a wasteland that finally claims the life of Mrs. Yeobright, stands against the imagined (though never visited) wonder of Paris—and these two settings frame the novel's oppositions. Accidents abound, such as the bizarre transfer of Mrs. Yeobright's money intended for Clym and Thomasin equally to Wildeve to Diggory (in dice games) and then mistakenly to Thomasin alone. Coincidence unites tragically with secret when Eustacia fails to answer the door upon Mrs. Yeobright's knocking because she is with Wildeve in the kitchen, a misfortune leading to Clym's mother's death walk across the heath. She dies because of the heat (and an adder bite); Eustacia and her unsuccessful rescuer Wildeve drown, all three of them victims of mimetic rivalries involving Clym. But the generator of the triangles, standing at the novel's center, is Eustacia, whose "great desire" is "to be loved to madness. . . . Love was to her the one cordial which could drive away the eating loneliness of her days. And she seemed to long for the abstraction called passionate love more than any particular lover" (75). This is misstated: her love is not object desire. It is mimetically directed, whether by Mrs. Yeobright or Thomasin.[87]

Hardy's most simple geometric novel is *Tess of the D'Urbervilles* (1891), with but a single triangle: Alec D'Urberville-Tess Durbeyfield-Angel Clare. The Durbeyfield family stands in double opposition to the other two families: poor, irrational Jack and Joan Durbeyfield versus middle-class, dogmatically evangelical Reverend Clare versus rich, depraved Alec. Nature, law, society, and justice all conspire together to condemn Tess: her life is a series of "ifs"—if only her father hadn't accidentally found he was a D'Urberville, if only Angel had found her letter to him explaining her past, if only her father hadn't died when she could turn to nobody except Alec to support her family. The tensions among the novel's opposing forces, as represented by the families' differences, magnificently culminate in Tess herself. Although Jack Durbeyfield and Alec die before her (D'Urberville by her hand), Tess is the chief and only "satisfying" sacrifice to the novel's capricious, insatiable forces.

Hardy's last and most pathetically tragic novel is *Jude the Obscure* (1895), which consists of three triangles: Richard Phillotson-Sue Bridehead-Jude Fawley; Sue-Jude-Arabella Donn; and (obliquely) Jude-Arabella-Cartlett. Hardy describes *Jude* in its preface as "a deadly war between flesh and spirit," a "tragedy of unfilled aims" (viii). The novel showcases the oppositions of isolation and reciprocity, convention and passion, despair and hope. The formation and collapse of a family triangle is repeatedly reconfigured in the mutating love triangles. When Arabella fears her rich suitor will reject her if he knows she once had a child, she sends five-year-old "Little Father Time" to live with his father Jude and Sue. Little Father Time's accidental overhearing of Sue's fatalistic musing that "children should never be brought into the world" leads him to hang himself and his two younger siblings. A pregnant Sue then gives birth to a dead baby and the novel closes with both her and Jude as victims: Sue returns to a torturous, masochistic marriage with Phillotson and Jude's weak lungs completely fail after a long trip to Sue in the pouring rain.

The procession of victims that these four novels offer to Nature and Civilization as sacrifices to the violent allows each work to end, as in *The Mayor*, on a respite of peaceful exhaustion or "an occasional episode" (327) of happiness. In *The Mayor*, the painful drama fittingly closes on a secret that is itself a revelation: the "secret" of happiness, Elizabeth-Jane finds, is that there is no secret of happiness. This is Fate's carefully hidden truth in all Hardy's work, the "secret" that happiness consists "in making limited opportunities endurable" and "in the cunning enlargement . . . of those minute forms of satisfaction that offer themselves to everybody not in positive pain" (405). Fittingly, this insight becomes integrated in "a reflex action" within Elizabeth-Jane's overall philosophy of life, for she finally sees no real difference between repute in the upper and lower strata of Casterbridge society—and no point in cultivating it in either. She has learned "the lesson of renunciation" (213), the same difficult education that young Hardy received during his unwilling boyhood surrender of the classics to architecture.

Yet *The Mayor of Casterbridge* as a "universe of radical opposition" is most sublimely expressed not in the practicality of Elizabeth-Jane's final thoughts, but rather in the "sacredness of [Henchard's] last words" (326). Those words mingle violence and desire and "bitterness" and longing in a scrawled statement of anguished grandeur made "of the same stuff that his whole life was made of." They also capture the paradoxical oppositions that Girard posits at the heart of the sacred itself, where not only violence but also another "directly contradictory element" coexist: "The sacred involves . . . order as well as disorder, peace as well as war, creation as well as destruction." "Tragedy might then be defined," concludes Girard, "as the dramatic execution of the sacred's destructive element."[88]

Or, as Hardy phrased it just one month before the serial publication of his "modern *Oedipus*," as if aware of the infernal triangle of desire's conflictual and arbitrary nature: "Tragedy. It may thus be put in brief: a tragedy exhibits a state of things in the life of an individual which unavoidably causes some natural aim or desire of his to end in catastrophe when carried out."[89]

This undated photograph of Ford Madox Ford was taken sometime during the 1930s, when the author was a widely recognized novelist, editor, and man of letters. It became widely identified with Ford as a result of appearing as the cover for the Dalkey edition of Ford's *The March of Literature* (1938).

CHAPTER FOUR

Ford's The Good Soldier

MOVEMENTS OF THE HEART

I don't know that analysis of my own psychology matters at all to this story. I should say that it didn't or at any rate that I had given enough of it.

JOHN DOWELL IN FORD MADOX FORD'S *THE GOOD SOLDIER*

I

The Good Soldier[1] has traditionally been approached as an exposition of the final breakdown of the traditional feudal order in Edwardian England, a novel of social criticism that assails the emptiness of aristocratic life and religious zealotry. Critics have typically stressed the work's "unique importance as an anatomy of the world of English society just before the first world war"[2] and judged it as pervaded by an irony that "expresses Victorianism in the final stage of self-consciousness with respect to the hypocrisies of its conventions."[3] Other readers have framed the novel's central issues in terms of a moral dilemma or an epistemological quest. Mark Schorer believes that "finally, *The Good Soldier* describes a world that is without a moral point, a narrator who is suffering from the madness of moral inertia."[4] To Samuel Hynes, the critical question is "what Dowell knows and how he comes to know—or fails to know."[5]

However much these perspectives illuminate crucial aspects of the novel and Ford's sociopolitical views and Impressionist aesthetic project, they do not finally seize what readers invariably testify to as their bewildering reading experience of *The Good Soldier*. Nor do they address adequately the underlying thematic tensions and oppositions that give rise to the work's overwhelming sense of a society on the vertiginous brink of exhausted self-consciousness[6] and of a narrator in the process of self-disintegration, desperate yet unable to "know." In the words of the subtitle, the novel is certainly "a tale of passion," with an extraordinary series of fantastic accidents (such as the recurrence of August 4), a chaotically digressive plot structure, several puzzling narrative omissions, and abrupt alterations in mood and tone between enflamed rapture and inconsolable despair. "It is so difficult to keep all these people going," narrator Dowell laments (148). "Perhaps all these reflections are a nuisance; but they crowd in on me" (139).

This chapter contends that *The Good Soldier*'s narrative incongruities and coincidences are not finally explainable in terms of Ford's political or aesthetic program; nor are they due to poor craftsmanship. Rather, this is indeed "a tale of passion" in the language of psychoanalytic theory.[7] Within the framework of libidinal development as described by Sigmund Freud and Melanie Klein, Dowell's narration of causally disconnected events and anecdotes and his deep-seated ambivalence toward his friend and hero Captain Edward Ashburnham become understandable when viewed as those of a fundamentally narcissistic personality engaged in an unconscious homosexual identification with an exalted father figure.[8]

The world of *The Good Solider* is the narrator's attempt to incarnate his "minuet de la cour" (11), a search to create his ideal family romance and to recapture his Paradise Lost. The narrative is a projection of Dowell's self, with the various characters serving as different aspects of Dowell's ego.[9] Dowell's reflection upon recalling Ashburnham's "monstrously wicked" sexual advances toward young Nancy Rufford is unwittingly accurate: "I tell you I see that thing as clearly as if it were a dream that never left me" (79). Despite Dowell's conscious demurrals, "analysis" of his own psychology does "matter," for Ford has written a dream-narrative that invites scrutiny of Dowell's self-admitted "dual personality" as storyteller and daydreamer. "Well, those are my impressions," he says in Part III. "I pieced it together afterwards" (79). He projects a narcissistic dream world in which he functions as both speaker and audience. Dowell, the novel's narrative consciousness, is in fact a collage of impressions operating according to the dream mechanisms of secondary revision, disguise, distortion, and displacement. It is, of course, doubtful that Ford deliberately crafted the novel as dream, though he does say in his introductory Dedicatory Letter to Stella Ford that *The Good Soldier* is the single work in which he invested "*all* that I knew about writing" and that it "hatch[ed] within myself for fully [a decade]," even though it was written "with comparative rapidity" (5).[10] Likewise, Dowell, though he professes to be "too-truthful" about his love for Edward, is quite unaware of his latent homosexuality.

For the aforementioned strictly textual reasons and because of the psychological issues embedded within this work, a psychoanalytic reading that interprets the novel as the enclosed world of a narcissistic daydreamer is warranted, since such an approach addresses directly the novel's "passion" and lends coherence to its seemingly anarchic narrative and mood "leaps."[11] The sociopolitical implications of the novel's national and religious motifs and Dowell's anguished outcries about his godless world also need not be limited to their immediate spheres: the husband-wife, parent-child, and landlord-tenant struggles may also be viewed in the psychosocial, phylogenetic terms of "repressive civilization" as developed by Freud in *Civilization and Its Discontents* and his other cultural investigations.[12] The price of civilization is the renunciation of our instincts. That exchange, said Freud fatalistically, represents an irreconcilable conflict for human beings as social and instinctual animals.

"Society," echoes Dowell, "must go on" (3): it is the "civilized" society in which the "normal" and "slightly deceitful" "flourish" and wherein "the passionate, headstrong, and too-truthful are condemned" (167). *The Good Soldier* is a stark exposition of the uncompromising struggle between the free gratification of man's instinctual needs and the development of civilization, a warring dialectic between (as Hynes puts it) "Passion and Convention."[13] In psychoanalytic terms, it is a rivalry between the pleasure and reality principles. Just as the perpetual inhibitions upon Eros ultimately weaken the life instincts and strengthen and release those destructive forces against which Ford's characters battle, Dowell, Edward, Florence, Leonora, and even Nancy are alternately sheltered (in their cozy "four-square coterie") and shackled together (in "a prison full of screaming hysterics") (11–12). Like a dream turned nightmare, the novel does seem driven toward death: the physical deaths of Edward, Maisie Maidan, and Florence; Nancy's madness and the hollow triumph of the "normal," rabbit-like Leonora and Rodney Bayham; and Dowell's psychic disintegration, in which he feels finally "alone—horribly alone" (12).

II

In his later modifications of the libido theory, Freud revised his original position that "libido" was the pleasure-seeking force of the sex instincts alone, a single force sharply distinguished from and opposed to the ego instincts. Beginning in "On Narcissism" (1914) and more fully formulated in "Libido Theory and Narcissism" (1917), Freud postulated the concepts of "narcissistic [or ego] libido" and "object libido."[14] In the latter, libidinal energy is invested in objects outside the self, whereas in the former it is withdrawn from objects and redirected toward the ego itself, a process also called "secondary narcissism." This state constitutes a mild re-creation of the infant's experience from his earliest developmental stage ("primary narcissism"), during which the narcissistic ego is integrated with the external world and in which the infant cannot distinguish self from others and feels the world as an extension of the self. "Narcissistic libido" occurs at the next developmental stage, before the differentiation of ego and id, and constitutes "the libidinal complement to egoism."[15]

All dreams are therefore fundamentally narcissistic or egoistic. As Freud explains in "Libido Theory and Narcissism," the mental activity manifested in dreams "is dominated by purely egoistic motives" during which "all object-cathexes, libidinal as well as egoistic, are given up and withdrawn into the ego."[16] The dreaming state restores "the primal state of the distribution of the libido," similar to narcissistic libido's attachment to the ego, which provides "satisfaction in the ego just as satisfaction is usually only found in objects."[17] This drive for the elevation and satisfaction of the ego marks a defining connection between daydreams (over which a dreamer usually has some conscious control, unlike night-dreams), and imaginative fiction. In "Creative Writers and Daydreaming," Freud indeed calls the poet "one who dreams in daytime," with "the hero of all daydreams and all novels" being "His Majesty the Ego." Both productions are fantasies whose "driving power" is the "fulfillment of a wish," whether ambitious or erotic or both.[18]

On close examination, *The Good Soldier* conforms to a daydream narrative, with a storyteller whose consuming though unfulfilled wish is the preservation and heightening of his dreamlike universe. Before the onset of Nancy's madness, and before Edward's suicide and Leonora's shattering revelations as to the circumstances behind them, Dowell would talk "by the hour, evolving my plans for a shock-proof world" (41). By his own definition, Dowell is a daydreamer-novelist: "If it's the business of a novelist to make you see things clearly. . . . I tell you I see that thing [Edward's attempted seduction of Nancy at the Casino] as clearly as if it were a dream that never left me" (79). Dowell ponders telling his "tale of passion" from the beginning, as if it were a straightforward narrative, a story told in sequence; but he rejects that approach and prefers instead to just "go on talking" (15). He finally concludes: "I console myself with thinking this is a real story and that, after all, real stories are probably told best in the way a person telling a story would tell them. They will then seem most real" (125).

So Dowell is obsessed with making his story seem "real." In fact, his characters are not so much separate persons with their own motivations (or even distinct characters in British society), as part-objects within Dowell's mind, which projects them as warring against one another. As Dowell insists, his story is not "The Ashburnham Tragedy"—not because it is not tragic, but rather because it is less about the Ashburnhams and Dowell's wife than about Dowell himself. "It is melodrama," he says, "but I can't help it" (80). In Freudian terms, day-dreamer Dowell belongs to that

> certain class of human beings upon whom not a god indeed, but a stern goddess — Necessity — has laid the task of giving an account of what they suffer and what they enjoy. These people are the neurotics. Among other things they have to confess their fantasies to the physician to whom they go in hope of recovering through mental treatment.[19]

Dowell constantly bewails the torments inflicted on him "by blind and inscrutable destiny" (41) as he "confesses" his "fantasies" to the "silent listener," his imagined "sympathetic soul opposite me" (15). His tale of woe is "the saddest story I ever heard," Dowell says in the novel's opening line. "Heard" is significant here. Sitting usually in Edward's old gun room, Dowell hears himself soliloquize his own sad story, and he is engulfed by it as both speaker and listener. He lives and narrates within a solipsistic world.

"You can't kill a minuet de la cour," Dowell pleads. Versailles and the Trianon may fall, he admits, but "surely the minuet — the minuet itself is dancing itself away into the furthest stars, even as our minuet of the Hessian bathing places must be stepping itself still" (11–12). The "minuet" is Dowell's metaphor for "the extreme intimacy" that he perceived to exist between the Dowells and Ashburnhams, and it is indeed "stepping itself still" as Dowell talks. For *The Good Soldier* is Dowell's wishful "minuet de la cour" turned "cri de coeur" with Dowell's often unconscious verbal echoes audible throughout in the descriptions of his "four-square house" and their movements. His story oscillates spasmodically between the mincing steps of an elegant AA'BB' minuet sequence and the flat-footed stomping of a merciless death march, between a wondrous "four-square house" and a horrific "prison full of screaming hysterics, tied down" (12). The story shifts abruptly from "heaven" and "Nirvana" (11) to "madness" (14) and "darkness" (14, 15), from the aristocratic stateliness of Act I of Mozart's *Don Giovanni* to the riotous, polyphonic futility of Charles Ives's *The Unanswered Question*. Dowell conceives the relationship of the two couples as a minuet

> simply because on every possible occasion and in every possible circumstance we knew where to go, where to sit, which table we unanimously should choose; and we could rise and go, all four together, without a signal from any one of us, always to the music of the Kur orchestra, always in the temperate sunshine, or if it rained, in discreet shelters. No, indeed, it can't be gone. (11)

Dowell does in fact desperately strive to preserve all this in his descriptions of specific characters and certain scenes. The first impression that he relates about Florence is, "Well, she was bright; and she danced." He goes on:

Ford Madox Ford is best remembered for his pioneering novel *The Good Soldier* (1915), which has been hailed as one of the great works of prose fiction of the twentieth century. It is included in the Modern Library's 100 Best Novels, and among *The Guardian*'s 1000 Novels Everyone Must Read. Set on the eve of World War I, *The Good Soldier* portrays the tragedy of two apparently "perfect" couples whose lives and relationships to one another are poisoned by a series of betrayals. In his "Dedicatory Letter to Stella Ford," a preface to the novel that honors his wife, Ford proudly reports that a friend declared *The Good Soldier* to be "the finest French novel in the English language."

The cover of the Penguin Classics edition of *The Good Soldier* depicts an image well suited to provoke reflection about the novel's characters and themes. We can imagine the couple in this scene engaged in the minuet dance that Dowell so frequently discusses, as if the image were the perfect objective correlative for the intricate interpersonal dance that the four main characters perform, namely that it evokes Edward Ashburnham and his lover Maisie Maidan engaged in the delicate steps of a minuet in a drawing room.

The image is a detail from *The Visit (Interior with Blue Sofa)*, painted in 1899 by the Swiss-born Parisian post-impressionist Félix Vallotton (1865–1925). The detail shows a living room furnished with a blue sofa, red chair, and green wall, on which hangs a cityscape painting. As in the case of the relationship between Ashburnham and Maisie, "the visit" is ostensibly from a man entering a woman's room and holding her in a tight embrace during a clandestine, intimate moment. Indeed, the scene is arguably more intimate than this cropped detail from *The Visit* allows. Vallotton's full painting shows an open door to a bedroom on the left, implying that the couple is soon headed there. Vallotton's suggestion is apparently that the couple are in each other's arms not just as dancers but lovers. The man seems to be guiding, perhaps quite insistently, the woman toward the bedroom door. Her blank visage discloses no emotions, mirroring suitably the ambiguities in Ford's novel, in which so many of the illicit rendezvous occur in sequestered rooms.

> She seemed to dance over the floors of castles and over seas and over and over the salons of modistes and over the plages [beaches] of the Riviera like a gay tremulous beam. . . . And my function in life was to keep that bright thing in existence. And it was almost as difficult as trying to catch with your hand that dancing reflection. (17)

Florence, "with her light step" (74), wanted above all "to be a great lady" (84), and Dowell suggests that she was attracted to the handsome, aristocratic British Captain Ashburnham largely because his Fordingbridge estate promised a return to "the home of her ancestors" (72). As if Edward were a prince entering a ballroom, Dowell remarks of him: "And that chap, coming into a room, snapped up the gaze of every woman in it" (27). Edward too is "an excellent dancer," for it was a "social duty to show himself at dances, and when there, to dance well" (110). Dowell sums up Maisie in a sentence: "She was very pretty; she was very young; in spite of her heart she was very gay and very light on her feet" (124). Leonora hoped Edward would tire "of the pretty little motions of her [Maisie's] hands and feet" (124). Leonora also tried to "put Nancy on a leash," but by then Edward is long past returning to his wife. Leonora's one chance to be in a man's arms occurred on her return from a hunt ball, but she burst out crying and ruined it (13). Given her repressive Catholic upbringing, she is no dancer. But she is (like Florence), Dowell exclaims, a "good actress . . . (By Jove she was good!)" who never reveals her dejection publicly (41). As if they had perfected the ceremonious curtsies, solemn bows, and graceful processioning of the minuet, Leonora and Edward behave with courtly grandeur even in the midst of torment. Before their partners, spectators, and friends, they perform stylized gestures. During those shining years with the Ashburnhams at the Nauheim spa, Dowell too dances and "fell into the habit of counting my footsteps."

> Yes, I could find my way blindfolded. . . . From the Hotel Regina you took one hundred and eighty-seven paces, then, turning sharp, left-handed, four hundred and twenty took you straight down to the fountain. From the Englischer Hof, starting on the sidewalk, it was ninety-seven paces and the same four hundred and twenty, but turning right-handed this time. (22)

Nauheim is indeed Dowell's dance floor, so "carefully arranged." He recalls: "I stood upon the carefully swept steps of the Englischer Hof, looking at the carefully arranged trees in tubs upon the carefully arranged gravel whilst carefully arranged people walked past in carefully calculated gaiety, at the carefully calculated hour" (21—22). He knows the scene as in a recurring dream: "That will give you the measure of how much I was in the landscape. I could find my

Published in 2010 and introduced by Sara Haslam, the Wordsworth Classics edition of Ford's *The Good Soldier* portrays on its cover two couples, as a lady looks on from behind—suggesting a scene of the Ashburnhams and the Dowells as Maisie Maidan (or perhaps Nancy Rufford) observes from a distance. The cover illustration for the Wordsworth Classics edition of *The Good Soldier* is *Woman in a Green Jacket* (1913), by the German expressionist painter August Macke (1887–1914). The scene blurs shape and color to express a mood, and it thus proves superbly pertinent to the novel's themes of emotional confusion, obscure hints and dim hunches, suspected betrayals, and bleary memory manifested in contradictory recollections. This image of four figures with a fifth detached also corresponds to the cast in Ford's novel, with its deadly quartet of two couples, plus either Maisie Maidan or Nancy Rufford (as the fifth). This closeness to the text lends the illustration a special credibility as a cover design.

way blindfolded to the hot rooms, to the douche rooms, to the fountain in the centre of the quadrangle where the rusty water gushes out" (22). Indeed the couples' relationship is "characterized by . . . taking everything for granted" (30). Even though there is among them "an extraordinary want of any communicativeness," they all seem to know what each of the others will do and what each wants.

Unbeknownst to Dowell, however, the couples' "four-square house" shows cracks from the start. The minuet begins with Edward's marriage to Leonora, which was "arranged by his parents" (47). Almost immediately Edward's attraction for other "partners" manifests itself and, as if observing etiquette, his "passions were quite logical in their progression upwards": "They began with a servant, went on to a courtesan, and then to a quite nice woman, very unsuitably mated . . . And after this lady came Maisie Maidan, and after poor Maisie only one more affair [Florence] and then—the real passion of his life [Nancy]" (47). Edward never consummates his passionate love, however, for when Florence "the great lady" captures her prince, it is the last dance—Florence commits suicide after secretly watching Edward's advances toward Nancy, and Edward's own suicide follows soon thereafter. The progress toward Edward and Florence's concourse thus advances through his series of partners and her affair with Jimmy to their final death embrace.

With his discovery of their affair and the rush of subsequent events, Dowell concludes his "goodly apple" was rotten, his "shock-proof world" was built with glass, and Europe all along was an "imprisonment." His "minuet de la cour" was actually a melancholic ode like the simple, mournful dirge Nancy plays on her "tinkly, reedy" piano:

> A silly, lilting, wavering tune came from before her in the dusk—a tune in which major notes with their cheerful insistence wavered and melted into minor sounds as, beneath the bridge the high lights on dark waters melt and waver and disappear into black depths. Well, it was a silly old tune. (149)

Dowell had thought that "the whole world ought to be arranged so as to ensure the keeping alive of heart patients" (40), and the regular summer meetings of his quartet, he now learns, were indeed so "arranged"[20] to facilitate the Edward-Florence affair. Not only do the revelations "close the harpsichord" and "shut up the music-book" (11) for Dowell, but they destroy "all the pleasantnesses that there were in my life" (42). But it is as if the game of musical beds simply ended on a wrong note, as if the right partners could have been easily matched if only the world were not so "queer."[21]

Here is another Vintage (U.K.) edition of *The Good Soldier,* introduced by Zoë Heller. The cover illustration is a suitable image to depict Florence, who is dressed in a long gown and sitting on a loveseat with a fan, complete with tassel, demurely positioned on her right knee. She is obviously in a pensive, perhaps even melancholy mood, doubtless searching for the truths of the past and uncertain about the future.

III

Freud compares daydreams to "romance" stories as fantasies occasioned by and developed through present experience, childhood associations, and past memory. "So past, present and future are threaded, as it were, on a string of the wish that runs through them all," Freud writes.[22] In the modern age, he believes, the writer tends to "split his ego by self-observation into many component egos, and in this way personifies the conflicting trends in [his] mental life" through many characters: "The 'good' ones are those who help the ego in its character of hero, while the 'bad' are his enemies and rivals."[23]

As we observed in Chapters One and Two, this propensity toward splitting, especially as it pertains to Dowell as narcissistic dreamer, also prevails in Melanie Klein's theory of the "paranoid-schizoid" position, which she considers the earliest stage of infantile development. Like Freud's concept of narcissistic libido, this stage occurs well before the differentiation of ego and id. According to Klein, the infant constructs a complex "inner world" of split-objects within himself, which he feels concretely. These objects are both loved and hated and they interrelate within the self and with one another. His obsessional fear is that he will lose the good objects (and thereby part of himself) or that the persecutory objects will overwhelm and annihilate the idealized objects (and the self). Thus the leading anxiety of psychic disintegration (death) is paranoid, and the state of the ego and its objects is characterized by splitting, which is schizoid. A Kleinian reading of *The Good Soldier* approaches Dowell as a narrator who reconstructs a story in which he projects his ego-ideal onto Edward, who is then "loved and admired because he contains the good parts of [Dowell's] self." Likewise Dowell projects his "bad parts" onto Edward (and Leonora and others too). Such impulses toward unconscious identification typify narcissistic object relations, which are characteristically shifting and unstable. Struggling desperately to steady, if not arrest, the convulsive movements of his interrelational "dance"—which repeatedly zigzags from stately minuet to fatalistic death march—a labile, paranoiac Dowell is driven to control his narrative by controlling his recalcitrant dance partners—that is, his own projected good and bad part-objects.[24]

According to Klein, when the external object is endangered, the internal object is felt to be in the same peril, and the result is "a feeling there is nothing left to sustain [the ego], and a corresponding feeling of loneliness." The paranoiac seems to lack anxiety, but this is "only apparent": "The feeling of being disintegrated, of being unable to experience emotions, of losing one's objects, is in fact the equivalent of anxiety," and his obsessiveness leads him to form a conception of either "extremely bad" and "extremely perfect objects" in this schizoid position.[25]

Dowell's "inner 'shock-proof world,'" consisting first of idealized "extremely perfect" objects like Ashburnham and later of persecutory objects leading to his feelings of loneliness and disintegration, can be further clarified within a Freudian and Kleinian framework. Dowell's obsessional wish is to actualize his "minuet de la cour" (or what Freud in his essay "Family Romances" [1909] called "the neurotic's family romance"), and his failure results in overwhelming despair and anxiety. Of course, Dowell remains unaware of this drive, but as narrator in control of his own story he is led to control the plot (through bewildering digressions) and others (into whom he has projected parts of himself) as a way to gain control of himself. Because his parents are "the source of all belief" to him, the small child's "peculiarly marked imaginative activity," says

Freud, focuses on his "most intense and most momentous wish": "to be like his parents (that is, the parent of his own sex)."[26] In later childhood, he recognizes his parents' (particularly his father's) fallibility and his "imagination becomes engaged in the task of getting free from the parents of whom he now has a low opinion and of replacing them with others who, as a rule, are of a higher social standing." His family romance is a "daydream . . . found[ed] to serve as the fulfillment of wishes and as a correction of actual life." As we saw also in the case of Godwin's Caleb Williams in Chapter Two, Freud's succeeding observations about the "young phantasy-builder" also evoke Dowell's world. Like Caleb, Dowell also builds his imaginative world by exploiting "any opportune coincidences from his actual experiences, such as his becoming acquainted with the Lord of the Manor or some landed proprietor if he lives in the country."

> These new and aristocratic parents [are] only an expression of the child's longing for the happy, vanished days when his father seemed to him the noblest and strongest of men and his mother the dearest and loveliest of women. He is turning away from the father whom he knows today to the father in whom he believed in the earlier years of his childhood; and his phantasy is no more than the expression of a regret that those happy days have gone. Thus in these phantasies the over-valuation that characterizes the child's earliest years comes into its own again . . . exalted personages stand for the dreamer's father and mother.[27]

Dowell describes Edward as "a painstaking guardian" (14), a "perfect maniac about children" (47) who would never even tell a dirty story. He was "an excellent magistrate, a first-rate soldier, one of the best landlords, so they said, in Hampshire, England" (14). With his penetrating gaze and paternal power he seems an object of perfection whose "gaze was perfectly level and perfectly direct and perfectly unchanging . . . the expression was that of pride, of satisfaction, of the possessor" (27). Together Edward and Leonora are to Dowell "the model couple": "To be the county family, to look the county family, to be so appropriately and perfectly wealthy; to be so perfect in manner—even just to the saving touch of the insolence that seems to be necessary. To have all that and to be all that!" (13).[28]

"As if she were listening, a mother, to the child at her knee" (41), Leonora listens for hours to Dowell's reveries about a "shock-proof world." Dowell is careful to stress that he "never had the beginnings of a trace of what is called the sex instinct" toward Leonora, and he "suppose[s]—no, I am certain that she never had it towards me" (29). Dowell believes instead that they share the passionate filial affection of a mother-son relationship. And like a protective mother, Leonora hides the truth about the Edward-Florence affair from Dowell.[29] Her treatment of him as an invalid and his own childlike (and dog-like) affection for Edward—Dowell even "trot[s] off" (169) dutifully with Nancy's telegram when Edward cuts his throat—suggest Dowell's deepest wishes, namely that he unconsciously identifies with all those creatures that Edward most loves—and that he wants to be loved by Edward in the same way that Ashburnham loves the weakest creatures.[30]

Of course, while Edward and Leonora are perhaps Hampshire's "Lord and Lady of the Manor," it is difficult at first to see how Dowell's "family romance" replaces and exalts his original parents. For while Dowell relates as much about the childhoods and families of most of the other characters, he reveals almost nothing about his own past. Yet this omission is itself significant. Both his descriptions in medieval chivalric terms of Ashburnham and himself, along with the little personal information that Dowell discloses, reveal how intense is his unconscious desire to erase his Yankee heritage by adopting new, aristocratic European parents.

From the beginning, storyteller-dreamteller Dowell sets his tale in relation to Provence, the land and language of southern France cultivated by the medieval troubadours and associated with romance. The bright moon of Provence, he says hopefully, presides over his story, "the Saddest Story" (8). Dowell describes Edward and himself in terms of real or fictional medieval figures: Edward (to Dowell and Nancy) is the Cid, the Lohengrin, and the Chevalier Bayard. (Dowell unwittingly, but fittingly, compares himself with Peire Vidal, the troubadour and "great poet" who pays court to La Louve, "the She-Wolf" who treats him "with indifference" [18].) Ashburnham therefore represents a pedigree and a tradition that Dowell cannot achieve himself as an American.

Despite an idiosyncratic fondness for his English Quaker roots, Dowell ridicules his wife as an "Anglo-maniac" (131) and claims her Anglophile craze manifests itself through her two main drives: to be a "great lady" and to be "installed in Branshaw Teleragh [the Ashburnham home]" (84). He maintains she attaches herself to Edward primarily because in him "she was sticking on to the proprietor of the home of her ancestors" (72). But Dowell has disguised and displaced his own Anglomania onto Florence because of the guilt and anxiety that he feels as an American.[31] "I am only an ageing American," he says resignedly at the novel's close (162).

While Dowell's statements could be read comically or as sarcasm belittling American habits in order to mock Florence's Anglomania, the more likely possibility within the context of Dowell's effort to construct a family romance is that they suggest his own dissatisfaction with his heritage.[32] His sense of America's (and thereby his own) inferior heritage is this childish daydreamer's "effort at replacing the real father by a superior one."[33] As he describes himself and his heroic paternal figure in terms of medieval chivalry, Dowell as narrator yearns "for the happy, vanished days" of childhood, the days of their "minuet de la cour."

To exalt "His Majesty the Ego," therefore, Dowell endows his narcissistic dream world with the trappings of feudal myth and monarchy. For myths, as Freud explains in "Creative Writers and Daydreaming," are "the distorted vestiges of the wishful phantasies of whole nations, the *secular dreams* of youthful humanity."[34] Dowell deprecates America in order to idealize Edward as an "English gentleman." He takes Edward's nobility and dignity "for granted" because "I guess I thought it was part of the character of any English gentleman" (69)—like a child dreamer who once saw "his father as the noblest and strongest of men and his mother as the dearest and loveliest of women." To be the son in this childless family is his "family romance."

So although Dowell is three years older than Edward and five years older than Leonora, *The Good Soldier* becomes the narrative quest of a "homeless" Dowell to replace the "good father"—and also the "good mother"—and the British heritage somehow lost in the past. Edward and Leonora are projections of idealized aspects of Dowell's self, alternately "extremely perfect" and "extremely bad" objects toward whom Dowell feels ambivalence. Dowell rightly considers himself, both physically and psychically, a "fainter" version of Ashburnham. "If I had had the courage and the virility and possibly also the physique of Edward Ashburnham," Dowell says, "I should have done much what he did" (168). With Edward, Dowell numbers himself in "the category of the passionate, of the headstrong, and the too-truthful" (168). Dowell is certainly a passive creature by comparison with Edward, but he correctly recognizes that "in my fainter sort of way, I seem to perceive myself following the lines" of Edward (157). While Dowell shows his own kindness in myriad ways,[35] in his mind Ashburnham is "the fine soldier, the excellent landlord, the extraordinarily kind, careful, and industrious magistrate, the upright, honest, fair-dealing, fair-thinking, public character" (69).

Leonora too is an idealized self-projection: she represents the austere aspects of Dowell's self. A straitlaced Irish Catholic, Leonora's thoughts are colored by her fear of the Almighty and church law. Dowell is also a fainter version of Leonora, a "strictly respectable person" and a Philadelphia Quaker. "For I solemnly avow," he says, that "not only have I never so much as hinted at an impropriety in my conversation in the whole of my days; and more than that, I will vouch for the cleanness of my thoughts and the absolute chastity of my life" (15).

Edward and Leonora also represent idealized bad aspects of Dowell's ego, the "extremely bad" persecutory objects by whom he feels threatened and who finally plunge his romantic daydream into a nightmare. Both Edward and Leonora are betrayers. Edward's passions lead him to practice marital and financial duplicity. The "normal," "slightly deceitful" Leonora virtually "buys" Maisie Maidan away from a loving husband to serve as Edward's mistress; she mercilessly taunts and persuades Nancy to yield herself to Edward's lust and thereby shatters the girl's love for Edward—and his will to live; and Leonora hides knowledge of the Edward-Florence affair from Dowell and insists that the liaison continue so as to prolong and deepen her husband's agony.

Unable to forge a family romance and unable to control his projected objects and thereby himself, Dowell suffers extreme loneliness and paranoid anxiety. "I sit here, in Edward's gun room all day," he says in the final chapter, "in a house that is absolutely quiet. No one visits me, for I visit no one. No one is interested in me, for I have no interests" (168). "I only know that I am alone, horribly alone," he cries (12). Ashburnham, Dowell says, was for years "my wife's lover . . . he killed her . . . he broke up all the pleasantnesses that there were in my life" (42), Dowell had conceived him "just exactly the sort of chap you could have trusted your wife with." "And," he says, "I trusted mine—and it was madness" (14). Leonora also makes Dowell suffer, not only by cloaking the Edward-Florence affair, but also by acting "the perfect British matron" when she presses his suit for Nancy and advises him to wait a year—even though Dowell (so he thinks) "loved Nancy very much—and Leonora knew it" (164). To prevent the happiness of Edward or Nancy, Leonora apparently would go to any length, even if it meant persecuting Dowell too.

But Leonora's treachery and ruthlessness, and Edward's deceit, have their counterpart, if again more faintly, in Dowell's own cruel machinations against Florence. He is apparently aware all along that she has been having an affair with Jimmy and that she has tired of "that fat and disreputable raven" (167). But Dowell uses her connection with Jimmy to thwart "the main idea of her heart" (167)—to get Edward and the Fordingbridge estate—and instead is delighted that she feels stuck and bored with Jimmy on the Continent. Although Dowell had said earlier that he wished he had not inherited Old Hurlbird's estate upon Florence's death, he implies that it was all part of a diabolical design in which he falsely sent her uncle "only the most glowing accounts of her virtue and constancy" (67). Dowell as narrator invariably gives the impression that he is unconcerned with material values and is the suffering, helpless victim of others' intrigues. Such passages expose his own calculating, flint-hearted nature. Not only do they establish his link with the persecutory objects in his narcissistic world, but they also point toward his obsessional drive to control himself by controlling others.

Yet if Dowell knew all along about Florence's affair with Jimmy, were his nine years before learning of Leonora's revelations truly a "paradise"? He claims: "You have the facts for the trouble of finding them; you have the points of view as far as I could ascertain or put them" (120). This cannot be true. Dowell shifts

Designed by the contemporary Manchester artist Stephen Raw, this cover of the Carcanet edition of *The Good Soldier* is based on a sketch created by Honoré Fragonard, the eighteenth-century French anatomist, who dissected a cadaver of a man riding a horse. This image of human and horse anatomy that Fragonard preserved decorates a wall at the Fragonard Museum in Paris.

The image strikingly captures the corrupted, deceitful characters in *The Good Soldier*, perhaps most especially the title figure himself, Edward Ashburnham. Fragonard's waxed cadavers were distinguished by human and horse skin stripped to reveal their muscles, blood vessels, and bone tissue. Raw conveys through this image the death-in-life of Ford's hollow men and women as they sleepwalk their macabre minuet.

back and forth so abruptly and unexpectedly from his state of mind before his final shattering discoveries to his present views (written during the succeeding six months, with the last chapter composed eighteen months later) that it is often near-impossible to pinpoint where past judgment ends and revised assessment begins. He claims to narrate events to which he was an eyewitness or with information "from the lips of Leonora or those of Edward himself" (15).

But he repeatedly attributes or surmises thoughts, behaviors, and actual conversations that he could not have personally witnessed and about which his alleged source could not have been informed. Dowell's narrative gyrates in overlapping circles, which introduce new evidence that not only illuminates earlier, unexplained events but that also directly contradicts them. While Dowell is seldom described by readers as cruel, deceitful, or even callous, we can now see how his storytelling discloses these weaknesses. His narrative tendencies toward questionable attribution, inexplicable digression, and repeated contradictions suggest that Dowell as narrator is not simply slipshod; nor is he presenting, as he claims, different "points of view." The "facts" are indeed here, but they suggest that Dowell's narration is orchestrated by his unconscious manipulation of his daydream world. Most daydreams possess unconscious and conscious elements,[36] and Dowell's casual reflection after Florence's death is revealing. He suddenly blurts out that he could now "marry the girl [Nancy]." His confession supports our line of inquiry, and he admits: "It is as if one had a dual personality, the one I being entirely unconscious of the other" (75).

Yet Dowell is unaware here of the underlying implications of his words, just as he is unaware of the implications when his affection for Ashburnham is expressed as a form of self-love. Dowell's "family romance" with the Ashburnhams is not merely filial devotion from an admiring child. Neither is it only "self-infatuation," as Mark Schorer has argued.[37] Just as Dowell twists ideas of medieval romance to his own purposes, he does the same with his family romance. If *The Good Soldier* is examined in light of how dream devices serve Dowell's unconscious identifications and "dual personality," both Dowell's unconscious repressions and the psychic origins of the incongruities in his narrative become clearer.

IV

The Good Soldier's narrative texture resembles dream material. After unconscious, threatening thoughts have undergone preconscious censorship to make them less intimidating to the ego, the sequence of dream events acquires a superficial, tenuous coherence. Extremely sensitive dream events are subjected to a "far-reaching," "tendentious" second round of censorship, which Freud calls "secondary revision," a follow-up process that completely "fills up the gaps in the dream structure with patches," so that the dream "approximates to the world of intelligible experience."[38]

According to Freud, less successful secondary revisions produce dreams in which "coherence rules for a certain distance, but the dream then becomes senseless or confused," though it may later "present an appearance of rationality."[39] The dream-work produces "absurd dreams and dreams containing absurd elements if it is faced with any criticism" in the dream-thoughts.[40] Although daydreams generally contain much more conscious material (compared to night-dreams), "so too are unconscious ones in great number, which have to remain unconscious because of their content and of their origin from repressed material." They share a "large number of properties" with night-dreams: wish-fulfillment, traces of infantile experience, and present-day associations. Their conscious elements result in the construction of an "idealized content" that frequently "arrange[s]" the constituent elements "in such a way that they form an approximately connected whole, a dream-composition.[41] The dream is given a kind of façade (though this does not, it is true, hide its content at every point)."[42]

As we shall see, Dowell's "family romance" is an elaborate "dream-composition" loosely connected by an associative patterning of events to present a "façade" of coherence. But it is only a façade, for the dream-work's linking and gap-filling are discernible in manifold and diverse ways: via the novel's content, point of view, and mood; by the narrator's indisputable contradictions and/or extraordinary coincidences with dating and numbers; through his seeming omniscience about others' behavior when he could not have gained knowledge of it; by the brilliantly clear, hallucinatory images describing certain important events; and from his characteristic preference for superlatives to describe events.

Dowell impresses us repeatedly with his scrupulous zeal in pinpointing events, specifying all kinds of extraneous information about ages, dates, and times. For instance, after telling us that the couples' acquaintanceship lasted nine years and giving their respective ages when they first met, he goes on: "Thus today Florence would have been thirty-nine and Captain Ashburnham forty-two; whereas I am forty-five and Leonora forty" (10).

Yet Dowell makes at least three significant "miscalculations" in dating events.[43] First, he reports in the novel's opening paragraph that he and Florence have known the Ashburnhams for "nine seasons" at Nauheim, the German retreat to which the Dowells repair every summer because of Florence's weak heart. Dowell later pinpoints the date of the couples' first encounter: August 4, 1904 (72). Pages earlier, however, Dowell dated the death of Mrs. Maidan as August 4, 1904 (59). This is impossible, for Mrs. Maidan died in the afternoon; on the evening of the couples' first meeting Leonora contritely asks Edward to escort Maisie to the Casino because she regrets slapping the girl (52). Moreover, Dowell had even earlier related that he saw "much of Mrs. Maidan during the first month of our acquaintance" with the Ashburnhams and that Maisie "died, quite quietly, of heart trouble" (42). And if Maisie died on the afternoon of the couples' "jaunt" to the ancient castle M——, that August 4 outing cannot have been the first occasion of the couples' meeting: Florence had already been "educating" Edward; the M—— excursion, as Dowell says, "would finally give her the chance to educate the whole lot of us together" (35). The day of the M—— trip was therefore not their first meeting, and there must have at least been one month separating the couples' introduction and the occasion of the M—— expedition. So, from the point of Dowell's dating of the couples' initial meeting and Maisie's death (72, 59), one must work back through the novel to identify the contradictions he advances. Nor is this carelessness on Dowell's part. A digression about Leonora's "acting" abilities produces an association which, Dowell says, "enables me to fix exactly the day of our going to the town of M——. For it was the very day poor Mrs. Maidan died" (53). And he recalls with Leonora on a date he claims is August 4, 1913: "I remember saying to her that on that day, exactly nine years before, I had made their acquaintance" (72).

Dowell's second dating error also involves over-attentiveness: he twice recollects the precise length of his "Nirvana" with the Ashburnhams and Florence before his fatal discoveries on August 4, 1913, but the periods differ. He first says his "long, tranquil life" crashed at the end of nine years and six weeks (11). But two paragraphs later he despairs that his "goodly apple" has gone rotten at the end of nine years and six *months* (12).

A third inaccuracy occurs in Part Four, when Dowell dates his writing of the novel's last two chapters. First he reports that he is working a "full eighteen months after the words that end my last chapter" (155): the November 1913 Glasgow telegram from Mrs. Rufford's lover promising to take her to Italy. But if Dowell is therefore writing the last two chapters in April 1915, why does he state two pages later that "eighteen months ago" at Branshaw Leonora brought him a letter explaining Nancy's mental illness? For we know that Nancy did not go mad until after she hears about Edward's suicide. She did not even *leave* Branshaw until *after* the Glasgow telegram was sent, apparently about a month later (161, 166). She traveled by boat to reach Brindisi, Italy, and then Ceylon, from which she sent her telegram, which precipitated Edward's suicide. Not until her return through Aden does she learn of his suicide. It is therefore doubtful that Dowell could have learned about her madness until, at the earliest, the late spring or summer of 1914—a "full" six to nine months later than his claim.

It is unlikely that Dowell's miscalculations are a result of Ford's oversights.[44] He revised the novel both after part of it appeared in the 1914 inaugural issue of Wyndham Lewis's periodical, *Blast*, and again for its 1927 reissue. In his 1927 Dedicatory Letter to Stella Ford, he notes that he had in the preceding months scrutinized the novel line by line because he translated it into French, which "forc[ed] me to give it much closer attention than would be the case in any reading however minute" (5).[45]

Dowell's historical inaccuracies are accompanied by a series of dating coincidences that reinforce the sense of *The Good Soldier*'s dreamlike ambience: the recurrence of August 4. On that day in 1874 Florence is born; she, Jimmy, and Old Hurlbird go on a European vacation that day in 1899; one year later Florence "had become a low fellow's [Jimmy's] mistress" (85)—and is seen by the "odious" Bagshawe leaving Jimmy's room in the early morning hours; the Dowells are married that day in 1901; three years later, Maisie dies, after the fateful trip to M—— reveals the Edward-Florence affair to Leonora—or on that day the couples make their introduction; and on August 4, 1913, Florence commits suicide after seeing Edward with Nancy and running into Bagshawe at the hotel. Dowell is aware that it is all "a curious coincidence of dates" (59). But he explains the European holiday as Old Hurlbird's birthday gift to Florence, and the marriage date could be explained as a conscious design by Florence. But the fact that Maisie's death, the crucial "protest scene" at M——, Bagshawe's witnessing Florence leaving Jimmy's room, Edward's "monstrous" advance toward Nancy, Bagshawe's introduction to Dowell, Florence's suicide, and Leonora's revelation of the Edward-Florence affair should *all* occur on an August 4 is an "impossible dream." Dowell concludes that the coincidences are either "the superstitious mind of Florence that forced her to certain acts, as if she had been hypnotized," or the "half-jocular and altogether merciless proceedings" of "a cruel Providence" (59).

The coincidences are by no means limited to events connected with Florence. The hypnotic narrative mind of Dowell is responsible for at least one of them, and the verbal echoes that resonate through Dowell's unconscious patterning of events as a minuet provide a clue. Just as he is unaware of the degree of his unconscious structuring of the novel in "minuet" terms, so too is he largely ignorant of coincidences and numerical repetitions beyond the obvious August 4 example—which he attributes to Florence or Fate anyway. The August 4 recurrences and the eerie repetition of the number "4" throughout reveal more deeply Dowell's "minuet" pattern of thinking: the eighth month, fourth day that haunts the two couples re-echoes so that it evokes the opening of a minuet, with its two repeating eight-bar strains, doubling to sixteen bars and being constantly repeated and redeveloped as the theme progresses.

We must remember that we hear these verbal echoes in *Dowell*'s voice: the choice of descriptions is his own. He describes the couples as a cozy "four-square coterie" living in a "four-square house" (11, 12). He refers twice to the Four Castles of Las Tours, mentions that Peire Vidal had four boat companions, says Edward had four medicine bottles in his case, notes that at 4 a.m. Florence became Jimmy's mistress (when he cannot know the precise time), and weds Florence at 4 a.m.[46] He structures *The Good Soldier* in four parts. He describes the villainous betrayals of the others in his "four-square coterie" in

Ford's *The Good Soldier* in the Barnes & Noble Classics series features an excellent introduction by Frank Kermode, the British scholar and man of letters. On the cover is a painting by William A. Breakspeare entitled *Dreaming*. It is a suitable illustration to help readers ponder a leitmotif of *The Good Soldier*. Spying, secrecy, hiddenness are all here: the foregrounded public personae vs. the backstage private shadows. The painting allows us to imagine Maisie Maidan's dreamlike attachment to Edward Ashburnham, the presentation of which is largely filtered through narrator John Dowell's misty voyeurism. It is as if Dowell lurks unobserved in the unlit rear of the room, as the scene spotlights Maisie Maidan, whose life is scarred and undermined by the welter of betrayals and deceptions that the Ashburnhams and Dowells commit in the novel. (Some visual details, in particular the man's shirt and trousers, render the painting an inappropriate choice, given that the clothes have an eighteenth-century appearance. This is unsurprising since Breakspeare [1856–1914] specialized in eighteenth-century reconstructions.)

numerical terms ("They were three to one [against me]" [54]), and as if he were half-consciously superstitious about the legion of coincidences and repetitions of "4," he says at the end of the novel that he now cares for another invalid (Nancy) and so has returned to "where I started thirteen years ago" (157). But this is a dating mistake. If he is writing these lines in February 1915, thirteen years earlier is 1902—whereas he married Florence fourteen years earlier in 1901.

These dating discrepancies and cabalistic numerical repetitions are not the only "accidents" that cast doubt on Dowell's credibility and point of view. Dowell's anxieties point to the dream-work's gap-filling: Dowell knows unconsciously that he is either inventing or manipulating "the facts," or surmising on the basis of no evidence. If the couples never really talk, how does he find out all the conversations between Nancy and Leonora, and those between Edward and Leonora? Dowell would have us believe that Leonora provided him with most of his information, but his descriptions of her make that doubtful: "She had been drilled—in her tradition, in her upbringing—to keep her mouth shut" (122).

If Dowell's narrative is indeed a macrocosmic rendering of his recollection about Edward and Nancy at the Casino—"I see that thing as clearly as if it were a dream that never left me" (79)—his contradictions and fantastically patterned coincidences, his questionable suppositions, and his phantasmagoric, idealized images become understandable as unconscious material arising from the id and forcing its way into the ego. According to Freud, in the id "there are no conflicts; contradictions and antitheses exist side by side."[47] The id has no conception of time and knows no values. As a result of the ego's resistance to the id, dreams become distorted, with persons or events condensed or displaced unrecognizably. Thus Dowell develops an inexplicable intimacy with the Ashburnhams without ever actually communicating with them because he does not recognize them as aspects of himself.

In Kleinian terms, the narrative gains coherence when viewed as the processes of a mind in the paranoid-schizoid position, a point at which the infant has not developed the capacity for "linking and abstraction" and can engage only in "disjointed thinking."[48] Narrator Dowell's miraculous coincidences, his abrupt digressions, and his chaotic associative patterns are the shifts of an unconscious mind that recognizes no orderly or sensible progression of events, of a paranoid personality that can engage only in "disjointed" thinking. His oddly eclectic omniscience alternating with constant denial ("Perhaps you can make head or tail of it; it is beyond me" [158]) is a desperate preconscious (or ego) attempt to impose narrative order, which the id overpowers by puncturing the patchwork with manifest improbabilities. As each narrative cycle rewinds, secondary revision attempts once again to smooth the façade, but the dream composition suffers more and more holes as Dowell's despair and anxiety mount in Part Four. Klein explains that one mode of the ego's attempt to master anxiety is to "get the better of the unconscious" by "overemphasizing all that is tangible, visible, and perceptible to consciousness."[49] So Dowell's occasional omniscience (as in the passage about Maisie in Edward's room) reflects the ego's frenzied overcompensation to fill narrative gaps. To Dowell, nothing is more tangible and visible than numbers; they promote the illusion of full control and finality—and almost every page of *The Good Soldier* contains needless references to dates, ages, times, street numbers, even the numbers of steps between buildings. "I wish I could put it down in diary form," Dowell says—and then immediately follows with eight sentences in diary style to bring news of his characters "up to date" so that none "get hopelessly left behind" (148).

Klein identifies this ego anxiety defense in *The Psychoanalysis of Children* as the "homosexual" mode. Narrator Dowell's repressed homosexual guilt is expressed in a twofold manner: first by his overwhelming self-doubts and displacement of narrative incongruities onto Florence; secondly, by his numerical contradictions and excessive dating scrupulosity. "I don't know," Dowell says repeatedly, "You never really get an inch deeper than the things I have catalogued" (32). "I know it is melodrama, but I can't help it" (80). He insists that his words are "from the lips of Leonora or from those of Edward himself" (15). But such explanations are merely ineffective anxiety defenses recruited to mask his unconscious manipulation of events that he has formed into his own impressionist aesthetic. After thinking that a story is most real when it is told chronologically, he revises himself by the time he reaches Part Four, when his anxieties about his distortions peak:

> I have, I am aware, told this story in a very rambling way so that it may be difficult for anyone to find their [sic] path through what may be a sort of maze. I cannot help it . . . when one discusses an affair—a long, sad affair—one goes back, one goes forward . . . I console myself with thinking that this is a real story and that, after all, real stories are probably told best in the way a person telling a story would tell them. They will then seem most real. (124–125)

Dowell's ego rationalization for his excessive emphasis on the tangible is apparent: "One remembers points that one has forgotten and one explains them all the more minutely since one recognizes . . . that one may have given, by omitting them, a false impression" (125). He attributes the recurrence of August 4 most often to Florence's "superstitious mind" or "hypnotic mind" or to Fate—whereas the numerical associations surely reflect Dowell's own habit of mind.

The two numbers most frequently mentioned by Dowell are four and nine,

Ford Madox Ford
The Good Soldier

OXFORD WORLD'S CLASSICS

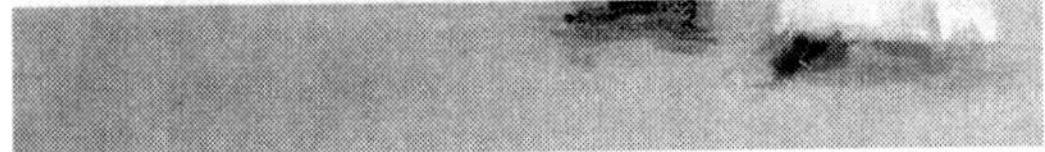

First published in 1990, the Oxford World's Classics edition of *The Good Soldier* is edited and introduced by Thomas C. Moser. Including perceptive commentary and valuable background information, the Oxford World's Classics edition features an impressionist-style image of Edward C. Ashburnham, the putative good soldier, and his wife Leonora. The image is a detail from *Luxembourg Gardens at Twilight* (1879), by John Singer Sargent (1856–1925). Originally part of the Palais du Luxembourg in Paris, built in 1620 for the widow of Henry IV, the gardens are located adjacent to the Latin Quarter. A public park beloved by Parisians, the area includes an English garden of lawns, a grove of orchards, picturesque terraces and fountains, and numerous gravel paths on which pedestrians stroll and enjoy strategically placed French sculpture.

In Sargent's twilight scene, whose fading light thematizes the murky relationships and dark, opaque obsessions of *The Good Soldier,* the people appear disconnected from one another and locked in self-isolation. Although the couple in the foreground walk arm-in-arm, they seem emotionally detached from each other: the woman, draped in a white sunshade, is preoccupied with holding up her skirt; the fashionably attired man casually smokes a cigarette and seems lost in thought.

representing for him what Freud and Adler termed "obsessive numbers."[50] Such numbers are often "quite unknown to consciousness," "related to the life of the person involved," and become a fixation if they are frequently connected with important events in one's life.[51] Numerical repetitions (such as four, nine, and August 4) are therefore not only manifestations of how the id perforates the narrative dream-work's façade. They also bear a deeper relation to Dowell's state of mind and the novel's themes. Freud states that the conscious and unconscious choice of numbers is no accident. Numbers in dreams "serve as allusions to matter that cannot be presented any other way":

> In this respect the dream-work is treating numbers for the expression of its purpose in precisely the same way it treats any other idea, including proper names and speeches that occur recognizably as verbal presentations.
>
> . . . Psychical events are determined. There is nothing arbitrary about them. . . . For instance, I may try to think of a number arbitrarily; but this is impossible; the number that occurs to me will be unambiguously and necessarily determined by thoughts of mine, though they may be remote from my immediate intention.[52]

In addition to other references to four, Dowell says twice that his "paradise" was lost precisely after nine years and six months (or weeks) minus four days. Apparently he does not mean four days sequentially, but four separate, tragic days: August 4, 1904, when Maisie dies; August 4, 1913, when Florence commits suicide and Dowell learns about Jimmy; November 12, 1913, when the events precipitating Nancy's leavetaking transpire; and the unspecified day of Edward's death two to three weeks later. Thus four is intricately bound up with the circumstances of the novel as a four-act tragedy.[53]

Dowell's unconscious identifications with these numbers disclose a relevant dimension of his psychic patterning, which posits a severely impartial, cosmic law of justice: "Is there then any terrestrial paradise where . . . people can be with whom they like and have what they like and take their ease in shadows and in coolness?" he asks. "Who the devil knows?" (158). Of course Dowell consciously believes that justice has not been "perfectly equal"—the "normal" Leonoras and Rodney Bayhams have triumphed over the noble Edwards, Nancys, and Maisies. But unconsciously he believes that "society must go on" and the "too truthful" ones received their sentences from Fate for their *hubris*. Many of the characters are spendthrifts or misers, most notably Edward and Leonora—and all in Dowell's "four-square coterie" are family betrayers. The *number* reveals these associations because Dowell's ego will not permit the material to be represented in any other way. Yet secondary revision cannot sufficiently cloak the coincidences and dating errors, which are not instances of the paranoid's disjointed thinking or the id's puncturing of the dream composition. For instance, Dowell makes the impossible association between his meeting Edward and the event of Maisie's death because Dowell identifies with her and wants to replace her as the object of Edward's love. So in fulfillment of his erotic wish, she "dies" at the moment he meets Edward. Similarly, his decision to backdate Nancy's suicide a full eighteen months prior to the probable time of the final two chapters' composition (February 1915) places Nancy (and his family romance) before not only Edward's suicide but also her departure for Brindisi. Dowell identifies with Nancy too, and his overpowering wish is to be united with Ashburnham and thereby erase the fact of Edward's suicide and her madness.

Both Dowell's narcissism and his driven need to forge a family romance extend beyond his unconscious identifications with Edward and Leonora. Consistent with Freud's concept of narcissistic libido, all the major characters are extensions of Dowell's ego, grafted libidinally onto "the ego itself and finding satisfaction [and distress] in the ego just as satisfaction is usually found only in objects."[54] Dowell constructs a remarkable series of unconscious identifications with Maisie, Nancy, and even Old Hurlbird, all of which confirm his latent homosexuality and illuminate his narrative distortions.

Dowell calls Maisie Maidan "the child" (52), and she behaves like one, "a nice little thing" with "a lisp and a happy smile" (42). Maisie has the poor peasant background that Dowell shares, which is alluded to obliquely as his "American" anxiety. He explicitly says that Edward and Florence consider themselves her surrogate "father" and "mother," (51) even to the point of Leonora "disciplining" her like a little daughter in the Schreibzimmer hotel. Thus Dowell identifies himself with Maisie as the child adored by the Ashburnhams and turns her into a sister in his family romance. He says he is "aware that I am a little in love with her memory" (43). What appeals to him most about Maisie is her "submissiveness"—expressed even to Dowell, a man whom "not the youngest child will ever pay heed to" (43). She is his younger sister and yet himself. Like Dowell, she is ignorant of the world's ways. "Oh, Mrs. Ashburnham," she cries in her letter to Leonora, "you knew the world and I knew nothing" (57). Despite Dowell's remark that she was "such a child that one has the impression that she would have hardly known how to spell 'adultery'" (38), that judgment could have been written by Dowell himself.

As she was for Ashburnham, Nancy is, Dowell claims, "the one" in his life. She is both "the girl," the official ward of Leonora and therefore a true child in the Ashburnhams' "country family," and "the real passion of [Edward's] life" (47). Dowell remarks on her extreme "rectitude" ("never seen surpassed" [89]), by comparison to which his own circumspection is a faint reflection. Even more so than Maisie, Nancy is a sister in his romance and Edward's love: she is a "legitimate" Ashburnham living under their roof and Edward's final, "real passion." Dowell also unconsciously identifies with Old Hurlbird, whom he considers a "poor, dear old thing" (65). Hurlbird goes to Europe upon retiring because he fears hearing that he is "the laziest man in Waterbury" (19). Florence's aunts call Dowell "the laziest man in Philadelphia" (17). Neither Hurlbird nor Dowell ever do any work, and Dowell alternately thinks him "extraordinarily lovable" and an old fool. He laughs at Hurlbird for wishing American women sexless, but he uses this same notion to cover his feelings of inferiority: he displaces his guilt for his sexual inadequacies onto Florence by interpreting the August 4 coincidences as products of her "superstitious mind." Dowell then splits himself and identifies with the hated Jimmy, whose function in traveling with Florence and Hurlbird was "to avoid exciting topics for him." Three paragraphs earlier, Dowell says that he too had to care for a heart patient, Florence, and "my whole endeavors were to keep poor dear Florence onto topics like the finds at Gnossos and the mental spirituality of Walter Pater" (18).

On this view, Mrs. Maidan, Nancy, Hurlbird, and Jimmy are all projections of good or bad aspects of Dowell's ego, unconscious identifications that reveal his psychic propensity toward homosexuality. Dowell identifies himself repeatedly as a woman and old maid (23, 26, 165), a solicitor (26, 165), a eunuch (15), and a male nurse (63). He desires to place himself in passive, feminine roles because the women he strongly identifies with are essentially submissive. He calls himself a solicitor not only for the professed reason that he listens with a lawyer's patience and understanding to his "client" Edward's troubles, but because he identifies La Dolciquita as a solicitor (111); and she is actually the woman in the novel toward whom Edward has channeled his strongest sexual passions. Dowell inherits Hurlbird's wealth and becomes, like him, a dupe of Florence and Jimmy. To combat his feelings of inadequacy and inferiority toward "that dreary boy," Dowell projects homosexual insecurities onto Jimmy and calls him fat, lugubrious, odious, square-shouldered, ominous, and craven. "Why, I was much the better man," he concludes (65). But it is potent Jimmy who sleeps with Florence; Dowell can repress that fact, but he cannot hide it from his unconscious self. Dowell thinks he would like to be a "polygamist" enjoying relations with Nancy, Leonora, Maisie, and possibly even Florence. The true nature of his unconscious links with these women, however, is not love but "mimetic desire": Dowell wants them because they are *Edward's* love objects or children.[55] Dowell sees the world in their terms, echoes their words, and undergoes similar patterns of depression to the extent that he experiences a fierce emotional doubling: he imagines that Edward feels passionately toward them and so he identifies with them and offers his conscious tale "just to get the sight out of [my] head" (11).

Dowell's psychic disintegration and impaired will to live exemplify his paranoid-schizoid anxiety, which represents, according to Freud, "what lies at the core of the conflict in cases of paranoia . . . [—]a homosexual wishful fantasy of *loving a man*."[56] Dowell unconsciously represses his hatred for Ashburnham, who "broke up all the pleasantnesses . . . in my life" (42) and has driven Dowell to "madness" (14). Instead Dowell metamorphoses his hatred into Ashburnham's purported nobility and "perfection," much as Freud describes five-year-old Little Hans as doing because of castration anxiety:

> His instinctual impulse . . . was a hostile one against the father. One might say that impulse had been repressed by the process of being transformed into its opposite. Instead of aggressiveness on the part of the subject towards the father, there appeared aggressiveness (in the form of revenge) on the part of the father towards the subject.[57]

Ashburnham's affair with Florence, his near-seduction of Nancy, and Dowell's obsession with numbers all manifest the sense of "revenge," which Dowell calls the work of "Fate." Dowell's bitterness and loathing toward Ashburnham has been transmuted (in Freud's formulation) into "a form that has undergone regressive degradation, to a passive, tender impulse to be loved by him [the persecutor] in a genital-erotic sense."[58] Dowell thus identifies with the women in order to merge his identity with Ashburnham's.

So both he and Edward are halves of the same "dual personality" (75), fancies Dowell. Just as Dowell blurted out "entirely unconsciously" (75) that he could marry Nancy when Florence was dead, it had somehow "come out" from Edward to advise Florence that Maisie accompany them from India to Europe. "He hadn't had the least idea of saying that to Leonora" (120). Although Dowell would no sooner have entered Florence's room than "burgl[e] a church," by the end of the novel he has "penetrated into [Edward's] private room" (66), his phallic "gun room" (168). Edward has once told him "how much the society of a good woman could do toward redeeming" a man and Dowell listened "like a woman or solicitor." This was his real romance: to be a "good woman" to Edward's "good soldier" (24). Although he has finally entered Edward's room, there is no identity with which to merge, for Edward is dead.

Dowell had yearned to believe in Edward as the hero of romance. He wanted to believe that Nancy and Maisie loved him because Dowell longs to be loved in the way he can romanticize that Edward loved them. His repeated deflection of sexual conflict into socio-religious categories disguises the intensity of his desire and the impossibility of his romance in a world where nationalism and religious difference breed hostility among peoples. Dowell thinks Edward's tears before the statue of the Virgin Mary are religiously inspired (even though

Edward isn't a Catholic [94]), that Leonora's Irish Catholicism underlies her terror during the M—— "protest scene," that she concealed the Edward-Florence affair because she is a troubled Catholic, and that he failed sexually with Florence because he behaved like a Philadelphia Quaker. He concludes that their typically "English acquaintanceship" (68) impedes communication between couples, attributes Florence's illness to her New England background, and loves Nancy Rufford "in my American sort of way" (87). Dowell would be willing to marry Nancy "to let her appreciate the meaning of an Anglican marriage service" (157), but he cannot because she is mentally unstable. He also believes that Florence and Leonora primarily desire Edward to get to Fordingbridge and to uphold their Catholic marriage vows.

Dowell's inflection of these interpersonal and emotional events onto a collective plane are comprehensible as desperate ego defenses, as narrative dreamwork aiming to disguise and displace the novel's sexual issues toward social and religious levels. Dowell's phrasing of the issues in socio-religious terms draws energy from his psychic ambivalence toward Ashburnham and rechannels it toward sociopolitical or religious issues (i.e., Americans vs. Britons, Catholics vs. Quakers).[59] Yet Dowell finally becomes aware that the "prison" in which the couples are locked is not simply a matter of their own betrayals. "Society must go on," he says, and Dowell recognizes a fatalism inherent in the fabric of his world that victimizes not only guilty Ashburnhams but also innocent Nancys and Maisies.

V

Why can't people have what they want?

JOHN DOWELL, *THE GOOD SOLDIER* (158)

Dowell's "minuet de la cour" partly fails because one cannot both live *in society* and construct "a shock-proof world"—one cannot dance a minuet alone. Nor can one ignore that the societal minuet, like its musical version, comprises "a whole collection of rules [that] applies to anybody,"[60] a socially established form of art or entertainment. As a Quaker, Dowell says that when he is invariably mistaken in England for an Episcopalian, "it is the cock that the whole of this society owes to Aesculapius" (32).

If the price of civilization is the renunciation of our instincts, as Freud argued in *Civilization and Its Discontents,* history demonstrates that humankind's struggles center upon "the single task of finding some expedient (i.e., satisfying) solution between individual claims and those of the civilized community."[61] Because community life requires the partial sacrifice of instinctual gratification and therefore incites rebellion, "every individual is virtually the enemy of society"—and vice versa.[62]

So a psychoanalytic approach to Dowell's "minuet de la cour" is not limited to the conflict of father figure vs. child. Rather, it also encompasses the social struggles between husbands and wives, landlords and tenants, Europeans and Americans, Catholics and Quakers, the collective and the individual. For Dowell is not only persecuted by Edward, Leonora, Florence, and Jimmy, but also by a society wherein the "normal" and "slightly deceitful" "flourish" (167). Like narrator-daydreamer Dowell's internal psychic battle of id against ego, *The Good Soldier* is a bitter war of pleasure principle against reality principle, in which Dowell's only period of contentment occurs during his fantasies of an illusory "shock-proof world," nestled within a "goodly apple" that was always rotten at the core. That shiny apple skin was the surface level of his dream-composition as family romance, which ultimately fails to furnish enduring narcissistic satisfaction.

In *Moses and Monotheism* and *Future of an Illusion*, respectively, Freud posits that religion springs from "a longing for the father"[63] and "a need for protection."[64] Civilization itself springs from the primal collective's reaction to the murder of the "primal father." This parricide was provoked by the oppression of the father, who achieved total gratification by imposing his iron will on others. Whereas parricide was possible if a strong man were confronted by his superior in battle, community life presupposes that a "number of men who are united together in strength superior to any single individual remain united against all single individuals."[65] The "Might" of the united body's strength is the proclaimed "Right," and any opposition is "brute force." Revolution thus invites even greater guilt than for the first assassins because it includes both the overthrow of "Right" and the "archaic heritage" of parricide, the latter of which is our species' "memory-traces" of repeatedly reenacted rebellions and parricides. Humankind's "memory-traces" resemble the individual's repressed unconscious thoughts. The implications for evaluating civilization, says Freud, are momentous:

> If we assume the survival of these memory-traces in the archaic heritage, we have bridged the gulf between individual and group psychology: we can deal with peoples as we do with an individual neurotic . . . After this discussion I have no hesitation in declaring that men have always known (in this special way) that they once possessed a primal father and killed him.[66]

The sense of Kafkaesque guilt pervading *The Good Soldier*—a guilt for something one did not do that is so ubiquitous that it devours even innocents like

Introduced by Zoë Heller and published in 2010, this Vintage Classics (U.K.) edition of *The Good Soldier* portrays John Dowell sitting next to Leonora Ashburnham, the wife of his admired friend Edward. Dowell pours out much of his misery to Leonora in this brilliantly subtle novel, which Ford had originally titled *The Saddest Story*. Dowell and his wife befriend Edward and Leonora Ashburnham, who appear to Dowell to be the utterly perfect couple. Theirs seems to be a marriage between a beautiful, intelligent woman and a much-decorated soldier and man of integrity. Yet the shiny, polished apple is rotten at the core; the Ashburnham marriage is dazzling on the surface and sinister underneath, and the tangled history of the couple's relationship to Dowell spawns the tragic drama that ultimately destroys all that he cherishes.

Maisie Maidan—is deeper than the characters themselves, woven into the tissue of civilization. *The Good Soldier* is not merely the decline and fall of a privileged aristocratic order, not just the "sack of Rome by the Goths," but also "the death of a mouse from cancer" (11). For community life oppresses both ideal "county families" like the Ashburnhams and the modest Maisie, who is just a "poor little O'Flaherty" with her husband of "country-parsonage" origin (44).

Of course, the physical and mental torment suffered by the wives and peasants is more apparent, and it is inflicted in the name of "Right" through both a social double standard and a perverted legal system. Dowell condemns Florence's adultery yet excuses Edward ultimately as a "fine fellow." Regarding Leonora's opinions, Dowell writes: "Man, for her, was a sort of brute who must have his divagations, his moments of excess, his nights out, his let us say, rutting seasons" (126). In Dowell's view, Leonora almost sees society as a primitive (or primal) horde after the father's death, in which the anarchy rules, women try to safeguard themselves and their children, and the liberated sons seek to gratify their passions with any available female. She heeds the words of the Mother Superior: "Men are like that. By the blessing of God it will all come right in the end" (126).

Indeed, Edward is a man of passion who observes "what was demanded by conventions and by the traditions of his house," whether social or religious, until his ignoble end (128). He suffers not only because his passions go unsatisfied but because he binds himself to the traditions of an English gentleman. He will not divorce Leonora to marry Nancy because he has "a violent conviction of the duties of his station" (47). He is willing to become a Catholic in order that his daughters can be raised as Catholics, but "his boys [must] be educated in the religion of their immediate ancestors," (i.e., the Church of England) (103). Dowell too, of course, frames many of his judgments in religious or social terms. He thinks Leonora's suggestion that Nancy wait a year before committing herself to marry Dowell is "one of the queer, not very straight methods that Roman Catholics seem to adopt in dealing with matters of this world" (164). The Hurlbirds consider Europe "a sink of iniquity" (58); Dowell considers it an "imprisonment" (4).

So Dowell's and the Ashburnham's angst is not explainable by their betrayals alone, for there is an invidious fatalism in *The Good Soldier* that renders their sins not only a cause for the wealthy's suffering but also a manifestation of the neurotic civilization in which they live. "At what, then, does it all work out?" asks Dowell. "Is the whole thing a folly and a mockery?" He asks if there is a higher natural law, but then quickly answers, "I don't know. And there is nothing to guide us" (15). Convention, Dowell believes, favors the "body politic" and works "blindly but surely for the preservation of the normal type." But it leads to "the extinction of the proud, resolute and unusual individuals" (158).

Such fatalism directly evokes Freud's conclusion in *Civilization and Its Discontents* that the central problem of man's existence as a social being lies in the "claim to individual freedom against the will of the multitude" and whether "a solution can be arrived at in some particular form of culture or whether the conflict will prove irreconcilable."[67] This is the ultimate question in Freud's cultural studies, and he was less than optimistic. Rather, in *Beyond the Pleasure Principle* and his later work, he postulated the concept of the Nirvana Principle, in which he considered Eros and Thanatos alike in their mutual tendency toward relaxation of tension. This principle actually serves the interests of the destructive instincts. It is not a matter of binding versus loosening energy, but of one principle tending toward the relief of excitation in opposition to the reality principle.[68] And so too, in a larger sense, Edward and Leonora are not destroyed or reduced to "rabbit-like" creatures by Florence, whom Dowell sees as the "contaminating influence" (125), or even by themselves. Their false gods, which demand allegiance both to an outworn code of honor and an exalted list of rules above concern for people, contain the seeds of their own destruction.

Dowell prays that somewhere there exists his "minuet de la cour," his ideal family romance, a "heaven where old beautiful dances, old beautiful intimacies prolong themselves," a "Nirvana pervaded by the faint trilling of instruments" (11). But by the end of the "Saddest Story," the "splendid personalities" have been "steam-rolled out" and the "normal" personalities (Leonora and Rodney) enjoy a "quiet, comfortable good time" (158, 155). "Life peters out" for Dowell, and the invalid Nancy can utter only two words: "Omnipotent Deity" (168). Dowell's conclusion is no more hopeful than his opening. Cast out of his paradise, his narcissistic "minuet de la cour," he anticipates only confusion and suffering:

> Is there then any terrestrial paradise where, amidst the whispering of the olive-leaves, people can be with whom they like and have what they like and take their ease in shadows and in coolness? Or are all men's lives like the lives of us good people—like the lives of the Ashburnhams, of the Dowells, of the Ruffords—broken, tumultuous, agonized, and unromantic lives, periods punctuated by screams, by imbecilities, by deaths, by agonies? (158)

Human civilization may never become a "terrestrial paradise," but the alternatives need not be so stark as Dowell draws them. Herbert Marcuse in *Eros and Civilization* challenges Freud's conclusions in *Civilization and Its Discontents* and argues that twentieth-century Western man has advanced to the stage at which technology can eliminate *Anake* (scarcity), a lack that provided the rationale for the repressive reality principle.[69] Technology has the potential to abolish the social demand for domination based on economic scarcity and therefore the need for repressive labor. Energy devoted to maintaining domination is then freed, permitting the development of non-repressive libido. Of course, whether or not Marcuse's vision is well grounded theoretically, Ford's world in 1915 had not progressed industrially even to the point of satisfying its citizens' minimal needs.

Yet if such a utopia is to come, humanity must one day concur that matrimonial (and class, national, and religious) relationships can no longer be characterized by Dowell's "one constant factor" (84)—a desire to deceive the person with whom one lives about our weaknesses. If a fully human civilization is to flourish on a worldwide scale, without the need of other nationalities or classes or religions to oppress, Society—unlike the case in *The Good Soldier*—must not extinguish persons such as Edward and Nancy. Rather, it must foster and nurture "those splendid and tumultuous creatures with their magnetism and their passions" (158).

CHAPTER FIVE

Lewis's Tarr

PORTRAITS OF THE FAILED ARTIST

The artist is relieved of the obligation of the practical man to lie: Why not retain this privilege to be one of the "truthful ones" of Nietzschean myth?

WYNDHAM LEWIS, *TIME AND WESTERN MAN*

I

Tarr (1918) is regarded by some critics of the modernist novel as a masterpiece of staggering originality, a literary achievement second only to Joyce's *Ulysses*, published four years later. Even for critics who do not hold this view, the novel is generally judged to be Lewis's most significant work of fiction. And yet *Tarr* is seldom read today. One reason for the novel's neglect is that its experiments in characterization, its unique style, and its highly cerebral quality render it quite unlike other leading works of British modernism. Its distinctiveness has induced critics to situate *Tarr* in the avant-garde German tradition of Thomas Mann's and Rainer Maria Rilke's "Nietzschean novella."[1] On this view, *Tarr* is a Nietzschean novel, that is, a work of philosophical fiction that anticipates and complements Lewis's philosophical *summa* of a decade later, *Time and Western Man* (1927).

Tarr is thus the literary half of Lewis's critique of the modernist convention of spatial time, a Teutonic novel of ideas that portrays his alternative: an existential, indeed superhuman, artist-hero. *Time and Western Man* represents a critical assault on the philosophical and literary exponents of the Western "time-mind" for their hypostatization of flux and the consequent undermining of the individualistic, superior, fully-conscious being. *Tarr,* whose title character represents Lewis's fictional counterpart, is an exploration of the place of the

This photograph of Wyndham Lewis in his early thirties, probably taken by his friend George Charles Beresford, portrays a bold and defiant artist on the eve of World War I. At this time Lewis was in his bohemian artist phase, specifically his Vorticism period. Lewis entered the war in 1917, after which he drastically altered his artistic and social outlook, becoming a sharp critic of bohemian values, as reflected in his pioneering first novel *Tarr* (1918).

artist, "the truthful one," in a "bourgeois-bohemian" society of conformist herd-men.[2] As the great exemplar of Nietzschean fiction in English modernism, *Tarr* "presents the development of the central hero, Tarr, marked out by his superior vigor and vitality, as he breaks through and transcends the sick and destructive forces which surround him."[3] Such a Nietzschean approach is invaluable in two respects: it both focuses attention on the young Lewis's philosophical roots in Nietzsche and positions Tarr's self-created values in opposition to a "normal" society breeding herd morality and bad faith.

Nonetheless, I believe that such a straightforward Nietzschean reading is misleading. It casts Tarr as a crowning exemplar of joyful wisdom and thereby overlooks his growing resemblance to the very corrupting forces he seeks to surmount. Indeed, such a reading is ironically itself a Nietzschean "lie," for it ignores Tarr's final inability to achieve a heightened synthesis for himself of the novel's central oppositions of art against life and work against sex. Nietzsche too was for Lewis a "'hollow, stagey' 'vulgarizer' of the 'notion of power and aristocracy.'"[4] Lewis claimed that Nietzsche "lived in a Utopia, and wrote in and for a Utopia, hoping to make Europe that Utopia by pretending that it was."[5] Treating *Tarr* as a Nietzschean novel therefore also misleadingly frames the novel's explicit artistic questions with regard to themes of power, thereby obscuring the fact that *Tarr* is a *Künstlerroman*, not a *Vollmachtsroman*, a novel about artists rather than one about the exercise of power.[6] The fact is that Tarr strives to be not a political but an artistic *Übermensch*, a post-Nietzschean man: "*the Artist* himself, a new sort of person; the creative man,"(29) declares Tarr.

Describing himself, Tarr adds that the "new animal" of his highly evolved self "will succeed the superman" (307).

If Lewis seeks in *Tarr* to surpass Nietzsche, indeed to out-Nietzsche Nietzsche, then to argue that the novel achieves "metaphysical gaiety" and that Tarr himself realizes "creative Selfhood" is misconceived.[7] That contention neglects the disunity and instability of Tarr's sex life, his emergent similarity to his foil Otto Kreisler, his guilt feelings towards Bertha, and the invariable testimony of readers that the tragic fate of Kreisler—not of Tarr—preoccupies them.

My reading of Lewis's novel inverts the Nietzschean conclusions: Tarr fails to achieve "creative Selfhood" and remains a "conflicted self." His ultimate "stillbirth" of full individuality is not best understood through a strict Nietzschean approach. Nor is it attributable to Lewis's oft-bemoaned loss of artistic control, anti-Shavian polemics, or nationalistic and cultural biases. Rather, *Tarr* is a literary artwork about visual artists by a literary and visual artist, and it is most appropriately interpreted within an explicitly artistic framework.[8] It is a tragicomic story plumbing the implications of growing self-consciousness and autonomous will, of "creative urge and personality development," words that are, significantly, the subtitle of psychoanalyst Otto Rank's landmark study of the creative being's struggle with Life, *Art and Artist* (1932). Like Lewis, although from a wholly different vantage point, Rank judges Nietzsche an "ultra-romantic"[9] and inverts his concept of the "will to power" by his own "will to art": the "integrative power" of the personality is fully realized only through relationships with others, and in community.[10]

II

This chapter proposes that, viewed within the Rankian framework of character development and typology, *Tarr* gains coherence as a fascinating series of successive "portraits of the failed artist"—in the course of which even Tarr, Icarus-like, finally falls. As we shall see, Rank's identification of three stages of character development (or three artist "types") parallels in significant ways *Tarr*'s triadic cast of characters: first, the "average" men Hobson, Butcher, and Lowndes, who adapt naturally to social convention and are at one with the world; second, Kreisler as "neurotic" or "conflicted" man, rejecting social conformity yet suffering terribly because he can neither accept the dictates of social convention, nor that of his father, nor yet affirm his own; and third and finally, Tarr himself is a potential Rankian "Artist" or "creative" man who aspires to make himself a work of art. But Tarr fails to reconcile and unite the human drive for separation from others with the concomitant drive for union through creative relationships with others. In Rankian terms, Kreisler suffers from the "fear of life," by which he dreads separation from established authority, the social order, and ultimately the womb; Tarr exhibits the "fear of death," by which he dreads loss of individuality and identity in union with Society or Woman and thereby defensively apotheosizes art in isolation from life.[11]

My aim here is, therefore, to offer a close textual reading of *Tarr* in the light of Rankian personality development. I believe that a Rankian approach to *Tarr* is especially fitting to illuminate Lewis's art. It honors Lewis's own philosophical emphases: it focuses directly upon the novel's central themes of creativity and individual consciousness in opposition to the unconscious "time mind" concepts that Lewis castigates—and Rank achieves this with a positive yet realistic treatment of impulse, will, and art. Largely neglected today, even in psychoanalytic circles, Rank alone among the early psychoanalytic theorists devoted sustained attention to the artist and the creative urge.

In Rank's view, Freud, Adler, and Jung interpreted creativity superficially as a negative concept rooted, respectively, in the sublimation of libidinal drives, in neurotic power urges to overcome biological inadequacies, and in unconscious religious archetypes.[12] Art for Rank is a positive, creative expression of the individual will. Thus, Rank's "Psychology of the Will" and "Will Therapy" theories are directly indebted to, and seek to synthesize, both Freud and Nietzsche. According to Rank, Freud fatalistically "denied the will" in his misguided view that repression could positively direct an instinct (rather than merely divert or suppress it), and by counselling clients to adjust to a sick reality.[13] By contrast, Nietzsche melodramatically overemphasized the will and "denied the guilt feeling." Even the "creative man" still needs relationships, and "guilt is an ethical problem found in every human relationship."[14]

All this resonates much more closely with Lewis's vision in *Tarr* than does a Nietzschean reading. The world of *Tarr* is a sick society to which Tarr's pseudo-artist friends adjust naturally and well, and in which a torn Kreisler suffers anguish. But Tarr too fails to become the Rankian Artist because in denying the challenge to synthesize his aesthetic doctrine and life through constructive relationships of his own making, he seeks to evade guilt and so misconceives what it means to be "*the Artist* himself, a new sort of person; the creative man" (29)—and thereby remains a divided self.

Extremely skeptical about the value of psychoanalysis, Lewis viewed Freud as the second great modern "vulgarizer" after Nietzsche.[15] But Lewis doubtless would have been more sympathetic to Rankian ego psychology, which elevates the conscious over the unconscious, individual will over repressed collective heritage. Born only two years apart, Lewis (1882–1957) and Rank (1884–1939) shared not just the same passionate youthful attachment to Schopenhauer and Nietzsche, but also a grand conception of the supremacy of the artist.[16] Indeed the familial and intellectual contexts of Lewis and Rank possess some striking similarities. Both Lewis and Rank were raised by tender mothers and without paternal love: Mrs. Lewis took young Wyndham from Canada to England after her separation from her American husband, and Rank's icy relationship with his father culminated in a cut-off in contact between them during his teens. Furthermore, while no evidence yet exists that either man ever read the other's work or was acquainted with it during their youths in the German-speaking world or later, their philosophical ideas and literary orientations, manifested in quite divergent creative fields and intellectual spheres, possess notable parallels.[17] As Lewis was beginning *Tarr* in Munich in 1907, Rank was completing *Der Künstler* (*The Artist*—a different work from *Art and Artist*) in Vienna. Lewis's rebellion against the literary establishment's embrace of psychological theorizing and mentalistic exploration, and thus its consequent rejection of visual precision and consciousness, along with his relative isolation and widespread dismissal by critics and fellow writers, broadly mirrors Rank's repudiation of Freudian orthodoxy and his consequent ostracism and neglect by the psychoanalytic community.[18]

Before examining *Tarr* as a series of "portraits of the failed artist" according to the three stages of Rankian personality development, however, let us place Rank's theories of artistic creation and the formation of the fully creative Self within the context of his concepts of the birth trauma, separation, individuality, and Will Psychology. This overview will better equip us to assess *Tarr* itself as an artistic success or failure.[19]

III

Otto Rank's psychoanalytical theorizing passed through several phases, not unlike that of his mentor Freud. Rank himself was the first to stress the great difference between his mature study of art and will, *Art and Artist* (1932), and his early period "completely under the influence of Freudian realism" and within "the biological-mechanistic terms of Freud's natural science ideology," which was exemplified by *Der Künstler* of 1907.[20] He identified the publication of *The Trauma of Birth* (1923) as his "decisive turning point" away from Freud, and it is Rank's mature thought that possesses chief relevance for our evaluation of *Tarr*.

According to Rank, humanity's conscious and unconscious struggles are rooted in the fact of our mortality, in our origin and destiny as creatures moving through life from the trauma of birth to the trauma of death. The birth trauma is analogous to Adam's banishment from Eden, for life consists in a ceaseless attempt to refashion the world into the unity and peace of the womb: "The Ego in its retreat from the confines of anxiety is constantly urged forward to seek

Paradise in the world formed in the image of the mother."[21] Each assertion of individuality repeats in essence the conflict of the birth trauma, for it reenacts the liberation from total biological dependence in the womb, to personal dependence on social institutions or an Other to, finally—if successful—the birth of a creative Self and Art.[22]

The birth and death traumas result in two fundamental, opposing, and interacting fears that shape human personality: the "fear of life" and the "fear of death." The former is the fear of separation, of loss of fellowship with others, of standing alone and acting independently—and its preponderance characterizes the "neurotic," "conflicted man." The life fear pushes us to seek mother surrogates on which we perpetually depend. It is the dread of differentiation from "the collective," the fear of becoming an individual. The death fear is the dread of "the All," of embracing union and rushing towards dependence, and of the demise of uniqueness and identity. To submit to such domination is also indicative of a "conflicted man" who seeks to perpetuate himself through productive action. Rankian man therefore struggles futilely to reconcile his two irreconcilably conflicting drives toward separation and union, toward individuality and collectivity. The life and death fears are likewise simply two sides of the basic primal fear:

> This ambivalent primal fear, which expresses itself in a conflict between individuation and generation, is derived on the one side from the experience of the individual as a part of the whole, which is then separated from it and obliged to live alone (birth); on the other side, from the final necessity of giving up the hard-won wholeness of individuality through total loss (in death).[23]

Nevertheless, although man cannot return to his maternal paradise, Rank is not a fatalist, for through the power of human "will" we can transform the outside world and be transformed in a creative interchange from passive object to active subject. While the life and death fears are never entirely reconcilable, since birth and death are the ultimate facts of life, one's level of character development consists in the degree to which one has attempted and achieved a constructive integration of inner conflicts. For Rank, "the problem of willing" in the philosophical sense of the word is "the central problem of the whole question of personality, even of psychology."[24] "Will" for Rank was not metaphysically real like Schopenhauer's blindly insatiable and evil will, or Nietzsche's powerful positive life force, nor was it simply the will of Romantic faculty psychology. It is principally but not entirely conscious and therefore similar to the Freudian "ego," but not a pawn of superego or id. Rather, it represents

> an autonomous organizing force in the individual which does not represent any particular biological impulse or social drive, but constitutes the creative expression of the total personality.[25]

"Will" is a "positive guiding organization and integration of self which utilizes creativity, as well as inhibits and controls, the instinctual drives."[26] First experienced negatively as "counter-will" in childhood, willing inevitably involves the burden of guilt, since willing is rejecting someone or something on which one has been dependent. In the act of willing consists "a kind of universal guilt problem," not the "moral guilt" of an explicit code violation but the existential or "ethical" guilt attendant with becoming an individual.[27] Ethical guilt can neither be avoided nor eliminated, and the extent of personality growth is based upon how successfully it is accepted and used affirmatively. Rankian Will Therapy is a process of strengthening the Will's autonomy in order to achieve a creative self-integration.

IV

Let us now turn to the three phases of Rankian character development—the "average man," the "neurotic," and the Artist—which will frame our depiction of *Tarr*'s cast of characters. In a letter to the editors of *The Egoist* in which he accepts their offer of serialized publication of the novel, Lewis concedes that its initial sections depict characters who in effect exemplify Rank's artsy "average men": "You must really consider the first three chapters as a sort of preface."[28] Given that each of these three chapters (the section is entitled "Overture") features an encounter between Tarr and one of his artist-acquaintances (Hobson, Butcher, Lowndes), it is as if Lewis is dismissing his opening Parisian scenes in the same offhand manner that Tarr (Lewis's self-described "mouthpiece") rebuffs his friends.[29]

Lewis's statement and Tarr's attitude suggest that "Overture" is mere prologue, an introductory *andante* movement in *Tarr*'s Haydn-like sonata. Each docile friend ("a substitute for this defective self") listens as Tarr develops a familiar theme: should he make a romantic "overture" of marriage to "the Lunken" (37)? "Overture" climaxes in a "fourth movement" when Tarr confronts his unofficial "fiancée" and they both recognize that their relationship must end. Of course, Tarr also serves as the "Overture"'s unifying consciousness, the common filter through which the narrative voice is expressed, through which narrative events cohere, and against which they must be measured. This makes a sympathetic or objective hearing of the "average men's" voices difficult.

Titled *Self-Portrait, 1920s,* this drawing was sketched in pencil and inscribed "W. Lewis." It is best known from the *catalogue raisonné* entitled *Wyndham Lewis: Paintings and Drawings* (1971), edited by Walter Michel. (Michel gave the sketch its title. He was unsure of the exact date, which prompted him simply to append "1920s.")

It also indicates that Lewis's negative position is essentially similar to Rank's attitude towards such men: they must be evaluated not in their own right but be set against the creative man, the Rankian Artist.

In his preface to *Art and Artist,* Rank announces his "intention" to define the relation between "two tendencies, inherent in art and creativity: the individual and the collective, the personal and the social, in their interaction, and correspondingly in their counteraction."[30] Lewis's conclusions in *Time and Western Man,* directed against the proponents of Bergsonian flux and process, exhibit a similar set of dichotomies:

> On every hand some sort of *unconscious* life is recommended and heavily advertised, in place of the *conscious* life of will and intellect . . . . [A] long time ago a battle was engaged between the *Unconscious* and the *Conscious*: and we have been witnessing the ultimate triumph of the *Unconscious* of recent years. . . . Inside us also the crowds were pitted against the Individual, the Unconscious against the Conscious, the "emotional" against the "intellectual," the Many against the One.[31]

Tarr's "average man" is the mechanical witness to the Pyrrhic victory of the Unconscious, for he harmonizes life's basic dualisms by his compliant yielding to authority and instinct. Seeking liberation from dependence within the womb, he resolves the dichotomous conflicts by surrendering to his clamoring internal voices: the Unconscious, the crowd, the emotional, and the Many. Hobson, Butcher, and Lowndes therefore exemplify the Rankian "average man" in two respects here: by their ready acceptance of both the external compulsion of authority and the inner compulsion of impulses, and by their identifications with role-playing and sham appearances, all of which betray the artist's vocation.

The Rankian average man never progresses beyond the first stage of liberating individuation from the womb, during which he "now wills what he was earlier compelled to, what externally or internally he was forced to do."[32] He "subordinates himself, both socially and biologically, to the collective" and his "ideal" is "to be as others are."[33] Alan Hobson, introduced in Chapter One through Tarr's eyes, is a counterfeit bohemian-artist, a trendy "Cape Cantabian"[34] philosopher with an aristocratic Cambridge education: "Hobson, he considered, was a crowd. You could not say he was an individual. He was a set. He sat there, a cultivated audience" (29). Hobson is "concentrated, systematic slop" (34), a mere "body," rather than an "intellect" like Tarr.

For Lewis, "the intellect is the individual"; Hobson is "livestock," a "cultivated audience" to which Tarr declaims about art and sex, a "friend" through whom Tarr "confesses his faults to the world when his self will not acknowledge or listen to them" (31). Like Rank's average man, Hobson succumbs not only in the face of external pressures (e.g., fashion, aristocratic tradition), but also to his own inner impulses. His credo is simple: "Surely, a man *is* his appetite" (26). He gives free play to his emotions like an animal, to "the sentimental Humor and worship of the ridiculous" that Lewis despises. Hobson "convulsed himself and crowed thrice," then "let[s] himself go in whoops and caws" (28) when the subject of sex arises, apparently incapable of discussing it in Tarr's "serious" terms.

Butcher too is regarded by Tarr as a "defective self" (31), a creature of impulse who behaves like a child, a schoolboy with a will perfectly pliant towards outer dictates and his own sudden urges. He is a "bloody wastrel, enamoured of gold and liberty," a "romantic, educating his schoolboyish sense of adventure up to the pitch of drama" (36). His new turn away from art and gypsies toward the automobile business reflects his mechanical nature, for he bears "the air of an Iron-Age mechanic, born among beds of embryonic machinery," and smiles "as though half his face were frozen with cocaine" (36). Hiccuping, belching, and guffawing like an animal, with "rheumy eyes" like "a dog" (39), Butcher is a mindless blob of "pure, unadulterated romanticism" (40). Like Descartes, Butcher is virtually a Skinner box, a cluster of predictable sensations that Tarr can manipulate as he chooses, for he can convince Butcher "of anything on earth within ten minutes" (39).

Lowndes also exhibits a "willed acceptance" of bohemian values not his own. He seeks to incorporate them by setting up a studio and working busily and quite conspicuously. He is "not very active," but has "just enough money to be a Cubist" (45), and is really nothing more than a fastidious, self-important creature of pretense. He prattles about his artistic ambitions and about "his work," yet he produces little (45). Like the Rankian average man who "finds the justification of his individual will in the similarly adjusted wills of the majority" and accepts their moral norms and religious projections, Lowndes apes the creative man's mature outlook.[35] He is no individual; he plays a role.

Lowndes's role-playing differs from the animalistic passions that Hobson and Butcher indulge, and it represents a second characteristic of the Rankian average man, who "always plays a role, always acts, but actually plays only himself, that is, must pretend that he plays in order to justify his being."[36] His acting is invariably transparent. Possessing little self-knowledge, he experiences few pangs of "ethical guilt" and is troubled more instead by the "moral guilt" of violating social norms or religious standards. So, although the average man "must always play a role to rationalize his being," he experiences no conflict unless his performance is judged unsuitable by his recognized audience.[37] His discomfort is not with a life of illusion; he is a herd-man content to remain in his Platonic cave, disturbed only by social disapproval, or if the light of individualistic values pierces the darkness.

Hobson's fraudulent posing mocks and vulgarizes the artistic vocation. When Tarr asks if he is idle or working as an artist, Hobson yawns. A pseudo-artist, he has "bought for eight hundred pounds at an aristocratic educational establishment a complete mental outfit, a programme of manners" (34). He is a "disciplined social unit," the very antithesis of Lewis's creative personality, the Individual or Artist (34). Tarr tells him:

> You are systematizing and vulgarizing the individual. You are not an individual. You have, I repeat, no right to that hair and that hat. You are trying to have the apple and eat it, too. You should be in uniform, and at work, *not* uniformly *out of uniform*, and libelling the Artist by your idleness. (34)

Seeking to buy the artistic vocation, Hobson fails because Lewis's Artist necessarily possesses the sensibility of aristocracy and individuality. Hobson is the "average man" whom Lewis bemoans in the "Nietzsche as a Vulgarizer" chapter in *The Art of Being Ruled*:

> The average, worldly man does not . . . get beyond the conception of "the struggle for existence." He has no creative surplus at all. . . . This bloody struggle he is determined to subsist in the midst of, and yet keep it at a distance. He outwardly, like Nietzsche, has a powerfully developed "falsification" theory and "will to illusion." Only (naturally) he is much more successful in the use of it than Nietzsche could be.[38]

According to Lewis, the average or worldly man is hated by Nietzsche only because he holds to his illusion so fully, and does not, like Nietzsche, commit himself "to just go on contemplating the horrors of existence."[39]

Hobson lives "harmoniously" with the world. He is "convulsed" by laughter "as though Tarr had been pressing him to perform" (28), and he does not recognize Tarr's authority to criticize his role-playing and is not shaken by Tarr's vitriol: "In any case, my hat is my business!" he concludes (35). And later: "My dear Tarr, you're a strange fellow. I *can't* see why these things should occupy you" (35). Tarr has just told him, he says, "lots of things which may be true or may not" (35), but Hobson has already concluded that "you know you don't mean all that nonsense" (34). He does not see beyond himself and his immediate actions, and through his casuistry he preserves his illusions. So Tarr tries vainly to puncture them. Revelling in a spontaneous adaptation of the Baudelairean fable in which the poet pummels a beggar but is himself attacked, Tarr knocks Hobson's hat off, the symbol of his pseudo-neediness and artiness. "Your hat, at least," he concludes, "will have had its little drama to-day" (35). Tarr's mocking gesture confronts Hobson with the role-playing that he refuses to see.[40]

Butcher flirts with different occupations, yet he is just another average man. He "actually plays only himself," a self that consists of roles without substance or foundation.[41] Abandoning the gypsy life, Butcher is suddenly "induced" (36) by Tarr into commerce. He mimics Tarr when speaking with him: "He talked to Tarr, when a little worked up, as Tarr talked to him. He didn't notice that he did. It was partly chicanerie and flattery" (43).

Lowndes, the "self-made man" (46) "with his friend Thornton," desperately strives to reach the Rankian average man's "ideal": "to be as others are." Having "risen ambitiously in the sphere of the Intelligence" (46), his aesthetic pretensions are obvious in his pitiable attraction to his "moth-like" admirer Thornton (45). Thornton praises Lowndes's intelligence, but Lowndes is an intellectual hustler, not a self-aware intellect. Plunged even more deeply than Hobson and Butcher into that sentimental world of "Humour," which "paralyzes the sense for Reality and wraps people in a phlegmatic and hysterical dream-world, full of the delicious swirls of the switch-back, the drunkenness of the merry-go-round" (43), Lowndes's "nether world" (46) is a staged illusion in which he plays both grand actor and adulating critic. "Biographically-minded," he foresees "analysis and fame" for himself (46). His specialty is the vain self-portrait; he is a Rembrandt of self-advertisement.

Because he respects Tarr as an authentic artist, Lowndes feels "always embarrassed" around Tarr, as if Lowndes senses that Tarr can indeed "see" through his congratulatory self-reviewing. Tarr "always embarrassed" him by his "mock curiosity" about Lowndes's work and by his ironic joking (46). So serious is Lowndes about his comic little dream world that he struggles to deliver "adequate and light" (47) repartees, he "undulate[s] himself as though for the passage of the large bubbles of chuckle" when he attempts a casually clever reply, and feels "disturbed" when Tarr does not laugh at his jokes and departs (48). Lowndes has only his pseudo-artist role. Even more so than Hobson and Butcher, he *is* the role he plays. Unlike Hobson, who feels no distress because he rebuffs Tarr's severe critique as "upside-downness" from an easily dismissed audience, Lowndes reveres Tarr, and so he agonizes about Tarr's indifference (35).

As we have seen, Tarr's "average" artist-acquaintances share two sets of behaviors: a surrender to the life of Instinct and a willed submission to others' standards via self-delusive role-playing. Their homogeneity as mere "livestock" extends even to their descriptions in animal imagery. Tarr muses aloud with Hobson how "one apes the forms of conventional life" (32)—obviously referring to Hobson himself—and Lowndes eyes his watch with "calculated, apelike impulsiveness" (48).

The re-echoing dog identifications are particularly noteworthy. Hobson, "meaner-spirited than the most abject tramp" (35), feels Tarr his "superior" (22). Devoted Butcher is "like a dog, with his rheumy eyes" (39). Lowndes "potter[s] about, like a dog" (46) and reveres Tarr too. The growing explicitness of the dog imagery announces the Bertha theme in "Overture," which modulates towards the Tarr-Bertha confrontation. Leaving Lowndes and nearing Bertha's flat, Tarr fancies that he is a top dog engaged on an amusing errand: "A big dog wandering on its easily transposable business, inviting some delightful accident to deflect it from maudlin and massive promenade. In his mind, too, as in the dog's, his business was doubtful" (50).

In "Overture"'s fourth movement, the appearance of Bertha witnesses the mundane and sentimental (she calls Tarr "Sorbet"), which builds in a crescendo. In Rankian terms, her façades "prove to be so false that [they] work through their complete spuriousness."[42] Tarr seeks to cut the string, but Bertha "had captured a bit of him, and held it as a hostage" (72). When Tarr broaches a separation, Bertha "sniffs softly" and Tarr feels "like a person who is taking a little dog for a walk at the end of a string" (59). Tarr departs, "suffering from something that came from Bertha," "wounded" by the "malady" of her love, which instills a "wasting and restlessness" (59). On this discordant note, "Overture" returns full circle. The section opened with an aria to Paris's "unscrupulous heroes" "largely ignorant of all but their restless personal lives" (21). It ends with a sombre coda that brilliantly connects and encapsulates Lewis's themes, and suggests that Tarr's own strutting canine "promenade" (50) is not quite the evolved Artist's path: "Something followed him like a restless dog" (74).

Because the "average men" in "Overture" do experience "a relatively harmonious working together of will and counter-will," they do not suffer excessively

The cover illustration for the Oxford World's Classics edition of *Tarr* is a Vorticist drawing by Lewis himself, who was one of the great Modernist masters in both literature and the fine arts. It is a detail from *Workshop* (1914–1915), which is one of only two artworks of this period sketched by Lewis himself. Lewis's original painting is currently at the Tate Gallery in London. Rumors have circulated for years that it was accidently discovered in a junk shop after having been missing for many decades, but today's scholarly consensus is that this juicy story is probably apocryphal.

The workshop may be the artist's place of work. Artists need light, and the blue square signifies the sky in the center. This painting includes structures that appeared in separate sketches during the war years. Architectural in inspiration, they feel like imagined urban structures; Lewis was an enthusiast for the urban at this time. The paint texture is deliberately rough, and the colors are meant to clash, or sit uneasily together, which reflects Lewis's aesthetic principle that colors should not be harmonious, as he explains in one of his short essays in *Blast 1* (1914).

Placing the novel in the context of the cultural politics and social fashions of the continental literary bohemia and expatriate beau monde, Scott W. Klein's introduction reflects Lewis's scorn for the hypocritical pretensions of the avant-garde and the smug self-satisfaction of the art world. Set in Paris on the eve of the First World War, Lewis's biting, often sarcastic narrative voice and sharp, almost staccato prose style in *Tarr* reflect his critical views on the art and literature of the period. This edition of *Tarr* in the Oxford World's Classics series also features Lewis's preface to the 1918 American edition.

from a Rankian fear of death or of life.[43] But they are mere pseudo-artists because, while their compromise in favor of the collective generates "fewer possibilities of conflict," it also "permits them fewer creative possibilities of any kind"[44]—as Hobson's "idleness," Butcher's vagrancy between art and commerce, and Lowndes's "inactivity" attest. By their willed surrender to cultural fashion and societal norms, they lead "the unexamined life"—an existence that Rank and Lewis deem far worse than the growing pains wrought by birth trauma anxieties from autonomously willed decisions. For Lewis, such people are never truly "born."

V

From the moment he is introduced and until his tragicomic end in the section titled "Holocaust," Otto Kreisler dominates *Tarr*. Kreisler becomes a divided, bathetic Hamlet, the novel's tortured psychopathic Fool. Kreisler's plight is that of Rank's "neurotic," the "conflicted" man of "divided will" caught in the second stage of individual development. This stage or "type" is

> characterized by the feeling of division in the personality, through the disunity of will and counterwill, which means a struggle (moral) against the compulsion of the outer world as well as an inner conflict between the two wills.[45]

Like Bertha's room, Kreisler's flat defines him: "Kreisler's room looked like some funeral vault" (77). We already know from the novel's section title that he is "Doomed, Evidently."

Kreisler is the chief presence in five of the novel's seven sections, yet the sections in which he appears—unlike Tarr's orderly Apollonian "Overture," with himself as the integrating consciousness—have no unifying central consciousness. They are a wild, chaotic Wagnerian opera with climactic recitatives, or Dionysian dithyrambs punctuating the narrative's dance, with scenes involving rape and a duel. Kreisler behaves in these scenes like "The Dithyrambic Spectator," a force whom Lewis identified elsewhere in an essay of that title. Only intermittently does Kreisler's consciousness filter the narrative voice. Kreisler can only react, not act. He cannot be an actively shaping and unifying consciousness because he too is a divided, abject self. The five Kreisler sections are consequently reported by a rather detached narrative consciousness.

Kreisler as Rankian "conflicted" man cannot transcend mere moralistic (or legalistic) and instinctual acceptance, because he can only conform or rebel, not struggle constructively to forge a new creative self from his inner divisions.

This type resembles a man restricted to inadequate one-word "yes" or "no" responses—in answer to questions he does not pose. For Rank, whereas the average man's ideal is "to be as others are," the "conflicted" man's ideal is "to be himself, that is, what he himself is and not as others want him to be."[46] His ideal self therefore is limited to a mere "is," rather than the Artist's "ought." But he still resembles the Artist more than even the "advanced" average type. Like the Artist, he is fundamentally committed to separation from the crowd. His tragedy is that he cannot unite his divided will and counter-will to achieve creative integration. So he knows neither the contented ignorance of the average man nor the triumphant exultation of the creative man, but only anguish. As if he were viewing Kreisler as the archetype for the "conflicted" stage, Rank terms him "the *artiste-manqué*."[47]

It is not only the appearance of his lodgings and his apparel that express Kreisler's internal war between submission and rebellion. His relationships, especially that with his father, also reveal conflicting tendencies of surrender to, and resistance against, inner impulse and external authority. Moreover, when the events of Kreisler's life "became too unwieldy or overwhelming," he "converted them into love [i.e., sex], as he might have done . . . into some art or other" (102). In this he embodies Rank's neurotic Romantic artist:

> Not only is he an individual-revolutionary in creation, but he confuses life with art; he is dramatic or lyrical, he acts the piece instead of objectifying it, or rather he is obliged to act it as well as merely objectify it. His art is as chaotic as his life.[48]

Of course, Kreisler utterly confuses art and life, and so completely converts the latter into a feeling of love (in practice expressed as sex) that he can only act upon, not objectify. No work of art emerges. Unproductive as an artist, "he had only lost [i.e., sold] one picture so far. This senseless solitary purchase depressed him whenever he thought of it" (81). Unlike Rank's Artist, who "strives to be deathless through his work," "the neurotic does not seek immortality in any clearly defined sense, but in primitive fashion as . . . accumulation of actual life."[49] Promiscuous Kreisler, the "sculptor of a mock-realistic and degenerate school" (102), has a remarkably impressive accumulation: seventeen children "in Munich alone," with "a small society . . . founded in Bavaria to care for Kreisler's offspring throughout Germany" (94).

Kreisler, like the "average men," is a creature of impulse. Womanizing is his arena. Women are "Art or expression for him" (101), "the aesthetic element in Kreisler's life" (102). A gifted "creator," it is rumored that "he only had to look at a woman for her to become pregnant" (94). "Not adept in the science of the heart," Kreisler feels "Woman" is "always connected with its [life's] important periods; he thought, superstitiously, that his existence was in some way implicated with *das Weib* [the female]" (102–103). He is correct, for each of his impulsive encounters in the three chief events of the Kreisler sections—the dance, the rape, and the duel—are prompted by Kreisler's uncontrollable passion for *das Weib*. On the basis of a single luncheon meeting with her, Kreisler fantasizes Anastasya Vasek into "an idée fixe" (107). He unsuccessfully seeks a "frac" (a dinner-jacket or tuxedo) in order to gain admittance and meet her at the Bonnington Club dance, but he goes anyway. He behaves outrageously to impress her, and his dancing suggests his urgent libidinal frenzy, "as though he mistook the waltz for a more primitive music" (148).[50]

Not only confusing art and life, but betraying art, Kreisler asks Bertha Lunken to sit and pose nude for him. Then he rapes her, using a ridiculous simile as his opening line: "Your arms are like bananas!" "But still he was an artist: it was natural—even inevitable!—that he should compare her arms to bananas," a hapless Bertha rationalizes (193). Kreisler then abruptly calls on Bertha, and now the urge to apologize becomes his instinct that must be satisfied: "He had not known what he had wanted with her, but the obvious pretext and road for the satisfaction of this impulse was the seeking of pardon" (200). Kreisler can only "act violently, in gusts. He did not know, when he began an action, whether he would be able to go through with it" (201).[51] Kreisler is no mere id, lacking consciousness like the "average men"; but when he attempts deliberate action, instinct invariably overcomes him: "Destiny had laid its trap in the unconscious Kreisler. It fixed it with powerful violent springs" (191). Next it snaps shut on Soltyk in their duel.

Harboring an immediate violent dislike for Louis Soltyk, Kreisler is furious to see him in Anastasya's company at the dance. He challenges him to a duel, and with characteristic impulsiveness, withdraws it on the condition that Soltyk kiss him. Soltyk rushes for Kreisler's neck, the German's gun accidentally goes off and kills the Pole, and Kreisler finally yields himself on an impulse to the French police.[52] Locked up in a cell at the police station, playing with a cord and the notion of hanging himself, "a sort of heavy confusion burst up as he withdrew the restraint" (285). His suicide resembles the duel, which had been "a whim, a caprice . . . as though, for instance, they had woken up in the early morning and decided to go fishing" (267). Kreisler's life is one comically accidental event after another.

Although Kreisler invariably yields to instinct, he can and does resist external authority. Despite the pressure of father, financial security, and mainstream society to abandon it, he persistently follows the artist's calling. His rebellions are, however, either overbalanced by or rooted directly in submission to authority or inner impulse. Despite his seeming defiance of his father, Kreisler still lives on a paternal allowance at the age of thirty-six. He quickly drops his hermit life when he meets the Lipmann set. His actions before and during the dance are done primarily from impulse or to impress Anastasya. And his sudden reversal toward Soltyk is prompted by fear and whimsy—indeed Kreisler's life seems a successive series of attachments and surrenders to others for social, financial, and personal security: to the Lipmann circle, to his father, to Volker, to Lowndes, and to Anastasya.

Women for Kreisler are the ultimate security. They are a "vast dumping-ground for sorrow and affliction—a world-dimensioned Pawn-shop, in which you could deposit not your dress suit or garments, but yourself, temporarily, in exchange for the gold of the human heart" (101). But Kreisler gets neither his frac nor Anastasya "out of hock." As he had done with Volker, Soltyk displaces him in Anastasya's affections.

The remarkable galaxy of associations between this group of characters (Volker, Anastasya, and Soltyk) and Kreisler's father and "stepmother" illuminate Kreisler's paradoxical behavior. If "Destiny" lies in the "unconscious Kreisler" (218), his unpredictable oscillations between rebellion and submission are not adequately explained by reference to cycles of defiance and resistance toward authority and impulse. Rather, the patterns of his chief relationships suggest Kreisler's impassioned search for a mother, for a return to the womb, to find a female "dumping ground" for his anguished self. These relationships highlight both the dynamics of Kreisler's neurotic personality and his Rankian quest to overcome the primal fear.

Herr Kreisler Sr. is "jealous, contemptuous and sulky" (81) toward Otto and uses his son's allowance to infuriate him and as leverage for getting his way in argument. So powerful is Herr Kreisler's authority that Otto refers to his father's girlfriend—a woman of approximately Otto's age (and his own former fiancée)—as his "stepmother." Otto is unable to imagine himself as his father's rival. He therefore distances his father's girlfriend by naming her his "stepmother" (though she can hardly substitute effectively for his dead mother). The "suffering" and "contempt" that Otto holds toward his father doubtless arise in part from his latent Oedipal feeling that Herr Kreisler stole his mother's love, just as he swiped his fiancée.

Kreisler is therefore not so much "the sort of man who would splice his sweetheart with his Papa" (94) as he is the powerless victim or pawn in an Oedipal battle that has been reenacted. His quest for security in *das Weib*, his perpetual student life, and his willed submission to institutional authority are all explainable in light of his chief, defining relationship to his father, who has abused him and kept him dependent. His idealization of Anastasya manifests his endless, enflamed pursuit both for the tranquil womb from which he was exiled and for the mother whose love was snatched away. By idealizing Anastasya, according to Rank, "neurotic" Kreisler idealizes himself. So when she rejects him, he is devastated and rejects a part of himself:

> The neurotic, no matter whether productive or obstructed, suffers fundamentally from the fact that he cannot or will not accept himself, his own individuality, his own personality. On one hand he criticizes himself to excess, on the other he idealizes himself to excess, which means that he makes too great demands on himself and his completeness, so that failing to attain leads only to more self-criticism.[53]

Anastasya becomes Kreisler's idealized good mother and, by extension, the good self for which he yearns. Soltyk, by contrast, who "physically bore, distantly and with polish, a resemblance to Kreisler" (90) is Kreisler's superior, thieving father, the bad self whom he despises. Soltyk is his "efficient and more accomplished counterpart," with a "handsome face" and "elegance" (90). But the Pole is actually just as "empty and unsatisfactory" (90) as Kreisler. Like Kreisler and his father, Otto and Soltyk harbour a mutual, innate contempt for each other: they "disliked each other for obscure physiological reasons: they had perhaps scrapped in the dressing rooms of Creation for some particularly fleshly covering, and each secured only fragments of a coveted garment" (90). Just as in the cases of Herren Kreisler Sr. and Jr., both Otto and Soltyk covet their neighbor's "*Weib*."

It is therefore unsurprising that the like-minded and more sophisticated Soltyk replaces Kreisler as Volker's favored beneficiary. But the possibility of also losing Anastasya to Soltyk, dimly connected with the loss of his fiancée to his father, sends Kreisler into a paroxysm of rage on seeing the pair together at the dance. "Anastasya was sitting there with Soltyk. With Soltyk!" (119). He fixes them in his mind as one: "Soltyk-Anastasya; Soltyk-Anastasya. That was a bad coupling!" (120). He then momentarily hallucinates the link between Volker and Herr Kreisler and between Soltyk (Soltyk-Anastasya) and his stepmother: "Behind Ernst and his parent, Soltyk and his stepmother stood" (121). He muses: "Soltyk, who had got hold of Volker . . . occupied a position not unsimilar to his stepmother" (121).

Although Kreisler consciously scorns Volker as a fool who is easy to exploit, he also idealizes him as the rich, generous good father whom he never had. Free with his allowance toward Kreisler, Volker arouses the tenderness in Otto that he wants to feel toward his father yet cannot: "Volker had been the ideal element of balance in his life" (93). Soltyk's new success with Volker is "the omen of the sinking ship, the disappearance of the rats" (93). Soltyk's triumph with Volker is therefore not only a financial setback for Kreisler, but the momentous triumph of his bad father over his good one. After Soltyk's capture of Anastasya (at least in Kreisler's eyes), Kreisler is again parentless, a helpless dependent without a dependency. He writes a note to his father, threatening suicide, but it is perfunctory. But why does Kreisler associate Soltyk, rather than Anastasya, with his stepmother? Or why not Soltyk directly with his father?

Kreisler's hatred for Soltyk is palpable. Feeling "endless dissatisfaction and depression," Kreisler is even "depressed" by Soltyk's "self-possessed and masterly signs of distinguished camaraderie" (150) with Volker and Anastasya. Kreisler "did not like him [Soltyk]. How it would satisfy him to dig his fingers into that flesh, and tear it like thick cloth!" (150). Kreisler's repressed identification of Soltyk with his stepmother, the former love object now distanced and desexualized, bursts forth in the duel scene: "A cruel and fierce sensation of mixed origin rose hotly round his heart. He *loved* that man!" (270). Kreisler immediately has a phallic dream-wish: "But because he loved him he wished to plunge a sword into him, to plunge it in and out and up and down!" (270). Suddenly Kreisler resolves to "kiss and make up": "Kreisler thrust his mouth forward amorously . . . as though Soltyk had been a woman" (272). At this affront, a crazed Soltyk rushes for Kreisler's throat. Soltyk's nails carve "six holes in the flesh and cut into the tendons beneath" (272), recalling not only Kreisler's desire to tear Soltyk's flesh but also the German's earlier identification of "Soltyk-Anastasya" as one, when, seeing this "bad coupling," "a sort of persecution complex seized him by the throat" (121).

Let us dwell here a moment on Kreisler's complex psychology. Traditional Freudian psychoanalysis would judge Kreisler's "persecution complex" as a father complex, with the series of character links viewed as unconscious identifications that disclose Kreisler's psychic propensity toward homosexuality and masochism. He "suffers" both before his father and even more before Anastasya: "But he wanted to suffer still more by her; *physically*, as it were, under her eyes. . . . he must excite in her the maximum of contempt and dislike" (124). "Contempt" and "dislike" are the very words used repeatedly to describe the mutual feelings of Otto toward his father and toward Soltyk, respectively. Kreisler's identification of Anastasya not only with Soltyk but also with his powerful father displaces Soltyk into "a position not unsimilar to his stepmother" (121). A classic psychoanalytic interpretation would propose that Kreisler unconsciously represses his own violent hatred toward his father, a deep-seated fear rooted in his Oedipal defeat, transforming him into a spectre of Vengeance—much as five-year-old Little Hans does because of castration anxiety:

> The instinctual impulse . . . was a hostile one against the father. One might say that impulse had been repressed by the process of being transformed into its opposite. Instead of aggressiveness on the part of

> the subject towards the father, there appeared aggressiveness (in the shape of revenge) on the part of the father towards the subject.[54]

From a Freudian viewpoint, "neurotic" Kreisler therefore wants to suffer and inevitably feels inferior because his chief relationship—to his father as vengeful Fate—defines all his other relationships: "All these people, allied with and privy to Fate, acted in an unexpected and malicious way" (138–139). Defending himself against a "homosexual impulse which has become too powerful,"[55] Kreisler displays classic *paranoia persecutoria*:

> There was a plot to deny his fermentations. His were the sensations of a simple man introduced for the first time into an official milieu,—a court or court-house—where everybody, behaving strangely, seems quite at home and born to it all. . . . He was the only one not in Fate's secrets. (139)

As with Little Hans's fear, Kreisler's hatred of his father gives expression, in a form that has undergone regressive degradation, to a passive, tender impulse to be loved by him in a genital-erotic sense. According to psychoanalysis, Kreisler inverts and disguises his homosexual love in a manner similar to his attempt to distance his fiancée by thinking of her as "stepmother." His passionate and ambivalent primary identification of Soltyk with his stepmother arises because Kreisler "*loved* that man!" (270)—and wants to be loved by his father in the way that he can romanticize his "stepmother" is loved.[56]

Equipped with this Freudian reading of Kreisler's condition, we are now in a position to grasp the radical difference between Freud and Rank, and the more satisfying explanation that a Rankian "life fear" approach to artistic creation affords.[57] A Rankian interpretation of the aforementioned character links does not deny Kreisler's latent homosexuality. Rather, it focuses upon his relationship with his mother figures and treats the paternal relations as secondary. Rank indeed speculates (but does not elaborate) in *Art and Artist* that the artistic nature (productive or obstructed) may be bisexual.[58] I contend that a Freudian reading, however, in its focus upon the father relation, overemphasizes Kreisler's paternal fear and hatred. It sidesteps the repeated references to *das Weib* as both the center of Kreisler's existence and the "dumping-ground" for his self. It also elides the fact that Soltyk is linked not only with his father but also with Kreisler's own bad self. His accidental but fated killing of Soltyk is the death of a part of himself, for Kreisler "questioned if it were not he that had died and not Soltyk, and if it were not his ghost that was now wandering off nowhere in particular" (279). Death confronts him like a "dive" into "deep water" (164). In fact, "he had got into life . . . by mistake: *il s'était trompé de porte*" (164).

Lewis's French is richly suggestive: "se tromper de porte" ("to take the wrong door") echoes the primary meaning of "tromper": "to betray." Kreisler unconsciously yearns to "dive" back into the "deep water" of the womb, for he has been forced out by his Oedipal rival. So Kreisler's life "might almost have been regarded as a long and careful preparation for voluntary death" (164).

In all this Kreisler corresponds to the Rankian "neurotic," whose efforts "to delay dying and to ward off death" only "hasten and strengthen the process of destruction because he is not able to overcome it creatively."[59] Thus Soltyk's death assists Kreisler's unconscious goal of return to the womb. His identification of Soltyk with his stepmother is important less for its homosexual undertones than because Soltyk is his hated but "better half" with whom he must reunite. He must kill Soltyk and himself in order to unify his divided self. Only then can he satisfy "the perpetual insatiable tendency to force one's way into the mother" and undo the trauma of birth.[60]

Kreisler's tragicomic gestures reflect his pathetic "neurotic" urge for what Rank terms "creative integration." His stepmother arouses intimate feelings as both a romantic attachment and a mother surrogate. But his way to her is blocked by his father, just as his way to his real mother is blocked by the fact of her death. Consequently, like the Rankian neurotic, for whom "actual production is only possible with the aid of a concrete Muse through whom or from whom the work is produced,"[61] Kreisler turns to Anastasya. Of course, his productive arena is not Art but Life, and every major action he takes—his seeking the frac, his behavior at the dance, his duel with Soltyk—is performed for her. She is both his idealized Muse and his passionate love object, and this duality represents the link between Kreisler's stepmother and Anastasya, or more precisely, "Soltyk-Anastasya."

Kreisler's "divided self" seeks reunion with *das Weib*—with his mother, his stepmother, and with Anastasya. Thwarted in his attempts with all three—even Soltyk is only "one of her [Anastasya's] many impresarios, who helped her on to and off the scene of Life" (150)—Kreisler rapes Art for Life by assaulting Bertha Lunken. But this is yet another unsuccessful attempt to satisfy his unconscious desire for reunion in the womb.

With his options to overcome the fear of life apparently exhausted, Kreisler must die. His pattern of willed suffering has unconsciously served to make his life "a long and careful preparation for voluntary death" (186). The Rankian neurotic's tendency to self-punishment

> has not so much the intention of granting him life as of escaping death, from which he seeks to buy himself by daily partial self-destruction. . . . In this way the lengthening of punishment is at the same time a drawing out of life, for as long as he punishes himself—feels pain, as it were—

> he still lives. This neurotic attitude of the individual towards death . . . is comprehensible only from the will psychology, which shows that the human being seeks to subject death, this original symbol of "the must," to his will, and as it were, at his own instigation transforms the death punishment that is placed upon life into lifelong punishment he imposes upon himself.[62]

The concept of the birth trauma as the foundation for Rank's psychosocial, phylogenetic theories places the father in the role of obstacle to the son's desire to return to the mother's womb. In *Tarr*'s closing pages, Kreisler repeatedly succeeds in penetrating the paternal "walls" that block his mother image, the prison, by submitting to them. As Kreisler flees from the French authorities to the German border after the duel, the border begins "to rise like a wall in front of him" (279).

Informed that he must face trial in Paris for Soltyk's death, Kreisler immediately associates the departure with the "walled" frontier and with his father, and so he prepares for his unconsciously willed physical death:

> This journey to Paris resembled his crossing of the German frontier. He had felt that it was impossible to see his father. That represented an effort he would do anything to avoid. . . . Noise, piercing noise, effort, awaited him revengefully. He knew exactly what his father would do and say. If there had been a single item that he could not forecast. . . . But there was not the least item. Paris was the same. (283–284)

In his dreary cell, Kreisler hangs himself, ending his unconscious quest for union with the mother, with "Soltyk-Anastasya": "[The cord's pressure] reminded him of Soltyk's hands on his throat." Finally: "It was the Soltyk struggle over again. But, as with Soltyk, he did not resist" (285).

Tarr is both right and wrong in his psychoautopsy of Kreisler's death. He is right that sex was Kreisler's "form of art" and that "the nearest [he] can get to art is *Action*" (302). Undoubtedly he "was an art-student without any talent, and was leading a dull, slovenly existence like thousands of others in the same case" (302). But Kreisler's suicide is not "an attempt to get out of Art into Life again," or as Tarr subsequently qualifies it, "*back into sex*" (302). Rather, Kreisler is a divided self whose overpowering life fear unconsciously drives him to a joint death with Soltyk. Before this occurs, he has failed to penetrate through images of his "warden" father so as to return to his "lost Paradise." He is the Rankian *artiste-manqué* who cannot unite his divided will and counter-will in creative integration, for even his suicide is merely the last of a series of willed, self-destructive acts of submission. Like the introductory and final notes in the Apollonian "Overture," this ending echoes the opening of the Wagnerian Kreisler sections (from "Doomed, Evidently—the Frac" to "Holocaust").[63] For Kreisler the ending is literally a return to origins. Kreisler (in German, "Kreis" = "circle")[64] comes full circle, from womb to tomb, from birth to death.

VI

Consider now the novel's protagonist, the title figure of Frederick Tarr, in light of Rank's psychology of art and neurosis. Tarr's "tragedy" is the failure of a potential Rankian Artist, that "exceptional being,"[65] to exploit fully his creative will and attain all he can. As we shall see, espousing an aesthetic that partitions art from sex and male from female, Tarr inadvertently and self-destructively ends as a "conflicted" Rankian man, battling in a "perplexed interior life"[66] between intelligent Anastasya and "average" Bertha. When the blockade separating Tarr's art and his sex life is finally lifted and he "marries" Bertha (for four hours per day) and cohabits with Anastasya, the choice represents in Rankian terms a developmental collapse, not a positively "willed" decision. It evades the messiness of life (in which male and female relationships cannot be fixed on canvas); it reflects Tarr's failure to engage in the creative effort necessary to synthesize constructively his conflicts. His oscillations between Anastasya and Bertha suggest finally that Tarr never does get "beyond A and B," for his dalliance with Prism Dirkes "represents the swing back of the pendulum once more to the swagger side," away from "cheerless and stodgy" Rose Fawcett (320).

Rather, Tarr becomes an increasingly fragmented self, ultimately unable to reconcile his aesthetic with his relationship to Bertha, or even to unify his sex life itself in opposition to art. Although his aesthetic manifestoes do not change much from beginning to end, his behavior in the novel's latter sections belies his words. As he shifts from an observer in "Overture" to a man who must deal with relationships and others' emotions, he cannot quite maintain his "*famous feeling of indifference*" (49). He cannot remain a disembodied intellect, and he grows to resemble the very characters whom he earlier despised. It is also not surprising that Tarr no longer serves after "Overture" as the novel's integrating consciousness through which the narrative voice is filtered and against which events are measured. As he becomes enmeshed in the interpersonal complications of daily human life, he cannot view it with the detachment that one might view disembodied art. He cannot be a central, unifying consciousness because, as he comes to resemble Kreisler and Bertha, he becomes a divided self. Still, more than any other character in *Tarr*, the title hero is periodically self-aware and in that respect approaches Rank's creative man. This third and highest level of development is characterized by a unified working together of the three fully developed powers, the will, the counter-will, and "the ideal-formation born from the conflict between them, which itself has become a goal-setting and goal-seeking force." Here "the human being, the genius, is again at one with himself; what he does, he does fully and completely in harmony with all his powers and his ideals."[67]

This "ethical ideal formation" entails an individual's willing to "free himself from the traditional moral code and to build his own ethical ideals from himself, ideals that are not only normative for his own personality but also include the . . . possibility of happiness."[68] Often he may in times of anxiety exhibit willed acceptance of external authority or inner impulse and become excessively compliant or rebellious, for the artistic path is a "continuous struggle against outer forces and a constant conflict with inner ones, in which the individual must live through for himself all stages of evolution."[69] According to Rank, whereas the "average" ideal is "to be as others are," and the "neurotic" ideal is to be "what he himself is and not what others want him to be," the artist's ideal is always "an actual ideal, which leads him to become that which he himself would like to be." This consistent, willed striving for the ideal, not artistic productivity or achievement, represents the defining criterion to ascertain the Rankian Artist. Although *Tarr*'s narrator says of Volker that "since arriving in Paris, he had blossomed prodigiously" (83), his development is external—just crass, bourgeois artistic success.

The first, and determining, sign of the Rankian creative man is not productivity, but rather his "nomination" of himself as an artist. Tarr at first appears to display this sign, though it is questionable finally that he ever does so. He clearly fails to exhibit the second sign, the development of a personal "philosophy of renunciation." As Rank explains:

> the creative type nominates itself at once as an artist . . . in the artist-type the creative urge is constantly related, ideologically, to his own ego . . . so that one can say of the artist that he does not practice his calling, but is it, himself, represents it, ideologically. . . . For the artist, therefore, his calling is not a means of livelihood, but life itself.[70]

Thus, the creation of his own personality is the artist's first work. It remains his *chef d'oeuvre,* since all other productions are at least partly the repeated expressions of this initial creation. Does Tarr accomplish this? Tarr does proclaim himself an evolved Artist, and knows that he must sublimate his energies in order to transform his own being into his first masterpiece:

> First, I am an artist. With most people, not describable as artists, all the finer part of their vitality goes into sex. . . . The artist is he in whom this emotionality normally absorbed by sex is so strong that it claims a newer and more exclusive field of deployment. Its first creation is *the Artist* himself, a new sort of person; the creative man. (29)[71]

"The creative impulse springs from the human urge for immortality," Rank explains. "Artists" seek "self-perpetuation through an artwork. Both are creations. But the latter is not only entirely individual, but an eternal legacy over which one (usually) has complete control."[72] Tarr himself is the "first-rate poet" whose "powers and moneys" are rechanneled "away from the immediate world" (29) toward aesthetics itself. This "will to self-immortalization," as Rank calls it, arises from "the fear of death." "In creation the artist tries to immortalize his mortal life. He desires to transform death into life, as it were, though actually he transforms life into death. For not only does the creative work not go on living; it is, in a sense, dead,"[73] that is, lifeless spiritually and psychologically, indeed almost inorganic.[74] Yet still it wards off the "fear of death" because it endures. Tarr's self-professed aesthetic reflects how Rank's death fear drives Tarr's urge for immortality:

> No, but *deadness* is the first condition of art. A hippopotamus' armored hide, a turtle's shell, feathers or machinery. . . . The second is absence of *soul*. . . . No restless, quick flame-like ego is imagined for the *inside* of it. It has no inside. . . . Instead, then, of being somewhat impelled like an independent machine by a little egoistic fire inside, it lives soullessly and deadly by its frontal lines and masses. (299–300)

As we have noted, the act of "nomination" or self-appointment is not alone sufficient for Tarr to become a Rankian Artist. Even Kreisler calls himself (along with "Boulevardier" and "Korpstudent") a "Rapin" (256). Because an artist *is* his or her calling, and represents it ideologically, nomination usually marks "the subordination of the individual to one of the prevailing art-ideologies," whereby the artist turns (consciously or unconsciously) to models from life or history for his "ethical ideal."[75] Tarr professes to admire Socrates and repeatedly echoes Nietzsche. Tarr's self-glorification and contempt for "the crowd" have Socratic roots; his misogyny bears a Nietzschean accent: "I prefer the *artist* to be free, and the crowd not be artists" (234), he tells Anastasya. Later he muses: "There was only one God, and he was a man. A woman was a lower form of life" (313). He declares: "I'm the new animal; we haven't found a name for it yet. It will succeed the Superman" (307). Tarr also intermittently speaks as if influenced strongly by Rousseau's romantic primitivism and Wildean aesthetics, echoing Vivian in *The Decay of Lying* (1889).

Tarr's failure does not lie in his renouncing his self-appointment as an "artist," but rather in his developmental arrest. This is a familiar hazard of "nomination," which often actually fosters a new dependence on an art-ideology. To develop further, the "mature" artist liberates himself from the ideological "bonds" that he accepted and helped to shape. The process is again a complex repetition of the trauma of birth, and excruciatingly difficult, not because it demands separation from persons and ideas one admires, but because "the victory is always, at bottom . . . won over a part of one's own ego."[76] In this battle, however, Tarr capitulates without ever actually "striving" for an ideal, since he willfully avoids developing "a renunciant view of life": a Rankian Artist sees that it is "not only impossible but perilous" to live out his ideology to the full "and can, willingly and affirmatively, accept the limitations" of "moral conventions and artistic standards, not merely as such, but as protective measurements against a premature and complete exhaustion of the individual."[77]

Mired in illusions, Tarr will not affirm his human limitations and so partitions art from life, male from female. Art is "life with all the nonsense taken out of it" (298), he insists, "ourselves disentangled from death and accident" (299).[78] A man without "*a vestige of passion*" in the sex "compartment" (31), Tarr takes up with his "pumpkin" Bertha (29) solely because the great artist, who seeks beauty not in women but rather in art, still needs an outlet for his vulgar nature.[79]

Tarr's conduct as an observer in "Overture" who needs only to talk and evaluate, not act, offers insight into why he later falters when confronted in his relationships with a choice between art and sex. Tarr has "no social machinery but the cumbrous one of the intellect" (23), which is just as mechanical as instinct when functioning alone: "full of sinister piston rods, organ-like shapes, heavy drills" (23). Although he resolves in the novel's first three chapters to give up humor, play, and then laughter, Tarr himself succumbs to "childish sport" (27) and sentimentality throughout the novel. Scorning the role-playing of Hobson, Butcher, Lowndes, and Bertha, Tarr never criticizes his own acting—or even seems aware of it. An objective narrator observes:

> When he solicited advice, it was transparently a matter of form. But he appeared to need his own advice to come from himself in public. . . . He was the kind of man who, if he ever should wish to influence the world, would do it so that he might touch himself more plastically through others. He would paint his picture for himself. He was capable of respect for his self-projection. It had the authority of a stranger for him. (38)

Tarr's delicious pleasure in acting the Baudelairean poet and knocking Hobson's hat off represents a grandiose act of self-projection. Rank notes that, in subordinating himself to an art-ideology, the individuality of the potential artist arrested at the "nomination stage" "vanishes."[80] Soon Tarr's "individuality" reemerges as Kreislerian conflict. Swimming in life's daily ooze "like an alligator" (27), Tarr loses his aesthetic distance and becomes "infected." Tarr senses that Bertha has captured part of him, but he cannot "escape": "The appeal of the *little* again. If only he could escape from *scale*" (73).

Unable to vault over the miniature—to escape "scale"—by returning to England, Tarr "marries" it. Of course, his four-hour-per-day union with Bertha is no partnership, just a legal bond. Tarr's "sentimental" self-justification rings inauthentic. In a defensive exchange with Anastasya, Tarr rationalizes his marriage to Bertha as follows—and she has the last word:

> "I have merely gone back a year into the past and fulfilled a pledge, and now return to you."
>
> . . .
>
> "That is sentimentality."
>
> "Sentimentality!—Sentimentality! . . . Sentimentality is a *privilege.* It is a luxury that the crowd does not feel itself equal to. . . . Besides, it is different in different hands."
>
> . . .
>
> "But the fact of your having married Bertha . . . will prevent your making anyone else your wife in the future. Supposing I had a child by *you*—not by Kreisler—it would be impossible to legitimatize him. . . . But you have given Kreisler's child what you should have kept for your own!" (318–319)

Tarr's "mutterings of reason" (314) tell him that Anastasya is right, launching a "counterattack" (312) against the impulses which ruled him during the Bertha proposal. He attempts to referee his intrapsychic conflict by appealing to reason itself:

> "'Why marry Bertha Lunken . . . ?' To keep faith with another person: and secondly to show my contempt for the world by choosing the 'premier venu' to be my body-servant and body-companion; my contempt for my body, too." (313)

Tarr is deceiving himself. He is caught in the web of Rank's "ethical guilt," which leads one to perpetuate dependence and "to tie down the individual in loyalty to the past."[81] Even Butcher muses exasperatedly that Tarr's affair with Bertha is a "disproportionately long" and "unique" (38) liaison. The decision to "keep faith" with Bertha (paradoxically both ennobling her as a "person" and denigrating her as a "body-servant") is filled with conflict, the conflict of "ethical guilt" that is rooted in the nature of willing and individuation:

> This loyalty to the past is itself opposed by a demand for loyalty to the artist's own self-development, which drives him onward. So the struggle of the artist against art is really only an ideologized continuation of the individual struggle against the collective.[82]

Tarr's claim to show his "contempt" (313) for the world by marrying Bertha signifies his misguided, willed surrender to the collective in the name of the "individual." His "sentimental" gesture is not one of strength but of willed resignation. The legal "tie" to Bertha is not significant in itself, as Anastasya notes in reference to the possibility of her having a child by Tarr, but rather for what it represents: Tarr's gradual succumbing to the values and persons whom he had once sought to transcend.

Unable to leave either Bertha or Paris, Tarr "persist[s] in his self-indulgent system of easy stages" (204). Magnetized by the values of the "crowd" and his "average" fianceé, Tarr increasingly resembles Kreisler, a "conflicted" man. "Belittled and guilty" (73) on leaving Bertha's room in "Overture," Tarr exacerbates his conflict by refusing to break definitively with her. He and Kreisler become rivals for Bertha and Anastasya together, even getting confused in one scene about which woman each man is now chasing.[83]

At the Cafe Souchet, Tarr is asked to be Kreisler's "second" in the Soltyk duel. He accepts only "temporarily," with the self-delusive explanation, "I am leaving Paris early tomorrow morning" (252). But Tarr is indeed already showing signs that he will become Kreisler's "substitute."[84] In her overvaluation of the Lipmann circle's social decrees, even Bertha inadvertently marks the two men as similar, differing only in degree: "Of Kreisler she thought very little. . . . Tarr to Kreisler. From bad to worse, for her friends" (181). Expecting visitors from the women's circle to her room, "at the knock [Bertha] thought of Tarr and Kreisler simultaneously, and welded in one" (181). And after "machine-like" Kreisler rapes her, Bertha believes "Tarr has been the real central and absorbing figure, all along, of course, but purposely veiled." Tarr, she thinks, "had been as really all-important, though to all appearances eliminated, as Kreisler had been of no importance, though propped up in the foreground" (198).

With Kreisler's death, Tarr moves into the "foreground." He marries Bertha, now pregnant with Kreisler's child, who would bear "some resemblance to Tarr" (320). If women do not become the "profession" of Tarr's life, they at least become his avocation. In his shift from observer of life to a participant, Tarr becomes the man of "swanky sex" (319). The sharp eye of "Overture" becomes the torn conscience of the section "Swagger Sex," by which time Tarr has abandoned his opening proclamation against sexual expression. He has forgotten his conviction in "Overture" that fatherhood coarsens and promiscuity putrefies "Form," the refined aesthetic, which "would perhaps be thickened by child-bearing; it would perhaps be damaged by harlotry" (30).

Whereas the true Rankian Artist "frees himself from the parallelism between his life and work,"[85] Tarr cannot. Experiencing how "impossible" and "perilous" it is to follow his ideological parallelisms uncompromisingly, Tarr instead denies Anastasya's personhood and the challenge of a full relationship with her. He fails to understand the underlying implications of his own aesthetic: "If you are going to work or perform, you must make up your mind to have dirty hands most of the time" (236). But the "dung" in life is not mere stage paint, as Tarr implies, "*put there for you*" the artist (236). It is life itself, and the order of his phrasing of the artist's problem reveals why Tarr cannot integrate his art within his life: "The conditions of creation and of life disgust me" (236). Tarr cannot truly accept the responsibility borne by Rank's creative man that to be in life is to be stained by it. One cannot remain an observer.[86] The Rankian creative man is more than an incorporeal intellect. The tragedy of Tarr's inflexible parallelisms regarding art and womanhood converge when he meets Anastasya, the intelligent woman who threatens him and toward whom a full human response would thrust him into Life: "Surrender to a woman was a sort of suicide for an artist" (214), he believes, thereby expressing his Rankian "death fear."

Still, he is attracted to Anastasya, and she is fully "*a woman*; not a man" (296), as she points out forcefully to him. Tarr admits that "it was chiefly his vanity that gave [him] trouble" (313) and causes him to reject Anastasya in order to marry Bertha; yet he can only comprehend her within his ideology by unsexing her: "There was only one God, and he was a man. A woman was a lower form of life. . . . Above a certain level of life, sex disappeared . . . . And, on the other hand, *everything* beneath that line was female. . . . [T]he line had been crossed by her" (313–314). Desexualizing her and making her the object of his "swagger sex," Tarr idealizes Anastasya doubly, even more that Kreisler had. She becomes Tarr's "perfect woman" (320)—a male in his artist's life and an object more beautiful and exciting than Bertha in his sex life.[87] Anastasya is his "Muse," a category of support in which Rank believes the aspiring (male) Artist sees "not so much the woman as a comrade of like outlook and like aims, who could equally well—and possibly better—be replaced by a male friendship."[88] As a result, he usually "needs two women, or several."[89] Tarr concludes that he married Bertha "to keep faith," yet he really loves Anastasya. According to Rank, this is another trap into which the arrested potential Artist characteristically falls:

> Because the Muse means more to him artistically, he thinks he loves her more. This is seldom the case . . . and moreover it is psychologically im-

> possible. For the other woman, whom, from purely human or other motives, he perhaps loves more, he often enough cannot set up as his Muse for this reason: that she would thereby become in a sense defeminized.[90]

According to Rank, the Mother, who originally gave life to the artist, is the artist's ultimate Muse, and the idea of her "is easily transferred in the course of life to another person."[91] This observation provides insight into Tarr's misogynistic splitting of Anastasya into Muse and object and his degrading of Bertha, for "he was the only child of a selfish, vigorous mother" and had "an enervating childhood of mollycoddling" (38). Rank would doubtless agree with Freud that such "unfavored children" demonstrate a peculiar self-assurance and an unshakable optimism that superficially resemble heroic attributes. Tarr, who "impressed you as having inherited himself last week" possesses "unparalleled" confidence (38).

But this "confidence" is really just an asexual form of swagger—which is why it so easily devolves into "swagger sex." I doubt that Tarr ever genuinely exhibits even the mature Rankian Artist's first sign of personality development, "nomination." Rather, Tarr's self-glorification is a continuation of his "elevated position" from childhood, in which he came "to feel prominence as a birthright."[92] His "long foundation of delicate trustfulness and childishness" from maternal mollycoddling have resulted in "a store of illusion to prolong youth" (38) and endlessly defer the inevitable day when he will no longer be the center of maternal attention. Only with the "fact" of Bertha's pregnancy does Tarr mildly re-experience the trauma of birth. Finally forced to end his "vague arrangement" with Bertha and marry her, Tarr swings endlessly like a pendulum, his aesthetic doctrine exposed as a self-delusive ideology fostered by dependence yet flaunted as "freedom."

If the "Overture" and Kreisler sections alternately approximate a Lewisian (and Rankian) Apollonian and Dionysian mode, Tarr's final fortunes are understandable in Rankian terms as a failure in the highest, "Kantian" mode: "We see these various levels of development toward ideal-formation in . . . three different ages, world views, and human types. The first is the Apollonian, *know thyself*; the second is the Dionysian, *be thyself*; the third is the Kantian, *determine thyself from thyself*."[93]

The "average men" are Apollonian. Their orientation is toward similarity to others and based on the Socratic formulation of the universal ideal. This is also the foundation of Freudian psychoanalytic therapy: not knowledge for the sake of self-actualization but rather for the sake of social adjustment. Kreisler's Dionysian condition exhibits a temperament that is not only antisocial but ridden with guilt, and therefore "leads to ecstatic-orgiastic destruction" when fully affirmed. The Kantian formulation, toward which Tarr might have striven, affirms "true self-knowledge" and "actual self-creation." Aware that the act of willing inevitably generates "ethical guilt," the Kantian man nevertheless practices a "renunciant" philosophy, whereby he lives fully in the world yet seeks to transcend its sick or limiting forces.[94] Beyond the Kantian type lies Rank's "new sort of person," his post-Nietzschean Artist-Superman, the creative person who will "no longer use art as the expression of his personality."[95] Developing a renunciant view toward art—renouncing not only his life fear but also his death fear—this new, ever-affirming, existential self will disclaim the "protection" afforded by art and devote his full being to creative, vitalistic living.[96]

This photograph portrays Lawrence and his wife Frieda in Mexico during the spring of 1923, shortly after the American and Spanish editions of *Women in Love* were published. Here the couple appears at their home near Lake Chapala, in the central Mexican state of Jalisco. At this time Lawrence began to pen *Quetzalcoatl*, a novel of the American continent, which was first formulated in Taos and served as the working title for what ultimately became *The Plumed Serpent* (1926), a novel about Mexican history.

The original draft features an Irish widow who has lost faith in political revolutions. Because Lawrence's publisher objected to the strange name of the Aztec god, Lawrence accepted the suggested alternative of *The Plumed Serpent*, a loose translation. Like *Women in Love*, it thematizes primitivism, "blood knowledge," freethinking, and the breaking of traditional sexual taboos.

CHAPTER SIX

Lawrence's Women in Love

THE ROLE OF MISS "DAWINGTON"

"What do you think of that figure there? I do want to know," Gerald asked. . . . He saw Minette in it. As in a dream, he knew her . . .

"It conveys a complete truth," said Birkin. "It contains the whole truth of that state . . ."

D. H. LAWRENCE, *WOMEN IN LOVE*

I

Until this point, we have been examining the rise of the modern British novel in light of the psychological theories of Freud and his European and American successors. In this closing chapter, addressing D. H. Lawrence's *Women in Love,* we turn to what might be thought of as a "Lawrentian" approach to psychology, emphasizing how Lawrence's ideas of race, gender, and culture—especially his concepts of "male-female polarity" and of Arctic or Nordic versus primitivist—feature in this novel. Lawrence's hostility to psychoanalysis in general and Freud in particular is well known, but it is crucial to stress that Lawrence by no means ignores familiar psychological issues related to eros and psyche. To the contrary, he developed his own form of what might be termed "Lawrentian psychology," which informed his fiction and, some critics argue, even preceded and therefore guided and shaped it.[1] In books such as *Psychoanalysis and the Unconscious* (1921) and *Fantasia of the Unconscious* (1922), Lawrence offers a psychological perspective rooted in his own experience as a man and artist, an outlook that vehemently rejects the Freudian unconscious and insists on addressing matters of the psyche via a visceral, body-based, nonrational, "blood" consciousness.[2] My aim in this final chapter is to draw selectively on Lawrence's psychological theories in order to enrich our understanding and appreciation of *Women in Love*.

Lawrence's thinking about Freud's work and the disease of the "terrible reducing activity of phosphorescent consciousness," as he calls it in the Prologue to *Women in Love*, was highly original on the Edwardian and Georgian intellectual scene. Lawrence had written at length about this "vice" in his correspondence and his fiction—and he had explored its connections to English literary life and Freud's own work. Although Freud's *Interpretation of Dreams*, published in German in 1900, was not translated into English until 1913, Lawrence already had access to sophisticated views about Freud's work as a result of conversations and active correspondence between Frieda Weekley, his paramour and future wife, and her former lover, the Viennese psychoanalyst Adolf Gross. Personally analyzed and trained by Freud himself, Gross wrote Frieda extensive letters in which he discussed their romantic relationship in light of Freudian theory.

Lawrence also had one other advantage: his early acquaintance with English translations of Nietzsche. The biographer of the young Lawrence, John Worthen, points out that Lawrence subscribed to the *New Age* in 1908–1909. Its editor, A. R. Orage, was known as one of the English Nietzscheans and had already published a popular book, *Nietzsche in Outline and Aphorism* (1907), which Lawrence probably read. As in the case of Adolf Gross and Freud via Frieda, Lawrence had been introduced to Nietzsche by women friends such as Helen Corke as early as 1909, according to her recollections in her memoirs. As Worthen points out, Nietzsche "appealed to English writers and artists" such as Lawrence as a revolutionary thinker who "was thoroughly unacademic" and hostile to metaphysical systems.[3]

Lawrence soon realized that Nietzsche could be a valuable counterforce defending vitalism and the body against Freud's cerebral, purportedly scientific psychology and over-emphasis on ego. As early as his manuscript draft in January 1910 for the story "A Modern Lover," Lawrence was pondering Nietzsche's influence on his own thinking: Lawrence's hero Cyril Mersham is a Nietzsche reader. In a manuscript passage of Lawrence's novel-in-progress, "The Saga of Sigmund" (1910), which by 1912 had become *The Trespasser*, Nietzsche is also cited.[4] Lawrence's poem "New Heaven and Earth" (1915), which marks his most explicit statement of the poison or "taint" of self-consciousness, inveighs against what Lawrence refers to later as "hyper-consciousness" in his critique of Freud in *Fantasia of the Unconscious*. The relevant passages of the poem warrant quotation at length:

> I was so weary of the world,
> I was so sick of it,

everything was tainted with myself,
skies, trees, flowers, birds, water,
people, houses, streets, vehicles, machines,
nations, armies, war, peace-talking,
work, recreation, governing, anarchy,
it was all tainted with myself, I knew it all to start with
because it was all myself.

When I gathered flowers, I knew it was myself plucking my own
flowering.
When I went in a train, I knew it was myself travelling by my own
invention.
When I heard the cannon of the water, I listened with my own ears to
my own destruction.
When I saw the torn dead, I knew it was my own torn dead body.
It was all me, I had done it all in my own flesh.

According to Lawrence, Freud served to legitimate such an unhealthy, excessive preoccupation with the mind. By contrast, Nietzsche fortified one to resist the allures of engulfing subjectivity.

Like most other avant-garde writers of his generation, Lawrence also endorsed what he termed Nietzsche's "demolition" of Christianity in *Thus Spake Zarathustra,* with its cry of "God is dead." But far more important for Lawrence's literary vision in general and his critique of psychoanalysis in particular was how Nietzsche, in John Worthen's formulation, "confirmed Lawrence's growing sense of the opposition between spirit, mental will and mental knowledge on the one hand, and body, instinct, blood and self on the other. In particular, Nietzsche provided a language for the almost inexpressible area of 'blood-knowledge' which, as a writer, Lawrence already inarticulately knew to be crucial to him."[5]

Nietzsche conceived the body itself to possess a "rationality," regarding the body not as a rapacious id, but rather as a "self." Zarathustra adds that the body exhibits a higher "rationality" than the "best wisdom" of the mind. In language that Lawrence adopted as his own to counter the concepts of Freudian psychoanalysis, Zarathustra asserts: "I love only what a person hath written with his blood. Write with blood, and thou wilt find that blood is spirit."[6]

It's hard not to imagine that passages like this formed the source of Lawrence's growing conviction about the value of "blood-knowledge." By the time of his composition of *Women in Love,* Lawrence was thoroughly familiar with Nietzsche, and he describes Gerald Crich as a man entranced by "the Will to Power" and determined to dominate his partner.

Tuesday

Now I can't stand it any longer, I can't. For two hours I have n't moved a muscle – just sat and thought ~~and suffered~~ I have written a letter to Ernst. You need n't, of course, send it. But you must say to him all I have said. No more dishonour, no more lies. Let them do their – silliest but no more subterfuge, lying, dirt, fear. I feel as if it would strangle me. What is it all but procrastination? No, I can't bear it, because it's bad. I love you. Let us face anything, do anything, put up with anything. But this crawling under the mud I cannot bear.

I'm afraid I've got a fit of heroics. I've tried so hard to work – but I can't. This situation is round my chest like a cord. It must n't continue. I will go right away, if you like. I will stop in Metz till you get Ernst's answer to the truth. But no, I won't utter or act or willingly let you utter or act, another single lie in the business.

I'm not going to joke, I'm not going to laugh, I'm not going to make light of things for you. The situation tortures me too much. It's the situation, the situation I can't stand – no, and I won't. I love you too much.

Don't show this letter to either of your sisters – no. Let us be good. You are clean, but you dirty your feet. I'll sign myself as you call me. – Mr Lawrence. And I love you and Gott, I'm sick of it. Don't be miserable – if I didn't love you I wouldn't mind when you lied.

Lawrence's letter to Frieda Weekley, 7 May 1912

Written during the time of his initial encounters and early fascination with the work of Nietzsche, whose vitalistic philosophy soon contributed to inspire Lawrence's ideas about "blood consciousness," Lawrence's May 1912 letter to Frieda Weekley urges her to break definitively with her husband Ernst. "No more dishonour, no more lies," declares Lawrence in a spirit of Nietzschean defiance.

All this attests to Worthen's observation that "Nietzsche became one of the most powerful of those multitudinous subterranean influences" on Lawrence.[7] Indeed "The Shades of Spring," in Lawrence's 1914 version of the story, shows the imprint of Nietzsche's subterranean influence. This story also reads like a veiled autobiography, echoing both Lawrence's later view about his relationship to Jessie Chambers and the relationship between Paul Morel and Miriam in *Sons and Lovers*. The hero of Lawrence's short story, writes Worthen, grieves that his " 'uncorporeal' relationship had left out so much of the person he was . . . ; His vividest life lay within his own consciousness, not outside it in experiences of what was Other to him. Such hyper-self-consciousness could never really acknowledge another person." Worthen adds that Lawrence develops both this theme and the tragedy of the child's growth into self-consciousness in *Fantasia of the Unconscious* in 1921. "But he had already carried the process of understanding one stage further when writing the 'Prologue' to *Women in Love* in the spring of 1916," where Lawrence describes Birkin's love for Hermione as utterly without "desire" or "passion" or "hot impulse." Rather, Birkin has only a debilitating "phosphorescent consciousness, the consciousness ever liberated more and more into the void, at the expense of the flesh, which was burnt down like dead grey ash."[8]

II

Let us now turn to *Women in Love* itself, and in particular to the important role of a typically overlooked secondary character, Minette Darrington. Although her presence in the novel spans little more than one dozen pages, Minette represents, in the phrase of critic H. M. Daleski, a "reductive force" advancing "in a straight line to the centre" of *Women in Love*.[9] That center is a vortex of "dissolution and decay." Minette, a frivolous, pregnant, vulgar blonde with a pageboy haircut, dwelling on the fringe of the decadent avant-garde scene, is an artist's model with tendencies toward cruelty and violence. She and the carved wooden figure of the African Negro woman "convey a complete truth," Birkin tells Gerald, "the whole truth of that state" (72): the voluptuary condition of aesthetic excess and degradation. As such, they embody for Birkin the essence of bohemian art and sensual corruption.

Because she exemplifies for Lawrence a distillation of mindlessness and sensuousness, Minette serves to reduce and clarify a triad of complex issues in *Women in Love*. A careful *explication de texte* of the subtle interconnections between Minette and several of the novel's other characters furnishes insight into Lawrence's larger ideas about male-female relationships, *Blutbruderschaft*, and the nature of evil. Within the broader context of Lawrentian thematics, a close reading of this purportedly minor secondary character proves worthwhile as a revealing instance of Lawrence's art and thought.

As we shall see, Minette's connection to the African statuette is noteworthy because it discloses her intense fear of black beetles. Birkin remembers that she had seen the Negro female statuette at Halliday's apartment, with "her diminished, beetle face, the astounding long elegant body, on short, ugly legs, with such protuberant buttocks, so weighty and unexpected below her slim long loins" (245). Moreover, the statuette's face (in Birkin's recollection) "was crushed tiny like a beetle's" and possessed an "astonishing cultured elegance." Birkin's vivid description continues:

> She had thousands of years of purely sensual, purely unspiritual knowledge behind her. It must have been thousands of years since her race had died, mystically: that is, since the relation between the senses and the outspoken mind had broken, leaving the experience all in one sort, mystically sensual. Thousands of years ago, that which was imminent in himself must have taken place in these Africans: the goodness, the holiness, the desire for creation and productive happiness must have lapsed, leaving the single impulse for knowledge in one sort, mindless progressive knowledge through the senses, knowledge arrested and ending in the senses, mystic knowledge in disintegration and dissolution, knowledge such as the beetles have, which live purely within the world of corruption and cold dissolution. This was why her face looked like a beetle's: this was why the Egyptians worshipped the ball-rolling scarab: because of the principle of knowledge in dissolution and corruption. (245–246)

Minette strongly identifies—and recoils from—the African statuette because she associates it with beetles, a connection that triggers her terror of Lawrentian "disintegration and dissolution." Yet this horrific fear is also opposed by a countervailing entropic force: Minette registers a powerful urge to "lapse" into "mindless progressive knowledge of the senses," a deeply felt desire to degenerate into an undifferentiated sensuality. Thus, she both cowers and yearns for the world of "corruption and cold dissolution" represented by the beetle. She is Janus-faced, but both profiles resemble the African carving whose "face looked like a beetle's" as it inscribes "the principle of knowledge in dissolution and corruption." That knowledge expresses itself in a violent destructiveness as well as in sexual abandon: for example, when Minette slashes the hand of an unnamed young man as she confesses her angst about beetles and professes her lack of fear about blood.

Minette's relation to Gudrun Brangwen also warrants scrutiny. Minette's resemblances to Gudrun in appearance and lifestyle are striking, and the introduction of Miss Darrington and her lover Julius Halliday in chapter VI foreshadows the disintegration of Gudrun's relationship with Gerald Crich. Moreover, the crude sexual encounter between Gerald and Minette represents a blatantly exploitative act, a classic instance in Lawrentian terms of mechanical "love." Viewed in this context, Minette becomes the reductive, indeed diminutive counterpart of the Crich miners ("Mine-ette" and "mine"), who themselves are "reduced to mere mechanical instruments . . . pure organic disintegration and pure mechanical organization" (223). Minette represents a reductive force in the novel, but she also anticipates and reflects the corrupt relationship of Gerald and Gudrun.

Critics have devoted scant attention to the London Bohemia section of *Women in Love*, and some have even proposed that these three chapters (VI, VII, VIII) should have been excised by Lawrence. The *locus classicus* of that view is F. R. Leavis's *D. H. Lawrence: Novelist*. Leavis suggests that these chapters could have been cut without sacrifice to the design and integrity of the novel. According to Leavis, this early trio of chapters, especially VI and VII ("Crème de Menthe" and "Totem") do not contribute to the novel's "thematic definition and development" and therefore "would have been better excluded" because they detract from a work that otherwise possesses "so complex and subtle an organization."[10] Even H. M. Daleski, despite giving extended consideration to the London Bohemia chapters, remarks that they are "relatively unimportant" and apologizes for having "dwelt at some length" on them.[11]

The present chapter challenges these views, arguing instead that Lawrence's portrait of the Bohemian milieu, which includes the initial conversations at the Café Pompadour, forms a crucial underpinning that illuminates the dense web of interconnections among the characters and events of *Women in Love*. My contention is that the Bohemia chapters are important precisely because, as Daleski acknowledges, "the circumreferential leads in a straight line to the centre" of *Women in Love*.[12] Unlike Daleski, my central claim is not, however, that "the rottenness of Bohemia . . . is an instance of the general rottenness in the state of England."[13] Rather, I hold that the secondary characters who dominate the London Bohemia chapters (Minette, Julius Halliday, Loerke, Libidnikov, and the unnamed young Russian) shed indispensable light on the thematics and major relationships in *Women in Love*, especially the connection between Gerald and Gudrun.

In considering the role of Minette Darrington in *Women in Love*, therefore, let us first examine how she relates to the African statuette and explore the nature of her relationship to the decadent playboy Julius Halliday, for it is herein that her significance as a female analogue to Loerke and her relationship to the novel's other characters emerges clearly.

III

Miss Darrington first appears in the "Crème de Menthe" chapter, and her voice and features seem as sweet and piquant as a creamy mint liqueur. By occupation she is an artists' model, and the narrator describes her as if she has been molded by a sensitive sculptor's hands into a living replica of a dainty bohemian statuette:

> [A] girl with bobbed, blonde hair cut short in the artist fashion, hanging straight and curving lightly inwards to her ears. She was small and delicately made, with fair colouring and large, innocent blue eyes. There was a delicacy, almost a floweriness in all her form, and at the same time a certain attractive grossness of spirit. (55)

On the surface, Minette appears to be a naïve, innocent girl. Her pronunciation is comically childlike ("terwified," "angwy," "Wupert," "afwaid"). "She spoke her r's like w's, lisping with a slight babyish pronunciation which was at once affected and true to her character" (55).

Yet it is not simply that Minette lacks sophistication or education. She has relinquished her *mind* to the sensual—and later her will to Gerald. Likewise, the miners have abdicated their wills and become instruments for the firm's leaders to direct. Something indefinably sinister festers in Minette's total lack of any sense of moral understanding. Gerald senses this absence at once, and it both excites and scares him. Minette turns to him at the bar table "with a curious, almost evil motion," and her eyes have "a furtive look, and a look of a knowledge of evil, dark and indomitable" (61).

Minette signifies carnal knowledge; Lawrence characterizes her as "demonic," evil personified.[14] Notably, in both the early manuscripts and the first English edition of *Women in Love,* Lawrence uses the name "Pussum" for Minette and darkens her features to correspond more precisely to the African statuette.[15] Gerald's initial reaction to Halliday's bawdy statuettes survives in the final version of the novel as a residue of the original name choice: "Aren't they rather obscene?" (67). Pussum, of course, obviously suggests obscenity.

But Lawrence's decision to change Pussum to Minette derived not chiefly from explicit artistic concerns but rather in response to objections that Minette represented a vulgar, transparent caricature of an acquaintance and her sexual encounters. And here we should pause and briefly address the biographical and satirical basis of the novel, which in numerous (and somewhat forgotten) respects is a *roman à clef.*[16]

It should be noted here that Lawrence based his portrait of Minette Darrington on the bohemian artist and Slade School of Fine Arts graduate Dora

Carrington, whom he disliked. (Minette's lover, Loerke, is chiefly based on Mark Gertler, her Slade School classmate and a close friend of Lawrence, who told Gertler that he had used his painting, *Merry-Go-Round* [1916], as the image of a "great granite frieze for the top of a factory."[17] Lawrence added that the character of Loerke in *Women in Love* is "not you, I reassure you" [46].)

Darrington was immediately recognizable as Dora Carrington by Lawrence's contemporaries, and the depiction of Carrington has understandably been viewed—given the verbal echoes between the two names—by both literary critics and Lawrence's acquaintances as a harsh satirical attack. The physical features of Minette correspond closely to those of Carrington. (Like several of her Slade School women classmates, Carrington adopted the masculine habit of using her surname only, dropping the name "Dora" ever after.) Carrington was a controversial female libertine in London's Bloomsbury Set between the wars. In 1915, when she was twenty-two and among the first women in London to sport a pageboy hairstyle, she met Lytton Strachey, who was immediately attracted by her boyish appearance. They attempted physical relations with no success, and then embarked on a platonic love affair that lasted until Strachey's death. Lawrence treats her disgust about sexuality and her Sapphic tendencies as the basis for Minette's corruption. (In the film adaptation, *Carrington*, directed and written by Christopher Hampton, Strachey catches a glimpse of Carrington through a window and pants with excitement: "Who is that ravishing boy?")

Carrington herself had a boyish figure, lisped "like a child confiding a secret," bobbed her hair (the more staid Virginia Woolf dubbed her a "crophead"), and even posed naked for a photograph as a "living statue," in her own words.[18] Unlike Minette, however, Dora Carrington, still in her teens, was a prize-winning art student in the years following Robert Fry's Post-Impressionist exhibition in December 1910. Her friend David Garnett, who edited her letters, noted that Carrington felt intense "shame about being a woman," especially about having a bosom and about female physical functions such as menstruation. Carrington cultivated androgyny—not only by lopping off her hair, but also by preferring to wear breeches and boots, courting and sleeping with numerous female lovers, and developing a lifelong passion and devotion for the homosexual writer Lytton Strachey. "How revolting women are," she once told Strachey. She wished that she had been a young man, not a "hybrid monster," because then she could have happily fulfilled both Strachey and her women friends.[19] She once described her happiest moment as having been "my daytime character" on a trip with Lytton, when she took a walking holiday with him as "a disguised female."[20] (A few weeks after Strachey's tragic death from cancer at the age of 51 in 1932, Carrington committed suicide at the age of 38.)

The androgynous personae projected by Carrington and a few of her Slade School friends, such as Barbara Hiles and Dorothy Brett, made them famous in London art circles in the 1920s. They became the subjects of many paintings, photographs, and even fictional portraits. For instance, Carrington herself is not only depicted as Minette in *Women in Love,* but also as Mary Bracegirdle in Aldous Huxley's *Crome Yellow*; as Greta Morrison in Gilbert Cannan's *Mendel*; as Betty Blyth in Wyndham Lewis's *The Apes of God*; as the painter-photographer Anna Cory in Rosamond Lehmann's *The Weather in the Streets*; as Eleanor Brooke in Pat Barker's *Life Class* and *Toby's Room*; and as the middle-aged, suicidal heiress in Lawrence's story "None of That" (published in *The Woman Who Rode Away and Other Stories*). By the 1980s, she had become what one art critic has called "a curious cult figure" with a growing mystique ("creeping Carringtonianism") whose life and death exert an equal measure of fascination because of her charm and her self-destructiveness.[21]

Lawrence casts her bohemian lifestyle and complicated sexual life in the most negative terms, presenting them as the "degenerate" counterpart to Birkin's (i.e., Lawrence's) life-affirming values. Jeffrey Meyers writes: "Like others who did not understand her inner life, [Lawrence] was confused and angered when she abandoned" Gertler and other heterosexual lovers "for the decrepit homosexual Strachey."[22] In his biography of Lytton Strachey, Michael Holroyd writes of Carrington:

> She was always hating men, hating all active maleness in a man. She wanted a passive maleness. . . . She could send out of her body a repelling energy to compel people to submit to her will . . . it was only in intimacy that she was unscrupulous and dauntless as a devil incarnate. In public, in strange places, she was very uneasy, like one who has a bad conscience towards society, and is afraid of it. And for that reason she could never go without a man to stand between her and all others.[23]

Carrington also felt antipathy toward Lawrence. In a 1924 letter to Gerald Brenan, she archly wrote:

> Lawrence was very rude to me of course, and held forth to the assembly as if he was a lecturer to minor university students. Apparently he came back this winter [from America] expecting to be greeted as the new messiah. Unfortunately very few saw his divination.[24]

Lawrence uses the destructive relationship between Carrington and Gertler to emphasize the thematic connection between the perversion of art and the perversion of love. In one respect, however, Lawrence modifies his antipathy toward Carrington by casting Minette in *Women in Love* as the victim of Loerke and the unscrupulous male world, whereas Lawrence believed that the true story was that Carrington was Gertler's victimizer and that she tormented the infatuated Gertler for years, finally denying him satisfaction. It can be argued, however, that Lawrence treated his friend Gertler far more cruelly than he did Carrington. He transformed Gertler into the sinister Loerke, whose mechanized industrial art and glorification of the machine in his German sculpture signify the corruption of the mining industry and the destructive principle of modern warfare.

IV

Further investigation of the biographical aspects of the novel are beyond our scope here. Of immediate relevance to our argument is that, even though legal considerations motivated Lawrence to alter the London Bohemia chapters of *Women in Love*, his decision to change Pussum to Minette (in response to objections that Halliday and Minette represented vulgar, transparent caricatures) was not, strictly speaking, a literary loss or capitulation. Lawrence's revisions also invest these chapters with meaningful new allusions. For instance, "Minette" is a type of igneous rock, which renders Miss Darrington's resemblance to the miners even more suggestive.[25] Lawrence makes this connection explicit in the "Coal Dust" and "Crème de Menthe" chapters. In the former chapter, one can detect within the miners "the strong dangerous underworld, mindless, inhuman. They sounded also like strange machines, heavy, *oiled*" (108, italics mine). Minette's mind is likewise empty, and her eyes seem similarly lubricated for a mechanical function:

> She was very still, almost null, in her manner, apart and watchful. . . . She had beautiful eyes, flower-like, fully-opened. . . . And on them there seemed to float a curious iridescence, a sort of film of disintegration, and sullenness, like *oil*. . . . (Italics mine, 57)

Furthermore, igneous rock is a fiery stone—hard yet flammable. Minette is similarly hard and cold; she unleashes an Arctic blast through Gerald's body, staring at him in a "heavy, ice-blank fashion" and then "unfold[ing] like some fair ice-flower in dreadful flowering nakedness." A powerful surge of dominant masculine energy wells up in Gerald as he beholds Minette, and he is suddenly enflamed with passion:

> [H]er fine mane of hair just swept his face, and all his nerves were on fire, as with a subtle friction of electricity. But the great centre of his force held steady, magnificent pride to him, at the base of his spine. (66)

One further clue that depravity lurks beneath Minette's childlike simplicity is her proclamation that she is "not afwaid of anything except black-beetles." Challenged by the Russian Maxim Libidnikov as to whether black beetles are truly her only dread, Minette responds pointedly, "Not weally. . . . I am afwaid of some things, but not the same." Then she adds: "I'm not afwaid of *blood*." That admission is revealing in light of Gerald's subsequent observation about Minette's presence in the Café Pompadour: "There was something curiously indecent about her small, longish, fair skull, particularly when the ears showed" (374).

While Minette may disdain the name "beetle" or "vampire," she shows no reluctance to suck the lifeblood and vitality out of Gerald and all others with whom she comes in contact. When one man questions her about her professed fearlessness in the face of blood, Minette "suddenly jab[s] a knife across his thick, pale hand" (63). Halliday screams, but the injured young man answers, "Don't give her the *pleasure* of letting her think she's performed a feat—don't give her the *satisfaction*" (italics mine). The imagery and language are suggestively sexual. Minette is a parasite whose pleasure is to perform and to relegate her male objects to obsolescence: she uses men "for the experience of it" and then discards them. For instance, she sleeps with Gerald largely for the satisfaction of arousing Halliday's jealousy. Gerald himself means nothing more to her than a weekend fling. Soon after his own night in bed with her, Gerald contemplates her relationship to Halliday and recognizes that intercourse with her unmans the male partner. Her "ice-flower" body is a bloody weapon: "Minette was becoming hard and cold, like a flint knife, and Halliday was laying himself out to her" (73). And curiously, when Minette stresses her aversion to black beetles, Gerald "laughed dangerously *from the blood*" (62).

These passages illuminate Gerald's observation in the Café Pompadour about Minette's vampire-like features, thereby also clarifying Minette's relationship to the African statuette. Indeed her connections both to black beetles and the statuette gain deeper resonance in light of Lawrence's much-discussed, controversial pronouncements on race and "blood knowledge." Lawrence harbored a marked preference throughout his work for the dark-skinned races and a skeptical wariness of the Caucasian and European peoples. The dark races possess "blood knowledge," contended Lawrence, and will finally triumph over the white "mind-conscious" civilization that has dominated and exploited them throughout the ages.[26] However skeptical we may remain about Lawrence's racial ideology—quite understandably, in view of both current scientific thinking about such polarized ethnological outlooks and the horrific genocidal campaigns (from the Holocaust to Serbian "ethnic cleansing") based on such views—it is undeniable that these aspects of Lawrence's *Weltanschauung* are crucial to the textual fabric and artistic design of *Women in Love*.

As we have seen, both in the Bohemia chapters and later, Minette's association with black beetles and the statuette is made quite explicit. Like the image of the sculpture, Minette too is a small, pregnant, sensual figure. (Notably, she never delivers, but only remains in a frigid state of perpetual unproductive pseudo-fertility.) Birkin recognizes her physical resemblance to the beetle, a symbol of dissipation, and he infers that Minette has devolved to the lowest, quintessentially dehumanized stage of corruption. Whereas the statuette is art, Miss Darrington is life; but as we have seen, it is as if the model has posed for this sculpture. Birkin recalls, in a passage to which we earlier alluded:

> There came back to him [Birkin] one [memory, that of] a statuette. . . . It was a woman. . . . Her body was long and elegant, her face was crushed tiny like a beetle's, she had rows of round heavy collars, like a column of quoits, on her neck. He remembered her: . . . her diminished, beetle face . . . the relation between the senses and the outspoken mind had broken . . . leaving the single impulse for knowledge in one sort, mindless progressive knowledge through the senses . . . in disintegration and dissolution, knowledge such as the beetles have, which live purely within the world of corruption and cold dissolution. (245–246)

Gerald, too, connects Minette to the statuette. ("He saw Minette in it. As in a dream, he knew her" [71].) The biblical usage is obvious. But Gerald disputes that the "obscene" carving should be dignified as "art":

> "Why is it art?" Gerald asked, shocked, resentful.
>
> "It conveys a complete truth," said Birkin. "It contains the whole truth of that state, whatever you feel about it."
>
> "But you can't call it *high* art," said Gerald.
>
> "High! there are centuries and hundreds of centuries of development in a straight line, behind that carving; it is an awful pitch of culture, of a definite sort."
>
> "What culture?" Gerald asked, in opposition. He hated the sheer barbaric thing.
>
> "Pure culture in sensation, culture in the physical consciousness, really ultimate *physical* consciousness, mindless, utterly sensual. It is so sensual as to be final, supreme." (71–72)

Miss Darrington's divorce of mind and senses functions as a kind of silhouette that anticipates Birkin's description of an exalted, richly edifying male-male *Blutbruderschaft* relationship, which fails utterly with Gerald because he is unfit to participate in it, and cannot—indeed *will* not—change. Gerald is described from the outset of *Women in Love* as cold-hearted, "mechanical," and "hollow." He is a fitting match—or victim-host—for parasitical Minette, and their symbiotic connection both reflects and accelerates his decay—and contributes to his failure to enter into a special, ritualized brother-lover relationship with Birkin. Gerald feels "a sort of fatal halfness" during his thoughts about *Blutbruderschaft* (199)—Minette has apparently sucked half the life from him. Birkin pleads with him to commit himself to an organic man-to-man union, but Gerald has already become involved in a sexualized pattern of parasitic symbiosis—first in his encounter with Minette and thereafter with Gudrun. He cannot extricate himself, and ends like Halliday, whom he despises and dismisses as a man with "a strange feel" (246).

This exchange between Birkin and Gerald gains power and scope later in *Women in Love* through Birkin's (and Lawrence's) racial ideology,[27] in particular Birkin's philosophical edict on the two great drifts towards racial/cultural death in the modern world. In both of these tendencies, an inexorable, entropic downrush into decay and dissolution is precipitated by a seismic rupture in the balance between mind and body. The cerebral excess is manifest in the "Arctic" way of the Northern peoples, "a hyper-consciousness whose characteristics are personified most clearly in Hermione Roddice and whose direction is exemplified by Gerald's icy death."[28] The somatic overstock is represented in the "African" way of pure sensuality, a self-destructiveness represented by Gerald. In *Women in Love,* Birkin foresees Gerald's death in the snow as a fulfillment of the fate of "Arctic man" (246), which is predicated on the "white" races "having the Arctic north behind them," while the African process is "controlled by the burning death-abstraction of the Sahara" (246). Birkin reflects:

> There remained this way, this awful African process, to be fulfilled. It would be done differently by the white races, having the Arctic north behind them, the vast abstraction of ice and snow, would fulfill a mystery of ice-destructive knowledge, snow-abstract annihilation. Whereas the West Africans, controlled by the burning death-abstraction of the Sahara, had been fulfilled in sun-destruction, the putrescent mystery of sun-rays. . . .
>
> Birkin thought of Gerald. He was one of these strange white wonderful demons from the north, fulfilled in the destructive frost mystery. And was he fated to pass away in this knowledge, this one process of frost-knowledge, death by perfect cold? Was he a messenger, an omen of the universal dissolution into whiteness and snow? (246–247)[29]

We shall soon also see how this Lawrentian metaphysics is also—in even more pointed and exaggerated form—exemplified by Minette and Gudrun, along with the secondary characters of the London Bohemia chapters of *Women in Love*.

V

Lawrence's treatment of Minette possesses significance not only for the novel's portrayals of Gerald and the miners. Her role also bears on other relationships in the novel, above all the Gerald-Gudrun connection. Minette is described in terms that amount to a degenerate version of Gudrun, who is a far more complex, multifaceted, fully realized Lawrentian character—not at all a female statuette. Yet their affinities emerge unmistakably by the close of *Women in Love*. Gudrun's deterioration ultimately approaches the level of Miss Darrington, a devolution suggested by Gudrun's relationship to Loerke, who represents the novel's male bohemian counterpart to Minette.

Like Minette, Gudrun is "soft-skinned, soft-limbed," and even has blonde hair. As *Women in Love* opens, Gudrun has just returned from London, where she has spent several years enrolled at an art school and "living a studio life." Both women lead an artsy, bohemian life: Minette the model, Gudrun the sculptress. Gerald explains to Birkin the slight difference in background between the two:

> I knew her [Gudrun] in London . . . in the Algernon Strange set. She'll know about Minette . . . and the rest—even if she doesn't know them personally. She was never quite that set—more conventional, in a way. (87)

The similarities are noteworthy, but far more important is the difference that Gerald overlooks: Gudrun aspires to be a creative woman—a sculptress, not a statue. Gudrun is a budding artist; Minette is a refined art object.[30] And yet Gudrun's mode of perception, both in art and life, is to also objectify in a taut, constricted, narrow fashion. Her sister Ursula perceives "the tightness, the enclosure of Gudrun's presence" (8). Gudrun has refined her sculptural work into a fixed, compact form, a concentrated, still-life art of miniatures. Indeed her art possesses a deathly stillness:

> She saw each one [of the guests at the wedding] as a complete figure, like a character in a book, or a subject in a picture, or a marionette in a theatre, a finished creation. She loved to recognise their various characteristics, to place them in their true light, give them their own surroundings, settle them for ever as they passed before her along the path

> to the church. She knew them, they were finished, sealed and stamped and finished with for her. There were none that had anything unknown, unresolved. (8)

Gudrun's epistemological and aesthetic modes are static. She frames both people and scenes in discrete frames, arresting them and rendering them inert. Like Gerald the industrialist—or Loerke the industrial artist—she thus reduces the animate to the inanimate: organic life becomes still life. Her art is all surface, no soul.[31]

On seeing Gudrun's sculptures, Gerald's first thought is to link them indirectly to Minette via their resemblance to the primitive carving. He reflects on how much they resemble the pregnant African statuette: "I thought it was savage carving again" (87). His revulsion toward its alleged obscenity is visceral, but Gerald's reaction is itself pregnant with meaning, for it foreshadows Gudrun's involvement with Loerke. Although Gudrun may be more "conventional" or socially respectable than Minette, a hint of corruption surrounds her from the moment she is introduced. Once again, her resemblance to the statuette is revealing: "Forward she went, through the whole sordid gamut of pettiness. . . . She felt *like a beetle* toiling in the dust. She was filled with repulsion" (italics mine, 5).

The most obvious similarity between Minette and Gudrun is their shared attraction to Gerald Crich. Gudrun is struck with wonder upon first seeing him:

> Gudrun lighted on him at once. There was something northern about him that magnetized her. . . . His gleaming beauty, his maleness. . . . And then she experienced a keen paroxysm, a transport, as if she had made some incredible discovery. . . . She was tortured with desire to see him again. (8–9)

Gudrun then repeats to herself: "His totem is the wolf." Appropriately, in "Totem," Gerald fulfills her suspicions when he sleeps with Minette, who at that moment also is "fascinated" by Gerald:

> He sat with his arms on the table. His sun-browned, rather sinister hands that were animal and yet very shapely and attractive, pushed forward towards her. And they fascinated her. And she knew, she watched her own fascination. (60)

Gudrun yearns to break loose from the perceived chains of bourgeois conformity, to become a less "conventional," more fully liberated young woman. Minette, as Birkin implies in his discussion of the statuette, has already ad-

Published in 1996, this Bantam Classics edition of *Women in Love* features a new introduction by Louis Menand. Exploring the complexities of human sexuality during the World War I era, *Women in Love* represents a subtle interweaving of sensual passion and sacred mystery, all of which is presented in the context of Lawrence's own experience of coal mines, factories, and the British working class. A masterpiece of erotic consciousness and spiritual psychology, the novel chronicles the intricate interrelationships between two male-female couples as they boldly explore the possibilities of love and monogamy.

The cover art for the Bantam Classics edition portrays the bohemian female artist of the novel, Gudrun Brangwen. Her head is positioned on her left shoulder and her eyes are downcast. The scene is a subtle mixture of the erotic and the chaste.

vanced (or devolved, in Birkin's estimate) in that direction. Yet Birkin also perceives that Gudrun is not "conventional" by nature, for just as Gerald is a "born lover," Gudrun is a "born mistress" (364).

Much of Gudrun's behavior springs from her obsession with novelty, her passion to encounter new things, to indulge and *"go the whole round of experience"* (italics mine, 403). She wants knowledge for its own sake—including knowledge of "evil, dark and indomitable" that Minette incarnates. Gudrun's insatiable curiosity leads to her downfall. The first discussion between Gudrun and her sister Ursula highlights Gudrun's restlessly insatiable and inquisitive nature. Their conversation anticipates what is to become Gudrun's fatal preoccupation:

> "One needs the *experience* of being married . . ."
> "Do you think it need *be* an experience?" replied Ursula.
> "Bound to be in some way or other," said Gudrun, coolly. "Possibly undesirable, but bound to be an experience of some sort."
> "Not really," said Ursula. "More likely to be the end of experience."
> "Of course . . . there's *that* to consider." (1)

But Gudrun does not consider it. Overwhelmed with jealousy when Gerald is dancing with one of the professor's daughters in "Continental," Gudrun fully discloses her hedonistic philosophy:

> They might do as they liked—that she realized. . . . So bestial, those two!—so degraded! She winced. But after all, why not? She exulted as well. Why not be bestial, and *go the whole round of experience*. She exulted in it. She was bestial. How good it was to be really shameful! There would be no shameful thing which she had not experienced. . . . Why not? She was free, when she knew everything, and no dark shameful things were denied her. (Italics mine, 403)

The vital difference between Gudrun's delusion of freedom and her sister's real freedom is that Ursula's freedom respects the dignity and autonomy of others; Gudrun's is founded on instrumentality, the exploitation and objectification of others.

VI

Gudrun finally does "*go the whole round of experience*" when she rejects Gerald and embraces Loerke. Although he is "the rock bottom of life," she prefers him to the repetitious tedium of her relationship with Gerald:

> Between any two people . . . the range of pure sensational experience is limited. . . . There is only repetition possible. . . .
> She [Gudrun] had farther to go, a farther, slow, exquisite experience

to reap, unthinkable subtleties of sensations to know, before she was finished.

. . . Gerald was not capable [of going further]. But . . . the fine, insinuating blade of Loerke's insect-like comprehension could [reach her]. (443)

Loerke is "a fellow craftsman, a fellow being" (450), acknowledges Gudrun. He tells her that "art should interpret industry, as art once interpreted religion" (415). But industry, of course, as presented in the novel, is utterly mechanical, lifeless; religion, in its larger, deeper sense, is organic and relational. Loerke (derived from Loki, the spirit of negativity)[32] is radically detached from everything: "He cared about nothing, he was troubled about nothing, he made not the slightest attempt to be at one with anything. He existed as a pure, unconnected will" (417). He is the culmination of Lawrentian "disintegration" in *Women in Love*. Gudrun feels a "certain violent sympathy for this "mud-child" of "the underworld of life," who swims, as Birkin says, "like a rat in the river of corruption" (418).

Loerke also epitomizes the frigid, "Arctic" mode of the northern European races in its most extreme, grotesque form. "Having the Arctic north behind them, the vast abstraction of ice and snow," the white races "would fulfill a mystery of ice-destructive knowledge, snow-abstract annihilation" (246). Loerke is also associated, however, with the degenerate forces of dark primitivism: he expresses admiration for "the West African wooden figures" and is also partial to "the Aztec art, Mexican, and Central American," prizing in all of them "primitive art" as it embodies "the inner mysteries of sensation" (439). As Ronald Granofsky points out, Loerke is a cosmopolitan and avant-garde Jewish artist who exemplifies "the process of racial decay" more than anyone else in the novel.[33] For Lawrence/Birkin, Loerke's Jewishness is an element of his dark corruption. Birkin calls him "'a little obscene monster of the darkness'" and suggests that he must be Jewish because, as a "rat" in "the river of corruption," he is far ahead in the process of dissolution (418).

Loerke is the epitome of Lawrentian "mental consciousness," which Lawrence derided in *Psychoanalysis and the Unconscious* as "a cul-de-sac" that "provides us only with endless *appliances* which we can use for the all-too-difficult business of coming to our spontaneous-creative fullness of being. . . . The mind as author and director of life is anathema."[34] Loerke, who considers "machinery and the acts of labour . . . extremely, maddeningly beautiful" (414), represents an Arctic, quasi-technocratic "cul-de-sac" in *Women in Love*. His frieze for a Cologne factory depicts "a fair, with peasants and artisans in an orgy of enjoyment . . . whirling ridiculously in roundabouts" (414).[35] This image is part

The Barnes & Noble Classics edition of *Women in Love* (2005) is introduced by Norman Loftis and edited by George Stade. The cover art of this edition is *Lovers (Man and Woman I)*, painted in 1914 by Egon Schiele (1890–1918). Schiele's painting depicts the artist and "Wally" (his mistress Valerie Neuzil) reclining together, utterly exhausted after sexual intercourse. The sharp-cornered, pointed bodies and square angles of the scene dramatize a decisive, harsh, and harrowing biographical moment, when Schiele, with cold indifference, announced their breakup and his intention to marry another woman. The couple's emotional distance is reflected in their gazes: Schiele stares straight, even defiantly, at the viewer; Wally kneels, with her arms clasped around her head, as if to buffer the deafening shock of Schiele's declaration. The exquisite cruelty of the scene captures the sadomasochistic element of the relationships between the pairs Gerald and Gudrun and Minette and Loerke in *Women in Love*.

of a network of shared affiliations with the "Arctic" way that discloses Loerke's intricately dense connections not only to Gudrun but also to Gerald. As J. B. Bullen observes, although Loerke is "physically and temperamentally very different from Gerald, he consciously articulates many of the ideals that Gerald holds unthinkingly or spontaneously."[36]

The repeated association of Gerald with ice and snow signals the downward trajectory of northern dissolution as the novel moves toward its bleak climax in the frigid waste of the high Tyrol. The collapse is motored by Gerald's systematic mechanization of ambition, action, thought, and emotion. Gerald, as a highly successful "Napoleon of industry" (56) and "the God of the Machine" (220), is the Lawrentian half-man of steel, a perfect mate for Gudrun, who is attracted to him precisely because of his machine-like prowess. (Revealingly, both Gudrun and Gerald degenerate into statue-like figures toward the novel's close.) When she later finds a superior "mate" in Loerke, her "shift of allegiance," as J. B. Bullen notes, is not so much a change in direction as "a focusing and concentration of the elements that drew her to Gerald."[37] In Lawrentian terms, Gudrun's movement away from Gerald and toward Loerke represents her definitive choice of the path of entropy and degeneration. Gudrun has decided that the only course remaining for her is "the obscene religious mystery of ultimate reduction, the mystic frictional activities of diabolic reducing down" (443).[38] She seeks her own rock-bottom level, a *reductio ad Minette.*

Assertive though both women are in pursuing the "dark shameful things," their bohemian experimentation is enacted in the form of a willfully submissive, depraved, "slave-like" (67) masochism. Minette first wants from Gerald "the experience of his male being" (60); later, in Halliday's apartment, she is "determined to have her experience" (59). Gerald quickly recognizes that he can master her just as he has taken control of the "slave-like" miners: "He felt, she must relinquish herself into his hands, and be subject to him. She was so profane, slave-like, watching him, absorbed by him" (59).[39] And after he has spent the night with her, Gerald reflects:

> Her inchoate look of a violated slave, whose fulfillment lies in her further and further violation, made his nerves quiver with acutely desirable sensation. After all, his was the only will, she was the passive substance of his will. (72)

The parallel here between the Gerald-Minette encounter and Gudrun's interaction with Loerke is apparent: after Loerke, also a sculptor, has shown Gudrun a carving of a nude girl—whose features closely resemble Minette's own—"she looked up with a certain supplication, almost slave-like" (420). By the conclusion of *Women in Love*, the "born mistress" has become very nearly Loerke's slave, though she still strives to maintain a repellent distance from him.

Nonetheless, it warrants emphasis that both female "slaves" (73) control their males at various moments in the novel. Gerald judges that Minette leaves him because Halliday is preferable as a half-man over whom "she could have complete power" (74). Halliday is desirable to Minette as a puppet with whom she can toy. Halliday came crying to her, "saying *he couldn't* bear it unless I went back to him" (60). Indeed she maintains that Halliday regularly behaved so. In similar fashion, hungry for love after his father dies, Gerald returns to Gudrun. She becomes the dominant presence that bolsters her broken man.

Ultimately, Gudrun arrives at a crossroads where the road forks in forever opposing directions: imitating her moral, proper, likewise rather "conventional" sister Ursula or descending to the insect world of beetle-like Minette. Gudrun takes the latter road, and her sister prophesies the path of her destruction accurately in chapter XXVII. Earlier, however, in Chapter One, Ursula views Gudrun's excruciatingly refined sensibility and lust for sensation as utterly "charming," even admirable. In "Sisters," Ursula judges Gudrun

> so charming, so infinitely charming, in her softness and her fine, exquisite richness of texture and delicacy of line. There was a certain playfulness about her too, such a piquancy or ironic suggestion, such an untouched reserve. Ursula admired her with all her soul. (4)

Yet by the time of the later chapter, "Flitting," Ursula disparages her sister as "rather common, really like a little *type*" (370). In the "Gudrun in the Pompadour" chapter, Gudrun herself treats Minette with hauteur and contempt, though by this point what separates them is merely Gudrun's superior air. Both women are now part of Birkin's "Flux of Corruption." Here Lawrence firmly establishes the connection between Minette and Loerke. In a conversation with Minette, Halliday reads Birkin's letter of advice to him aloud:

> "And if, Julius, you want this ecstasy of reduction with Minette, you must go on till it is fulfilled. But surely there is in you somewhere . . . when all this process of active corruption, with all its flowers of mud, is transcended. Minette, you are a flower of mud. . . ."
>
> "Thank you—and what are you?"
>
> "Oh, I'm another surely, according to this letter. We're all flowers of mud—*Fleurs*—hic! *du mal*!" (375)

Loerke is described by Gudrun as "a mud-child," "the very stuff of the underworld of life. There seemed no going beyond him" (417–418).

Taken at the Fontana Vecchia in Taormina in 1926, this image shows an apparently casual Lawrence, though he was suffering terribly at this time from tuberculosis. Here Lawrence was inspired to write *Lady Chatterley's Lover,* which would prove even more controversial and indeed scandalous than *Women in Love*. The main protagonist of the former novel, Constance Chatterley, is an even more extreme and defiant libertine than the bohemian characters in *Women in Love*—including Gudrun, Gerald, Loerke, Halliday, and Minette—whom Birkin terms "flowers of corruption—*fleurs du mal*."

The character of Constance Chatterley was based on an Englishwoman living in Taormina, an eastern Sicilian resort town, during Lawrence's stay there. Indeed, according to a local rumor, Constance was based on Frieda's affair with an illiterate Sicilian. The alleged lover, Peppino D'Allura, announced in 1990 that he had been Frieda's lover in the early 1920s, when he visited the Fontana Vecchia and suddenly encountered Frieda in the nude. He claimed that she then offered herself to him.

Lady Chatterley's Lover (1928) was first published in Italy to avoid censorship. The novel remained banned in many countries, including Britain and the USA, until the 1960s. Many obscenity trials occurred in various countries, during which famous literary critics and writers testified on behalf of Lawrence's work as art, not pornography.

By the closing pages of *Women in Love,* all these characters—Gudrun, Gerald, Loerke, Halliday, and Minette—represent the flowers of evil that Birkin warns Ursula about in "Water Party":

> "You mean we are flowers of corruption—*fleurs du mal*? I don't feel as if I were," she protested. . . .
>
> "I don't feel as if we were, *altogether,*" he replied. "Some people are pure flowers of dark corruption—lilies. But there ought to be some roses—warm and flamy." (164)

Birkin and Ursula are right: they resist the entropic impulse that drives Gerald and Gudrun. The two pairs of characters diverge, moving in opposite directions. Gerald and Gudrun do not finally stand with Birkin and Ursula. Rather, they devolve from roses to lilies as they follow the descents of Minette, Halliday, and Loerke. But Minette prefigures it all, for she is already a fully reduced, subhuman creature. She is death-in-life, *the whole truth of that state*—indeed, like the African statue, "the whole truth" and nothing but the naked truth.

Notes

The English-language translations of the works of Sigmund Freud have appeared in various American and British editions, some of them abridged and in paperback. Wherever possible, I have cited the so-called *Standard Edition of the Works of Sigmund Freud,* translated by James Strachey and originally published in the 1950s and 1960s by Hogarth Press in the UK. It has been reissued several times, most recently in a Vintage edition that is widely available.

Even more accessible is the online edition of the *Psychological Works of Sigmund Freud,* which is available in a PDF format numbering more than five thousand pages. Edited by Ivan Smith, this edition is available on several websites aimed at making the works of major writers and thinkers readily accessible digitally.

One of the best known such sites is the Internet Archive, a 501(c)(3) nonprofit that was founded to build a web library. Among its purposes is to facilitate convenient use of digitized scholarly collections to researchers, students, and the general public. Smith himself states that his goal is to render leading authors "available to anyone interested" in a reader-friendly format.

The Smith edition of Freud (uploaded 2000, 2001, 2010) is adapted from the original, authoritative English translation by Strachey, completed and published by Hogarth in 1961. The online version is a near-exact transcription of the entire twenty-four volumes of the Strachey edition, departing occasionally from it only to recast infelicitous phrasing, clarify "Germanic"-sounding sentences, and simplify select psychoanalytic concepts and Freudian usage that may impede the common reader's understanding of Freud's work.

INTRODUCTION

1. I am reminded here of an exchange that occurred between Columbia colleagues Lionel Trilling, the literary critic, and Richard Sennett, the political theorist. These two distinguished men of letters were good friends and exemplary liberal humanists, but

they sometimes differed sharply in their ideological outlooks, less in their ultimate convictions than in their approaches to problems. Sennett once recalled a conversation with Trilling that encapsulates their difference. The main title to my book is a veiled act of homage to Trilling's point of view:

> "You have no position," Richard Sennett once upbraided Trilling. "You are always in between."
>
> Trilling replied: "Between is the only honest place to be."
>
> QUOTED IN JOHN RODDEN, *LIONEL TRILLING AND THE CRITICS* (LINCOLN: UNIVERSITY OF NEBRASKA PRESS, 2000), 375

2. Lawrence's dictum is "a cardinal principle of modern hermeneutics from Freud and Nietzsche to Lévi-Strauss," according to David Lodge (*After Bahktin*, London, 1990). Whatever its philosophical value or influence, however, Lawrence's statement represented a simple distinction: the tale is what the author writes. The teller or artist is the author who makes claims about what he has done. His work may or may not be what he claims to have done. Sometimes it is, but sometimes he does what he does not realize.

Lawrence actually wrote: "Never trust the artist. Trust the tale. The proper function of the critic is to save the tale from the artist who created it." The tale must be saved from the artist because, of the two opposing claims to trust directed at the reader, the artist's cannot be trusted. He can't be trusted because, as Lawrence has told us a few paragraphs earlier, the artist is usually a "damned liar" and his art, if it is art, gives us the only truth there is, which Lawrence refers to as "the truth of his day."

When Lawrence tells us to trust the tale rather than the artist, he does so in the specific context of his argument in *Studies in Classic American Literature*. According to Lawrence, the "classic" American writers can't be trusted because they are divided men: their purpose, philosophy, or metaphysics is at variance with their passion and inspiration. But in Lawrence's view, not all novelists are divided against themselves in this way. Some novelists have managed to keep their purposes and their passions harmonized. Their novels are the work of their whole being. In such cases there is no question of having to save the tale from the artist, because no split in the artist has occurred to divide them.

3. My decision to close this study with Lawrence and his generation of British modernists (such as Ford and Lewis) owes simply to the fact that my analysis of "the rise of the novel" across a full century and a half seems more than sufficient to indicate the evolution and recurrent patterns of British psychological fiction. Certainly one could select numerous other, more recent British novels that would reward careful psychological exploration. For instance, several novels of the 1950s come to mind, ranging from the novelistic saga of C. P. Snow to the so-called "kitchen sink" school of fiction. Such novels are often treated exclusively from a documentary perspective as wooden narratives that portray "social problems," and are thereby dismissed by critics as tractarian reactions to various topics of the day or prisoners of outworn genres (e.g., works such as Lynne Reid Banks's *The L-Shaped Room* or John Braine's *Room at the Top*

or Alan Sillitoe's *Saturday Night and Sunday Morning* and *The Loneliness of the Long-Distance Runner*).

4. Such mentalistic hyperawareness "provides us only with endless *appliances* which we can use for the all-too-difficult business of coming to our spontaneous-creative fullness of being. . . . The mind as author and director of life is anathema." D. H. Lawrence, *Psychoanalysis and the Unconscious*, 126–127. According to Lawrence, the European mind is a diseased specimen of the Arctic, technocratic sensibility, lodged in a "cul-de-sac" to which excessive mentalism inevitably leads. Loerke's Jewishness, like the phenomenon of Jewish intellectualism generally, is incribed in this overdeveloped, corrupted form of intellect. The repeated association of Gerald Crich with ice and snow also points to the fact of Arctic (or Nordic) dissolution. The frigid Arctic mode characterizing the Northern European races represents a destructive form of abstract, deadened knowledge that Lawrence brands degenerate.

5. Ian Watt, "Serious Reflections on the Rise of the Novel," 213.

6. Ibid. This phrasing, set in the context of Watt's adamant, long-standing disagreement with the New Critics, reflected his position that critical understanding is necessarily extra-literary, not only literary. For Watt, aesthetic works are not verbal icons or well-wrought urns existing autonomously of each other or best approached only in formalistic terms apart from such considerations as history and social background, but rather widely and inclusively, embracing also nonliterary contexts.

7. Or as the Irish novelist John Banville, who shares the familiar contempt of the empirical Brits for "head shrinking," likes to say upon hearing critics mention the word "psychology" in relation to the novel: "I reach for my revolver." Quoted in Joan Acocella, "Doubling Down," *New Yorker*, 16 October 2012, 106. Banville's allusion to Hermann Goering's notorious remark about *Kultur* reflects the intense cynicism felt toward psychology by so many writers and intellectuals of the British Isles. It is hard to imagine any other artistic or literary issue in which such a nonpolitical man of letters as Banville would readily echo the sentiments of a Goering.

My own attitude toward the value of psychology for illuminating art and literature mirrors the stance of Robert Penn Warren: "There is no *one, single, correct* kind of criticism, no *complete* criticism. You only have different kinds of perspectives, giving, when successful, different kinds of insights." *Writers at Work: The Paris Review Interviews*, ed. Malcolm Cowley (New York, 1958), 293.

8. Moreover, it warrants emphasis that Watt's historical frame is restricted to the three authors of the eighteenth century named in his subtitle. *Between Self and Society* aims to combine psychological interpretation with social criticism and tell the story of the British novel's rise through the early decades of the twentieth century. Whereas Watt is concerned with the Augustan Age and thus with the rise of literary realism, *Between Self and Society* treats the novel across a century and a half with a special focus on its psychological dimensions. Watt's seminal contribution to literary studies was his integration of history, philosophy, and sociology with formalist criticism. My hope is that *Between Self and Society* may fill a gap not covered by Watt or as yet fully addressed in British Studies: the relation of the novel to psychoanalysis and affiliated developments in psychology.

9. Let me illustrate this richness and depth of the literary artist's approach to so-

cial observation. Reflecting a distinctive accent on concrete particulars rather than the social theorist's emphasis on abstract generalization is the following pair of statements, eloquently expressed by two very different German-language contemporaries of one-time key members of Freud's inner circle (e.g., Carl Jung and Otto Rank).

I quote here the poet-novelists Rainer Maria Rilke (1875–1926) and Hermann Hesse (1877–1962). First let us attend to Rilke, whose rare poetic sensibility never failed to address "the single human being" and yet issued forth in daring philosophical flights. Such flights were not seldom accompanied by stormy jeremiads, as the passage below attests. It is cited from his lone work of long prose fiction, *The Notebooks of Malte Laurids Brigge*, an autobiograpical novel in which "Brigge" is largely a mouthpiece for Rilke himself. The last clause—"Simply because there is nobody else"—means no one besides Rilke-Brigge.

> Is it possible that in spite of inventions and progress, in spite of culture, religion, and worldly wisdom, that we have remained on the surface of life? That at least would have been something! But is it furthermore possible that we have simply pulled an incredibly dull slipcover over life's surface, so that it looks like living room furniture during the summer vacation?
>
> Yes, it is possible.
>
> Is it possible that the whole history of the world has been misunderstood? Is it possible that the past is false because we have always spoken of "the masses," as if we were telling a story about a gathering of multitudes, instead of honoring the real story: that these onlookers are all circled around a single human being whom they have viewed as somehow different and has died?
>
> Yes, it is possible.
>
> Is it possible that we speak of "the women," "the children," "the boys," and yet don't realize (despite our advanced educations) that for ages none of these words have any longer had a plural, but only countless singulars?
>
> Yes, it is possible.
>
> Is it possible that people voice the word "God" and imagine that they thereby share something in common? Consider two schoolboys: the first buys a knife, and the same day the other purchases one just like it. A week goes by and they show each other their knives—and already they bear only the remotest resemblance to each other, so differently have they developed in different hands . . .
>
> Yes, it is possible.
>
> Yet if all this is possible, indeed bears even the possibility of possibility . . . then . . . something must happen. The first person to harbor this disconcerting thought must begin to discover whatever has been missed and to restore or transform some measure of it. This must be so even if he is just someone who happens to come along, not the ideal or best qualified person—simply because there is nobody else.
>
> RAINER MARIA RILKE, *THE NOTEBOOKS OF MALTE LAURIDS BRIGGE* (NEW YORK: NORTON, 1964) (TRANSLATION MINE)

Also note how Hesse, also proceeding from the singular to the universal, possesses the artist's sensibility that the "uniqueness, individuality, and distinct specialness" of "every thought and every art form" "strive diversely toward the same ultimate end." Hesse writes:

> The more sensitively, and the wider the scope and appreciation for rich interconnections that we cultivate in our capacity for reading, the more we begin to see every thought and every art form in their uniqueness, individuality, and distinct specialness. What also results is that we grasp how all beauty and stimulating charm is founded on precisely such a uniqueness, and we also see ever more clearly how all the thousands and thousands of voices of a people strive diversely toward the same ultimate end, how under whatever the name they call upon the same gods, how they dream the same wishes and undergo the same sufferings. As the reader glimpses the tiniest, finest threads of the densely woven web of the countless languages and books across the past several thousand years, he beholds a wondrously sublime and surreal chimera: the face of a human being, magically transformed from a thousand conflicting features into a unity.
>
> HERMANN HESSE, QUOTED IN HEINZ ALFRED MÜLLER, *PSYCHOLOGIE DES LESENS* (LÖRRACH: DRUCK, 1958), 141 (TRANSLATION MINE)

10. Speaking to his community of fellow literary critics in the mid-1950s, Louis Fraiberg voiced a concern that is a *locus classicus* for my thinking about this book:

> If we are to derive the greatest benefit from psychoanalysis in our study of the creative process—or any other literary problem for which it has relevance—we must always keep before us the difference between our way of looking at literature and the psychoanalyst's. Since they are not the same, this means that in order to make intelligent use of psychoanalytic findings and theories, we need to understand where they came from and how they were arrived at. To put it bluntly, we must know psychoanalysis as well as we know literature and criticism.
>
> LOUIS FRAIBERG, "LITERATURE AND PSYCHOLOGY: A QUESTION OF SIGNIFICANT FORM," *LITERATURE AND PSYCHOLOGY*, VOL. 5 (1955), 77

CHAPTER ONE

1. Citations throughout refer to the 1979 edition of *Roderick Random*, which for many years served as the standard edition and is also widely available as an Oxford paperback (reissued in 1999). The most recent edition of the novel (eds. James G. Basker and O. M. Brack, assisted by Boucé and Nicole A. Seary) was published by the University of Georgia Press in 2012.

2. Robert Alter, *Rogue's Progress*, 76: "What is both surprising and frustrating for a reader of Smollett's novel is the discovery that nearly the entire last third of this long

book moves in a most unpicaresque world . . . . On the technical level, the picaroon does not ordinarily possess enough inner life to enable the author to involve him convincingly in great love. The later chapters of *Roderick Random* make it painfully evident that Smollett floundered with this difficulty."

3. As Ernest Baker writes in *The History of the English Novel*, the structure is "a string of episodes, with no connection except that they happen to one personage" (quoted in M. A. Goldberg, *Smollett and the Scottish School*, 49). See also Donald Bruce, *Radical Doctor Smollett* , 167: "To write a chapter on the structure of Smollett's novels is rather like writing the chapter on the snakes of Iceland which Dr. Johnson boasted of knowing by heart: 'There are no snakes to be met with throughout the whole island.'"

Ross has argued that the critical mistake in viewing *Roderick Random* has been to look for narrative structure and ignore thematic structure, which he insists is a "vision of moral disorder" that permeates the book and is rendered by verbal repetition (Ian Campbell Ross, "Language, Structure, and Vision in Smollett's *Roderick Random*," 55).

4. Goldberg, *Smollett*, 36.

5. Paul-Gabriel Boucé, *The Novels of Tobias Smollett*, 114.

6. Alter, *Rogue*, 76.

7. Grant, *Tobias Smollett: A Study in Style*, 45–46.

8. At least one scene in *Peregrine Pickle* was taken virtually verbatim from William Battie's *Treatise on Madness* (1748). Smollett also wrote many articles for the *Critical Review* on current medical research in psychiatry. See Hunter and Macalpine, "Smollett's Reading in Psychiatry." According to John Sena, Smollett's "depiction of Narcissa's aunt . . . is derived almost entirely from contemporary medical theories of hysteria" ("Smollett's Portrait of Narcissa's Aunt: The Genesis of an Original," 270). Particularly interesting in connection to my argument is Sena's finding that Freud's work in dreams and psychoanalysis had its "genesis" in his joint research on hysteria with Josef Breuer (*Studies in Hysteria*, 1895).

9. James Highsmith contends: "We have, in essence, a narrative-within-a-narrative, in which the ghost [Miss Williams] addresses a dreamer-listener [Roderick]." Roderick serves as a "bridge between the ghost's words and the real world, *represented by himself*" (italics mine). "The presentation of Smollett's heroine seems to have received reinforcement from the tradition of mirror literature," such as *The Mirror for Magistrates* (Highsmith, "Smollett's Nancy Williams: A Mirror for Maggie," 117).

10. Boucé, *Novels*, 41: "It is rare for a critic not to use the word 'autobiography' when writing of *Roderick Random*."

11. Of course, the use of twentieth-century psychoanalysis to interpret an eighteenth-century novel is immediately open to the charge of historical anachronism, i.e., to the argument that such an approach represents a crude superimposition of a modern theoretical paradigm on an early modern fiction. My contention is, however, that the psychodynamics of Smollett's novel can be illuminated by recourse to Freud and Klein—quite apart from considerations about the era when they wrote their works—because the psychological insights that their models provide are not derived from or limited to any particular historical context. That is why, for example, theorists

of depth psychology such as Freud and Klein can have something valuable to say about classical dramas such as Sophocles's *Oedipus Rex*.

12. Because my chief aim in this chapter is to furnish new insight into *Roderick Random*, a full-scale conceptual reconsideration of the picaresque is beyond my scope here. But the work of scholars such as Mary Jo Kietzman, especially her valuable study of the seventeenth-century Englishwoman Mary Carleton, is directly pertinent to the matter.

Much as in the case of Carleton, Roderick's subjectivity becomes "less authoritative and more fragmented" when he is subjected to new or increased situational pressures. Carleton was ultimately executed when she ventured into criminal activities in order to survive. Like her, Roderick frequently enters worlds in which "getting a living becomes a matter of skilled, opportunistic feigning." Peter Linebaugh describes this social condition as the state of the "picaresque proletariat," which must sustain itself without a defined station in life and must instead engineer favorable circumstances or "platforms" for self-interested action. To do so, the *picaro* changes "location, situation and identity with often dizzying frequency," in Kietzman's phrase. Quite commonly, the personages whom the *picaro* deploys become ever more "random" and lacking in subjective control. The successful *picaro* manages to rise above the collective experience of the proletariat and call attention to himself as an individual in possession of the ingenuity that warrants a secure station in life and the requisite authority that comes with it. Smollett's Roderick succeeds in this fashion, representing himself as the author of his own picaresque narrative: i.e., the authoritative voice in his own first-person story of his lived experience.

Like Carleton, Roderick is also a trickster, a protagonist "capable of assuming whatever disguise is required by his situation." As such, Smollett's novel and its hero exemplify the intersection between eighteenth-century criminal biography and realistic fiction. In the former, we enter a murky underworld; in the latter, we encounter a sympathetic representation of a mobile and interiorized protagonist. This convergence discloses the similarities between the character's illegal practices and the narrator's activities of trade and authorship. For J. Paul Hunter, the feature that distinguishes "the new fiction of the eighteenth century" from earlier narrative is "its attempt to display the inner life of its protagonists, and its characteristic first-person point of view that probes selfhood in ways never so fully explored previously in narrative and not yet recognized as possible in extended, public literary forms." In this sense, as Kietzman explains, "the novel combines a biographical mode of discovery (through its narrative perspective) with an autobiographical mode of self-discovery (through the character's perspective, words, and actions)."

The coexistence of narrator and character in the same historical fiction is a distinguishing feature of the realist aesthetic. This aesthetic is partly based on a mode of character structure linked to mobility, and this dynamic inevitably works against the establishment of hierarchical social patterns, especially those in the family. Noting that a majority of characters in realistic fiction are orphans, Elizabeth Ermarth writes: "People in realistic fiction have to recognize that their identity depends on themselves and their actions, rather than on family, class, or some other such 'mark' of identity that has nothing to do with their wills or self-consciousness."

See Kietzman, *Mary Carleton*, 28–36. The quoted passages from Linebaugh, Hunter, and Ermarth are in Kietzman, 28–29. Kietzman also notes that, according to Ulrich Wicks, when the *picaro* as narrator feels desperate, "he assumes yet another role and becomes a trickster of narration, a verbally manipulative rogue" (36).

For a more extensive engagement with these and related issues, see Linebaugh, Hunter, Ermarth, and Wicks. See also Manning.

13. For an informed theoretical discussion of how the psychoanalytic process itself may be conceived as a narrative art, and more particularly how posited Freudian structures of the mind bear affinities with several literary conceptions of dramatic structure, see Fred M. Sander.

14. Sigmund Freud, *Civilization and Its Discontents*, 21.

15. One Kleinian scholar-therapist has written: "Melanie Klein chose the term position to emphasize the fact that the phenomenon she was describing was not simply a passing 'stage' or 'phase,' such as, for example, the oral stage; her term implies a specific configuration of object relations, anxieties, and defences which persist throughout life" (Hanna Segal, *An Introduction to the Work of Melanie Klein*, xiii).

16. Melanie Klein, "Notes on Some Schizoid Positions," 210.

17. Melanie Klein, "Contribution to the Psychogenesis of Manic-Depressive States," 268. Technically speaking, this characteristic is even more typical of what Klein calls the "depressive" position, rather than the paranoid-schizoid position. But the depressive position grows out of the paranoid position and never fully supersedes it. Often the individual oscillates between the two. Roderick does indeed oscillate between the two, but I have emphasized the paranoid position both because he more closely conforms to it and for the sake of clarity within space restraints.

18. Ibid., 271.

19. Michael Rosenblum observes: "The only fathers in sight in *Random* are bad fathers, men who victimize the young under the guise of helping them. Crab, the Horatian innkeeper, the money-dropper, schoolmaster, the French sergeant, the Scottish priest, and most sinister of all, Lord Strutwell, who preys upon Roderick's belief that a young man of merit will be rewarded with disinterested patronage . . . . Good fathers allow their sons to grow up, i.e., to become fathers in their turn" ("Smollett as Conservative Satirist," 563, 572). Of course, this is the beatific prospect emerging at the end of *Roderick Random*, as Roderick is about to become a father himself (and already is the beloved patriarch of his estate, which he obviously superintends with paternal care and affection).

20. For an interpretation of Narcissa's relation to classical myth (and to Smollett's heroines in *Peregrine Pickle*), see Jerry C. Beasley, "Amiable Apparitions: Smollett's Fictional Heroines."

21. Some critics have interpreted Roderick's "irresistible desire to know" about Don Rodrigo in homosexual terms. See, for instance, Steven Bruhm, "Roderick Random's Closet."

22. Klein, "Contribution," 268.

23. Ibid., 262–289.

24. Goldberg implies that one can distinguish clearly between Roderick's two

"roles," claiming that Roderick's "statements of self-insight scattered throughout the novel . . . reveal a signal lack of understanding, both of self and the external world" (*Smollett and the Scottish School*, 34).

25. Grant, *Tobias Smollett*, 45.

26. "The marvelous ambiguity of the autobiographical, or reputedly autobiographical, novel is therefore triple: the I of *Roderick Random* represents at once Roderick, Smollett and the reader" (Boucé, *Novels*, 42).

27. Segal, *Introduction*, 70.

28. Freud, *Civilization*, 22.

29. Melanie Klein, "Mourning and Its Relation to the Manic-Depressive States," 354.

30. Segal, *Introduction*, 14.

31. Klein, "Contribution," 277.

32. Klein, "Mourning," 351.

33. For an extended analysis in neo-Freudian terms of the *sui generis* project, see Brown (1962).

CHAPTER TWO

1. For instance, see Harvey Gross, "The Pursuer and the Pursued: A Study of *Caleb Williams*," *Texas Studies in Language and Literature* 1 (1959): 401–411; also Gerard A. Barker, "Justice to Caleb Williams," *Studies in the Novel* 6 (1974): 377–388; and D. Gilbert Dumas, "Things As They Were: The Original Ending of *Caleb Williams*," *Studies in English Literature* 6 (1960): 575–597. For recent scholarship that raises valuable questions in similar terms, see Daniela Garofalo, "'A Left-Handed Way'": Modern Masters in William Godwin's *Caleb Williams*," *European Romantic Review* 17 (2) (April 2006): 237–244; Evan Radcliffe, "Godwin from 'Metaphysician' to Novelist: Political Justice, *Caleb Williams*, and the Tension between Philosophical Argument and Narrative," *Modern Philology: A Journal Devoted to Research in Medieval and Modern Literature* 97 (4) (May 2000): 528–553; and Ken Edward Smith, "William Godwin: Social Critique in *Caleb Williams*," *Studies on Voltaire and the Eighteenth Century* 263 (1989): 337–341.

2. George Woodcock, *William Godwin*, 120.

3. D. H. Monro, *Godwin's Moral Philosophy*, 86–108.

4. On this theme, see also Glynis Ridley, "Injustice in the Works of Godwin and Wollstonecraft," in Lang-Peralta, Linda (ed.), *Women, Revolution, and the Novels of the 1790s* (East Lansing, MI: Michigan State University Press, 1999), 69–88; Gary Handwerk, "Of Caleb's Guilt and Godwin's Truth: Ideology and Ethics in *Caleb Williams*," *ELH* 60 (4) (Winter 1993): 939–960; and James Thompson, "Surveillance in William Godwin's *Caleb Williams*," in Kenneth W. Graham (ed.), *Gothic Fictions: Prohibitions/Transgression* (New York: AMS Press, 1989), 173–198.

5. Woodcock, *William Godwin*, 119, 122.

6. Nor did Godwin set out to portray his characters and their relationships in psychoanalytic terms, let alone to write a "Freudian" or "Kleinian" novel: such claims

would obviously be anachronistic. Yet the degree to which Godwin's literary imagination inspired a fictional world that anticipated certain Freudian themes and concepts is—to use a psychoanalytic term—"uncanny."

7. P. N. Furbank, "Godwin's Novels," 215.

8. Two psychological readings of the novel have been published. See, for instance, Joel Faflak, "Speaking of Godwin's *Caleb Williams*: The Talking Cure and the Psychopathology of Enlightenment," *English Studies in Canada* 31 (2–3) (June–Sept 2005): 99–121. But Faflak concerns himself largely with the role of speech, the analyst-analysand dynamic, and the psychological climate of the Enlightenment as they relate to psychoanalysis, not to narrative issues or the reading experience of *Caleb Williams*, let alone to topics such as introjection in Kleinian or object relations theory.

A second psychological treatment of *Caleb Williams* is Charles J. Rzepka, "Detection as Method: Reconstructing the Past in Godwin and Freud," *Literature Compass* 2 (1) (January 2005). But Rzepka approaches the novel as detective story and confessional fiction, utilizing Freud to evaluate psychological evidence and to draw distinctions between psychological and biographical truths.

For three insightful essays on Godwin's narrative technique as it relates to issues of power and resistance, see Eric Daffron, "'Magnetal Sympathy': Strategies of Power and Resistance in Godwin's *Caleb Williams*," *Criticism: A Quarterly for Literature and the Arts* 37 (2) (Spring 1995): 213–232; Kenneth W. Graham, "The Politics of Narrative: Ideology and Social Change in William Godwin's *Caleb Williams*" (New York: AMS Press, 1990); and Kenneth W. Graham, "Narrative and Ideology in Godwin's *Caleb Williams*," *Eighteenth-Century Fiction* 2 (3) (April 1990): 215–228. For a study of the reading experience of the novel by readers during the Romantic era, see Kristen Leaver, "Pursuing Conversations: *Caleb Williams* and the Romantic Construction of the Reader," *Studies in Romanticism* 33 (4) (Winter 1994): 589–610.

9. A standard approach to the theme of passion in *Caleb Williams* is to frame it in political and/or ideological terms. See, for instance, Alex Gold Jr., "It's Only Love: The Politics of Passion in Godwin's *Caleb Williams*," *Texas Studies in Literature and Language* 19 (1977): 135–160; Afshin Hafizi, "Ideology and Utopia in William Godwin's *Caleb Williams*," *Interdisciplinary Literary Studies: A Journal of Criticism and Theory* 4 (2) (Spring 2003): 94–109; and Andrew M. Stauffer, "Godwin, Provocation, and the Plot of Anger," *Studies in Romanticism* 39 (4) (Winter 2000): 579–597.

10. Ford K. Brown, *The Life of William Godwin*, 47.

11. Sigmund Freud, *Civilization and Its Discontents*, 21.

12. Melanie Klein, "Notes on Some Schizoid Positions," 192.

13. Melanie Klein, "Contribution," 268, 271.

14. Sigmund Freud, "Family Romances," 238.

15. Ibid., 237.

16. Ibid., 238–239.

17. Ibid., 239.

18. Ibid., 240–241.

19. Rudolf Storch, "Metaphors of Private Guilt and Social Rebellion in Godwin's *Caleb Williams*," 194.

20. Has Caleb consciously or unconsciously adjusted Collins's reportage for his own uses? He insists that "scrupulous fidelity restrains me from altering the manner of Mr. Collins's narrative" but carefully notes that he "cannot warrant the authenticity" of Collins's words (123). If he has not changed the "manner," has he changed the "content"? Despite Caleb's seeming familiarity with romance stories, "the case seemed entirely altered when the subject of those passions was continually before my eyes" (123). Caleb "brood[s]" over the story and it becomes "mysterious" as he "turn[s] it a thousand ways" (123).

21. Sigmund Freud, "*Interpretation of Dreams*," 490.

22. Ibid.

23. Hanna Segal, *An Introduction to the Work of Melanie Klein*, 70.

24. Klein, *The Psychoanalysis of Children*, 260.

25. If Laura or the reader could fully hear "both sides of the story," *Caleb Williams* would more properly be viewed not as a "half-told" tale but rather as a "twice-told" tale. But neither Falkland's *History* nor Caleb's novel can completely explain events or persuade the audience as to the tragedy's real victim or villain.

26. On these correspondences, see also Alex Gold's analysis of the novel as a dream in "It's Only Love: The Politics of Passion in Godwin's *Caleb Williams*," 141–144. Also relevant is Robert Uphaus, "*Caleb Williams*: Godwin's Epoch of Mind," *Studies in the Novel* 9 (1977): 279–296.

27. Sigmund Freud, *Inhibitions, Symptoms, and Anxiety*, 106.

28. Ibid., 105.

29. Alex Gold, "It's Only Love," 144. Dean T. Hughes views the novel's interludes of romance as narrative defense mechanisms: "Each of Godwin's novels is an experiment in human psychology. A mind is studied during a time of crucial pressure or difficulty . . . each novel is interrupted by interludes of 'romance,' in Godwin's term, which avoids psychological probing." See Dean T. Hughes, *Romance and Psychological Realism in Godwin's Novels, Dissertation Abstracts International* 33, 2330A, 1980.

30. Freud, *Inhibitions*, 85.

31. Sigmund Freud, "Libido Theory and Narcissism," 426.

32. Ibid.

33. Ibid., 429.

34. Sigmund Freud, "Dostoevsky and Parricide," 185.

35. Freud, "Libido Theory," 424.

36. Sigmund Freud, *Civilization and Its Discontents*, 61.

37. Sigmund Freud, "Instincts and Their Vicissitudes," 72.

38. Freud, *Civilization*, 620.

39. Freud, *Moses and Monotheism*, 82.

40. Even Godwin's choice of the name "Caleb" for the protagonist reinforces the religious resonance of the novel. Caleb literally means "dog" in Hebrew (i.e., "faithful"), and Caleb certainly considers himself faithful to Falkland and to his oath until the last pages. In the Old Testament, only Caleb and Joshua were to be permitted to see the Promised Land. Moses reports Yahweh's words: "Not one of these men, this perverse generation, shall see the rich land that I swore to give to your fathers, except Caleb. . . .

He shall see it. To him and to his sons, I will give the land he has set foot on, for he has followed Yahweh in all things." See Deuteronomy 1.30, *The Jerusalem Bible*, ed. Alexander Jones (New York: Doubleday & Co., 1968), 189. Caleb is also known in Volumes Two and Three of the scurrilous Falkland *History* as "Kit," a diminutive for Christopher, which means "bearing Christ."

41. Freud, *Civilization*, 59.

42. Freud, *Moses*, 100.

43. Freud, *Civilization*, 61.

44. Ibid., 121.

45. Sigmund Freud, *Beyond the Pleasure Principle*, 54–55; Smith, 3756.

46. For an excellent critique of Marcuse and a fine summary and analysis of Freud's psychosocial thought, see also Robert Bocock, *Freud and Modern Society* (Middlesex, Great Britain: Thomas Nelson & Sons, 1976).

47. Freud, *Civilization*, 70–71.

48. Ibid., 70.

49. Ibid., 71.

50. Ibid., 90.

51. Ibid., 143–144.

52. William Godwin, *Thoughts on Man*, 125.

CHAPTER THREE

1. Duane Edwards, "*The Mayor of Casterbridge* as Aeschylean Tragedy," *Studies in the Novel* 4 (1972): 608–118. Edwards sees *Tess* as Hardy's version of Euripides's *Hippolytus* because "the two central characters find themselves victims of their own and one another's passion" (609). Voicing a lone dissent, Edwards holds that *Jude the Obscure* (not *The Mayor*) is Hardy's *Oedipus Rex* because the central character's motives and errors occur in a particular situation to force a tragic choice in the present. *The Mayor of Casterbridge* is Aeschylean tragedy, specifically *Agamemnon*, because "what Henchard did in the past is more important than what he does in the present" (609).

2. Swinburne is quoted in Florence Hardy, *The Later Years of Thomas Hardy* (London: Macmillan, 1930), 40: "Balzac is dead, and [except for Hardy] there has been no such tragedy in fiction—on anything like the same lines—since he died." Swinburne was speaking particularly of *Jude*.

3. D. A. Dike, "A Modern *Oedipus*: *The Mayor of Casterbridge*," *Essays in Criticism* 2 (1952): 169–179. See also John Paterson, "*The Mayor of Casterbridge* as Tragedy," *Victorian Studies* 3 (December 1959): 151–172; Frederick Karl, "*The Mayor of Casterbridge*: A New Fiction Defined," *Modern Fiction Studies* 6 (Autumn 1960): 195–213. Karl writes: "Henchard is an Oedipus who, instead of marrying his mother after twenty years, marries Susan after a similar lapse in time" (196).

4. L. Starzyk, "Hardy's *Mayor*: The Antitraditional Basis of Tragedy," *Studies in the Novel* 4 (1972): 594.

5. See, for instance, Paterson. See also John Cooley, "The Importance of Things

Past: An Archetypal Reading of *The Mayor of Casterbridge*," *Massachusetts Studies in English* 1 (1967): 17–21; Julian Moynahan, "*The Mayor of Casterbridge* and the Old Testament's First Book of Samuel: A Study of Some Literary Relationships," PMLA 71 (1956): 118–130; and Robert Schweik, "Character and Fate in Hardy's *Mayor of Casterbridge*," *Nineteenth Century Fiction* 21 (December 1966): 249–262.

6. Thomas Hardy, *The Life and Death of the Mayor of Casterbridge, A Story of a Man of Character* (New York: New American Library, 1962).

7. J. Hillis Miller's excellent *Thomas Hardy: Distance and Desire* (Cambridge: Harvard, 1970) assesses the value of this criticism on Hardy. See pages 29–76 and 237–271.

8. Miller, *Thomas Hardy*, 23, 34–35. The most ambitious psychobiographical reading is by Lois Deacon and Terry Coleman, *Providence and Mr. Hardy* (London: Hutchison, 1966). Miller concludes about their reconstruction project: "It is probably an exaggeration . . . to make so much of his work an oblique dramatization of his love for Tryphena" (23).

9. Miller, *Thomas Hardy*, xii.

10. Ibid.

11. F. B. Pinion, *A Hardy Companion* (London: Macmillan, 1976), 40.

12. Hardy makes these observations about the craftsmanship of his fiction in the preface to the fifth edition of *Tess*, which he wrote to defend his freethinking novel against those critics who condemned it for its celebration of paganism and contempt for Providence.

On Hardy's preface, see *Tess of the d'Urbervilles* [1891], ed. Juliet Grindle and Simon Gatrell (Oxford: Clarendon, 1983), 6. For a rich discussion of the themes of religious heresy and ritual in relation to James Frazer's *The Golden Bough*, see Damon Franke, "Hardy's Ur-Priestess and the Phases of A Novel," *Studies in the Novel*, 39 (2) (2007): 161–176. See also John Rodden, "Of 'Nater' and God: Pagan Joan Durbeyfield and Reverend James Clare in Hardy's *Tess of the D'Urbervilles*," *English Studies* 92 (3) (2011).

For a stimulating general appreciation in the anthropological literature devoted to Hardyean folklore and Hardy's treatment of seasonal change, see the short piece by the French cultural ethnographer Solange Pinton, "Passage par la Creuse," *Ethnologie française* 21 (4) (1991): 366–368.

13. For a related application of Girardian theories to love triangles in medieval literature, specifically in the work of Chaucer and John Fletcher, see Jacek Mydla, "Triangles of Desire: From *The Knight's Tale* to *The Two Noble Kinsmen*," *The Same, the Other, the Third* (Katowice, Poland: Wydawnictwo Uniwersytetu Slaskiego, 2004), 215–232. See also Michael Kidd, "Triangular Desire and Sensory Deception in Francisco de la Cueva y Silva's *Trajedia de Narciso*," MLN 110 (2) (1995): 271–283.

14. Or rather than "musical chairs," one might characterize the plot of *The Mayor* as a ritual dance in the form of *la ronde*. On the complex interconnections in *The Mayor* among primitive ritual dance, seasonal rhythms, agricultural community, and social disintegration, see Langdon Elsbree, "The Purest and Most Perfect Form of Play: Some Novelists and the Dance," *Criticism: A Quarterly for Literature and the Arts* 14 (1972): 361–372.

Franke's comment about *Tess*'s plot is also apropos of *The Mayor*: their narratives illustrate "the buried cliché that history repeats itself with a difference" (163). Franke's citation of J. Hillis Miller's work on *Tess* likewise applies fully to *The Mayor.* Like *Tess,* it too "is a story about repetition," and the "relation among the links in a chain of meanings . . . is always repetition with a difference, and the difference is as important as the repetition" (163).

15. Indeed, as we shall see, Girard's main preoccupations recall the themes and analytical method of Frazer's *The Golden Bough,* which explains Aryan fertility rites as a custom of worshipping a slain god largely in terms of a bloody succession ritual (i.e., slaying the high priest of Diana, the reigning "King of the Wood").

Although he does not relate *The Golden Bough* to *The Mayor,* Bruce Johnson discusses Hardy's use of the past throughout his oeuvre in terms of ritual succession patterns in Frazer that echo Girard strikingly. Johnson notes that "[we] have lost the meaning [of the] murder of the priest in the grove, [but] it can be recovered through penetration of the strata that comprise its particular formation and by a comparative mythology that aids that penetration" (259).

See Bruce Johnson, "'The Perfection of Species' and Hardy's *Tess,*" in *Nature and the Victorian Imagination,* ed. U. C. Knoepflmacher and G. B. Tennyson (Berkeley: University of California Press, 1977), 259. (Critics have established that Hardy read Frazer's *The Golden Bough,* first published in 1890.) Of course, Girard's main topics also resemble earlier discussions of slain gods and ritual sacrifice by thinkers such as Robertson Smith.

16. For a thoroughgoing exploration of the novel's narrative structure in light of its architectural motif, see Tomas Monterrey, "Architecture in Thomas Hardy's Narrative Method," in *Traditions and Innovations: Commemorating Forty Years of English Studies at ULL* (1963–2003), ed. Manuel Brito and Juan Ignacio Oliva (Tenerife, Canary Islands: Revista Canaria de Estudios Ingleses, 2004), 325–333; Norman D. Prentiss, "Compilation and Design in *The Mayor of Casterbridge,*" *Thomas Hardy Journal* 11, no. 1 (Feb. 1995): 60–74.

17. J. Hillis Miller, *Thomas Hardy: Distance and Desire,* xii.

18. Schweik (see note 5), however, has attempted to trace out *The Mayor*'s "movements," picturing the novel as a sort of overblown symphony running out of steam at its close: "The largest elements in *The Mayor* are four relatively self-contained and structurally similar 'movements' of progressively diminishing lengths, roughly comprising chapters 1–31, 31–50, 51–53, and 54–55. . . . Each provides a variation on a common pattern: an initial situation which seems to offer hope is followed by events which create doubt, fear and anxious participation for an outcome that follows, originally, as a catastrophe" (250). But Schweik offers no structural criteria for his chapter divisions, nor does he place the novel in a dramatic context as tragedy.

A perceptive study is by V. J. Emmett, "Marriage in Hardy's Later Novels," *Midwest Quarterly* 9 (1968): 331–348. Emmett notes the presence of "romantic triangles" in *The Mayor* and Hardy's "later novels" (*Native, Tess, Jude*). But he does not see the opposing family triangles, especially in *The Mayor,* nor the psychosocial dimension of the triangular configuration. Instead the triangles for him indicate Hardy's "concern with marital problems" and reflect "the moral disorder of the universe." Emmett makes no attempt to treat the functional and dynamic nature of the triangles as structuring agents in Hardy's work.

19. For a general discussion of the role played by love triangles in Hardy's fiction, see H. M. Daleski, "Figures in the Carpet," *Victorian Literature and Culture* 19 (1991): 257–275. Limiting her analysis to *Tess*, Judith Weismann has pursued related issues in "*Tess of the D'Urbervilles*: A Demystification of the Eternal Triangle of Tennyson's *Idylls of the King*," *Colby Library Quarterly* 11 (1975): 189–197.

20. The middle three acts are not precisely equal in chapter length, with Act II and Act IV containing twelve chapters and Act III having fourteen chapters. Act I and Act V contain two chapters each.

21. Virginia Woolf once called Hardy's style "blundering and gauche." Joseph Beach lamented: "In plot he out-Herods Herod in his Victorian fondness for mystery and complication," adding that Hardy is "inordinately fond of coincidence" and that *The Mayor* has "an almost ridiculous air" to it because of its plot devices. Finally, James Baker deplores Hardy's "unstable manipulation of plot" in *The Mayor*. See *Twentieth Century Literature* 1 (1955): 13–16.

22. René Girard, "Myth and Ritual in Shakespeare: *A Midsummer Night's Dream*," in *Textual Strategies*, ed. Josue Harari (Ithaca: Cornell, 1977), 201.

23. Ian Gregor, *The Great Web: The Form of Hardy's Major Fiction* (London: Faber and Faber, 1974), 170–180.

24. René Girard, *Deceit, Desire and the Novel* (Baltimore: Johns Hopkins, 1965).

25. René Girard, *Violence and the Sacred* (Baltimore: Johns Hopkins, 1977).

26. René Girard, *"To Double Business Bound"* (Baltimore: Johns Hopkins, 1978).

27. *Violent Origins: Walter Burkert, René Girard, and Jonathan Z. Smith on Ritual Killing and Cultural Formation*, ed. Robert G. Hamerton-Kely (Palo Alto: Stanford University Press, 1988).

28. René Girard, *A Theatre of Envy: William Shakespeare* (New York: Oxford University Press, 1991).

29. René Girard, *Oedipus Unbound: Selected Writings on Rivalry and Desire* (Palo Alto: Stanford University Press, 2004). See also Girard's related work in *The Girard Reader*, ed. James G. Williams and René Girard (New York: Crossroad, 1996); and in René Girard, *Mimesis and Theory: Essays in Literature and Criticism* (Palo Alto: Stanford University Press, 2008.)

30. See Girard, *Violent Origins*, 106–107.

31. Girard, "*Double*," ix.

32. Ibid., 201.

33. Ibid., ix.

34. Ibid., x.

35. Girard adds: "The great writers apprehend intuitively and concretely, through the medium of their art, if not formally, the system in which they were first imprisoned with their contemporaries. In the great works, human relations conform to the complex process of strategies and conflicts, misunderstandings and delusions that stem from the mimetic nature of human desire. Implicitly and sometimes explicitly, these works reveal the laws of mimetic desire." *Deceit*, 3.

36. Girard, *Violence*, 81.

37. Ibid., 221.

38. According to Girard, "the mimetic process detaches desire from any predetermined object, whereas the Oedipus complex fixes desire on the maternal object. The mimetic concept eliminates all conscious knowledge of patricide-incest, and even all desire for it as such; the Freudian proposition, by the contrast, is based entirely on the consciousness of the desire" (*Violence*, 180).

39. Girard, *Violence*, 36.

40. Ibid., 72.

41. Ibid., 73.

42. To my knowledge, no scholar has yet addressed in Girardian terms either Hardy's oeuvre generally or *The Mayor* in particular. One critic has discussed imitative desire and triangulation in Hardy's *The Return of the Native* (1878). See Jeff Massey, "Why Wildeve Had to Die: Mimetic Triangles and Violent Ends in *The Return of the Native*," *Hardy Review* 3 (Summer 2000): 11–26.

With passing reference to Girard, however, J. Hillis Miller has emphasized that "the law of mediated desire" is central to Hardy's fictional design. Miller cites "the presence of a third person" as "the most important and pervasive barrier between Hardy's lovers," noting that his entire corpus "might be defined as an exploration of the varieties of mediated love." H. M. Daleski alludes to this claim by Miller, only to dismiss the role of "mediated desire" as of "minor importance in Hardy." But Daleski does affirm that "the pattern that came to dominate [Hardy's] work" is the "simple and traditional figure of the love-triangle."

See Miller, *Distance and Desire*, 158–159; and H. M. Daleski, "Figures in the Carpet," *Victorian Literature and Culture* 19 (1991): 260, 272.

43. Gregor, *Great Web*, 176.

44. According to Sartre, "[There is] one privileged mediation which permits it to pass from general and abstract determinations to particular traits of the single individual . . . existentialism . . . believes that it can integrate the psychoanalytic method which discovers the point of insertion for man and his class—that is, the particular family—as a mediation between the universal class and the individual." Jean-Paul Sartre, *Search for a Method* (NY: Vintage, 1963), 61–62.

45. *The Mayor* invites a psychosocial approach, for Hardy is concerned both with love and marriage and with class conditions. Lennart Bjork sees "an intimate relationship between a . . . psychosocial vision and social criticism" throughout Hardy's fiction, based in large measure upon Hardy's debt to Fourier's social criticism, which was "inseparably linked to his view of human personality." Bjork notes that Hardy's psychological vision is rooted in social interests spiritual and intellectual in nature, rather than in economic and political issues of the day. See "Psychological Vision and Social Criticism in *Desperate Remedies* and *Jude the Obscure*," in *Budmouth Essays on Thomas Hardy*, ed. F. B. Pinion (Dorchester: Hardy Society, 1976), 92, 94.

46. Girard, *Double*, 67.

47. Freud, *Inhibitions, Symptoms, and Anxiety*, Vol. 6, 105.

48. Girard, *Double*, 64.

49. See also Tod E. Jones, "Michael Henchard: Hardy's Male Homosexual," *Victorian Newsletter* 86 (1994): 9–13; and Robert Langbaum, "The Minimisation of Sexuality in *Mayor of Casterbridge*," *The Thomas Hardy Journal* 8 (1) (February 1992): 20–32.

50. Adds Girard: "If homosexuality is a dead weight, it is because it always appears to aim at a 'father substitute' rather than at the present rivalry. The regression of psychoanalysis, its Oedipal fetishism, the primacy of difference, and the inability to spot the working of mimetic rivalry all demonstrate the same shortcoming." *Double*, 54.

51. The phrase is Tony Tanner's, from an essay on *Tess*. See "Colour and Movement in Hardy's *Tess of the D'Urbervilles*," *Critical Quarterly* 10 (Autumn 1968): 226.

52. Girard, *Violence*, 46.

53. For a very different approach from my own to the architectural motif of the novel, see Julian Wolfreys, "Haunting Casterbridge; Or, 'the Persistence of the Unforeseen,'" in *The Mayor of Casterbridge*, ed. Julian Wolfreys (New York: St. Martin's, 2000), 153–169.

54. Miller, *Distance and Desire*, xii.

55. Ibid.

56. Girard, *Deceit*, 9.

57. Ibid.

58. Girard, *Violence*, 146.

59. For a valuable Girardian treatment focusing on the theme of envy, see Ed Block, "The Plays of Peter Shaffer and the Mimetic Theory of René Girard," *Journal of Dramatic Theory and Criticism* 19 (10) (2004): 57-78. On a similar pattern in Othello from a Girardian perspective—how male rivalry facilitates the spreading infection of jealousy—see Rob Wilson, "Othello: Jealousy as Mimetic Contagion," *American Imago: Studies in Psychoanalysis and Culture* 44 (3) (Fall 1987): 213–233.

60. Girard, *Violence*, 114–115.

61. Ibid., 82.

62. Ibid., 84.

63. Ibid., 216.

64. Ibid., 149, 79.

65. Ibid., 158.

66. Technically, this is not the case if one considers the full title, *The Life and Death of the Mayor of Casterbridge*. Farfrae, of course, does not die. But the novel is usually not referred to in its full title.

67. Girard, *Violence*, 69.

68. For a Derridean approach that focuses on this aspect of Farfrae's character, especially his memory and the significance of this topic in the novel, see Earl Ingersoll, "Writing and Memory in *The Mayor of Casterbridge*," *English Literature in Transition (1880–1920)* 33 (3) (1990): 299–309.

69. Girard explains:

> In the temporal plan of the system there is not a moment when those involved in the action do not see themselves separated from their rivals by formidable differences. . . . That explains why the antagonists only rarely perceive the reciprocal nature of their involvement. Each is too intensely engaged in living out

> his nonreciprocal moment to grasp the whole picture, to take in several of these moments in a single glance and compare them in such a way as to penetrate the illusory quality of singularity that each moment . . . seems to possess. (*Violence*, 158)

70. Girard explains:

> The model for the same sex, soon to be a rival, designates for the subject an object of the opposite sex. It is quite evident that the subject's interest cannot be displaced from the heterosexual object toward the rival of the same sex without giving the impression of a "homosexual tendency" at work.
>
> This mimetic formation of "neurotic" desire . . . [shows] why everything interpreted as "latent homosexuality" appears pervaded with "masochism." Masochism . . . is nothing but the fascination exercised by the obstacle in his capacity as potential and then actual model. The homosexual tendency is indeed present; it is not at all a matter of denying it. . . . What must be supposed is that beyond a certain threshold, the truly libidinous element of desire will in turn desert the object and become invested in the rival. (*Double*, 53–54)

It should again be noted that mimetic rivalry normally is *not* conscious. It is clear in *The Mayor* that neither Henchard nor Farfrae (nor any of the other characters) are consciously aware of the nature of their desire. A second point is that Farfrae, until near the novel's close, does not ever appear consciously aware of the *fact* of the rivalry itself with Henchard, which the rest of Casterbridge clearly sees. Lucetta makes reference to it after Donald disputes her statement that "Scotsmen are always lucky": "I was only speaking in a general sense, of course! You are always so literal" (239). Significantly, her offhand remark comes when Farfrae has admitted for the first time his awareness of a hatred borne by Henchard towards him. Farfrae, the modern man, is a success because he is completely "desymbolized" in his outlook. Newson shares the same attribute, as when Henchard lies to him about Elizabeth-Jane's death: "He had not so much as turned his head. It was an act of simple faith in Henchard's words—faith so simple as to be almost sublime" (288).

71. On the Henchard identity as it is shaped by both social and religious morality, see Jane Adamson, "Who and What Is Henchard? Hardy, Character and Moral Inquiry," *Critical Review* 31 (1991): 47–74.

72. Girard adds that they are "exterior or marginal individuals, incapable of establishing or sharing the social bonds that link the rest of the inhabitants. . . . But what about the king? Is he not at the very heart of the community? Undoubtedly—but it is precisely his position at the center that serves to isolate him from his fellow men, to render him casteless. He escapes from society, so to speak, via the roof, just as the pharmakos escapes through the cellar" (Girard, *Violence*, 12).

73. Ibid., 13.

74. Ibid., 107.

75. Ibid., 8, 14.

76. Ibid., 297.

77. Ibid., 23.

78. Ibid., 299.

79. Ibid., 307.

80. For a rich interpretation of how violence emerges from organized religion, see William Mishler, "Mimetic Violence and the Sacred in Ibsen's *The Pretenders*," in *Proceedings: VII International Ibsen Conference* (Oslo, Norway: Center for Ibsen Studies, University of Oslo, 1994). See also Andrew McKenna, "Uncanny Christianity: René Girard's Mimetic Theory," in *Divine Aporia: Postmodern Conversations about the Other* (Lewisburg, PA: Bucknell University Press, 2000).

81. Girard, *Violence*, 258.

82. The phrase is G. W. Sherman's. See *The Pessimism of Thomas Hardy* (Madison, NJ: Farleigh Dickinson, 1976), 404–450.

83. Hayden White, "Ethnological 'Lie' and Mythical 'Truth,'" *Diacritics: A Review of Contemporary Criticism* 8 (1) (1978): 3.

84. Sherman claims that Maeterlinck and Bergson actually had very little influence on Hardy, since their translated work did not appear until the first quarter of the twentieth century. And despite the close connections often drawn between Hardy's outlook and the work of von Hartmann and Schopenhauer, Sherman believes they too had little direct influence upon Hardy. He did not read the latter two until after writing *Jude*. Biographical evidence supports his view that Hardy's philosophy was shaped by his reading before this date. Likewise his outlook on his experiences in Wessex and London was established long before the work of such thinkers as Maeterlinck, Bergson, von Hartmann, and Schopenhauer was available in translation.

Hardy did, however, read Darwin's *Origin of Species* as a young man in 1865. At that time and also later, he recorded in his journals his preference for Darwin, Spencer, and Comte over the German idealists. When Hardy finally did read Bergson in his later years, he disagreed with most of what the Frenchman said. But his encounter with Bergson was stimulating, and so Hardy was in some ways influenced by him, according to Sherman. Of course, the issue of "direct" influence is in part a red herring; many of the fatalistic ideas reflected in Hardy's work were certainly "in the air." He was influenced by them even though he had not read their authors' work.

85. White, "Ethnological 'Lie' and Mythical 'Truth,'" 3. This entire issue of *Diacritics* is devoted to Girard's work and serves as an excellent introduction to his literary theory and psychosocial thought.

86. For an application of Girard's theories about love triangles and their relationship to sacrifice in the work of Spanish writer Francisco de la Cueva y Silva, see Michael Kidd (note 13). A stimulating earlier study of the role of women and mimetic desire in Cervantes's *Don Quixote* is Ruth El Saffar, "Unbinding the Doubles: Reflections on Love and Culture in the Work of René Girard," *Denver Quarterly* 18 (4) (Winter 1984): 6–22. The interconnections among sacrifice, law, judicial authority, and capital punishment are explored in Jody Lyneé, "The Execution as Sacrifice," in *Evil, Law and the State:*

Perspectives on State Power and Violence, ed. John T. Parry (Amsterdam, Netherlands: Rodopi, 2006). See also Henri Tincq, "What Is Happening Today Is Mimetic Rivalry on a Global Scale," *South Central Review* 19 (2–3) (Summer–Fall 2002): 22–27.

87. Following Girard's distinction between "externally" and "internally" mediated relationships, Jeff Massey notes that the first two triangles lead to violence and death for their participants. By contrast, Diggory Venn escapes a violent end; he belongs only to the third, externally mediated triangle, which remains "peaceful" because the subject has no direct contact with any potential model or rival. All the other triangulated characters in *The Return of the Native* meet fatal outcomes, according to Massey, because they collide in internally mediated, triangulated relationships, whereby the distance between subject and model narrows and dissolves, activating rivalries and retaliatory violence. Massey, "Why Wildeve Had To Die," 119–120.

88. Girard, *Violence*, 258.

89. Florence Hardy, *The Early Life*, 23

CHAPTER FOUR

1. Ford Madox Ford, *The Good Soldier* (New York: Norton, 2012), 73. All further references are to the second Norton Critical Edition, edited by Martin Stannard.

2. Barry Bort, "*The Good Soldier*: Comedy or Tragedy?" *Twentieth Century Literature* XII (4) (1967): 195.

3. Paul Wiley, *Novelist of Three Worlds: Ford Madox Ford* (Syracuse, NY: Syracuse University Press, 1962), 174–176. On the novels as a critique of the Imagist/Vorticist strain of modernist aesthetics, see also Damon Marcel DeCoste, "A Frank Expression of Personality? Sentimentality, Silence and Early Modernist Aesthetics in *The Good Soldier*," *Journal of Modern Literature* 31 (1) (Fall 2007): 101–123. Robert M. Robertson regards the novel as not only an example of modernism, but also of emerging postmodernism. See Robert M. Robertson, "The Wrong 'Saddest Story': Reading the Appearance of Postmodernity in Ford's *Good Soldier*," *Postmodernism Across the Ages: Essays for a Postmodernity That Wasn't Born Yesterday* (Syracuse, NY: Syracuse University Press, 1993), 171–187.

4. See Mark Schorer's introduction to Ford, *The Good Soldier*, xiii.

5. Samuel Hynes, "The Epistemology of *The Good Soldier*," *Sewanee Review* 27 (1961): 234.

6. On this topic, see Robertson (note 3).

7. For an alternate approach to these issues in social terms, see Robert Micklus, "Dowell's Passion in *The Good Soldier*," *English Literature in Transition (1880–1920)* 22 (1979): 281–292.

8. Karen Hoffman has broached these issues in somewhat different terms in "'Am I No Better Than a Eunuch?': Narrating Masculinity and Empire in Ford Madox Ford's *The Good Soldier*," *Journal of Modern Literature* 27 (3) (2004): 30–47.

9. For an interesting treatment of the narrator's psychological issues in light of the novel's shadow symbolism, see Julie Gordon-Dueck, "A Jungian Approach to Ford

Madox Ford's *The Good Soldier*: John Dowell Meets the Shadow," *Journal of Evolutionary Psychology* 25 (1–2) (March 2004): 40–45.

10. Although an autobiographical reading of the psychology of *The Good Soldier* lies outside the scope of this chapter's main argument, such an approach to the novel's staggering welter of betrayals, as well as to its religious motifs, would also prove rewarding in light of Ford's own nervous breakdown in 1904, his marital hardships (including his extramarital affairs and subsequent divorce during this period), and his tortuous battle with his Catholic faith. A literary comment of Ford's from his 1927 Dedicatory Letter to Stella Ford even provides an as-yet unexplored biographical analogue to the familiar view of the novel as the passing of a social order: "At the date when *The Good Soldier* was finished, London at least and possibly the world appeared to be passing under the dominion of writers newer and much more vivid" (4). On Dowell as an unreliable narrator and his treatment of Catholicism, see Vincent J. Cheng, "Religious Differences in *The Good Soldier*: The 'Protest' Scene," *Renascence: Essays on Values in Literature* 37 (4) (Summer 1985): 238–247.

11. For a different and valuable approach to the narrative issues, see John G. Hessler, "Dowell and *The Good Soldier*: The Narrator Re-Examined," *Journal of Narrative Technique* 9 (1979): 53–60. See also Kenneth Womack, "'It Is All A Darkness': Death, Narrative Therapy, and Ford Madox Ford's *The Good Soldier*," *Papers On Language and Literature* 38 (3) (2002): 316–333; Frank G. Nigro, "Who Framed *The Good Soldier*? Dowell's Story in Search of a Form," *Studies in the Novel* 24 (4) (1992): 381–391; and Carol Jacobs, "The (Too) Good Soldier: 'A Real Story,'" *Glyph* 3 (Spring 1978): 32–51.

12. Sigmund Freud, *Civilization and Its Discontents*.

13. Hynes, "Epistemology," 234.

14. Freud, "Libido Theory and Narcissism," 413; Smith, 3461.

15. Ibid., 415; Smith, 3462.

16. Ibid., 417; Smith, 3462.

17. Ibid., 418; Smith, 3462.

18. Freud, "Creative Writers and Daydreaming," in *On Creativity and the Unconscious* (New York: Harper & Brothers, 1958), 51; Smith, 126.

19. Ibid., 47; Smith, 126.

20. Even Florence in her suicide is "lying, quite respectably arranged" (75).

21. As Dowell reflects: "It is a queer and fantastic world. Why can't people have what they want? The things were all there to content everybody; yet everybody wants the wrong thing" (158). Moreover, it is as if Nancy's doleful tune were the melodic line of Dowell's minuet and meditations, with the minor chords finally drowning out all else in a series of digressive movements pounding over and over again. If *The Good Soldier* is explainable as Dowell's narcissistic minuet played upon projected characters, Nancy's melody running through Dowell's mind also is understandable in psychoanalytic terms. As Freud writes:

> Dreams *hallucinate*—they replace thoughts by hallucinations. In this respect there is no difference between visual and acoustic presentations. The meaning of a series of musical notes in one's mind . . . becomes transformed into a hal-

> lucination of the same melody; while if he [the dreamer] wakes up again—and the two states alternate more than once . . . the hallucination gives way in turn to the mnemonic presentation, which is at once fainter and qualitatively different from it.
>
> . . . Dreams construct a *situation* out of these images. (Freud, *The Interpretation of Dreams*, 50; Smith, 559)

The lyric couplet that Nancy sings is from "To the Willow Tree" by Robert Herrick, a poem apparently unknown to Nancy. Both Nancy's dirge and Herrick's final stanza close on a somber note. Nancy's song ends as it turns "dusk; the heavy, hewn, dark pillars that supported the gallery were like mourning presences; the fire had sunk to nothing" (149). Likewise Herrick's lines about two ill-fated lovers descend into a prison-like darkness:

> And underneath thy cooling shade
> When weary of the light
> The love-spent youth and love-sick maid
> Come to weep out the night.

22. Freud, "Creative Writers," 49; Smith, 1925.

23. Ibid., 51; Smith 1927.

24. Melanie Klein, "Notes on Some Schizoid Positions," *Developments in Psycho-Analysis* 27 (1946): 13.

25. Ibid., 15, 16.

26. Freud, "Family Romances," 238; Smith, 1987.

27. Ibid., 237; Smith, 1988, 1990.

28. In the first three chapters of Part One alone, Dowell describes persons and events with the extreme degree of exaggeration that characterizes dream distortion and the paranoiac's idealization tendency. Leonora's comment to Dowell about her trip home from the hunt ball is "the most amazing thing I had ever heard" (13). Florence's aunts call him "the laziest man in Philadelphia" (17). Old Hurlbird is "extraordinarily lovable" with "quite an extraordinary kind of heart" (17, 20). The Ashburnhams are in every respect the "perfect" country family, and Leonora's complexion has "a perfect clearness, a perfect smoothness" (23). Edward exhibits a "perfect expression" with "extraordinary" fair hair in a wave; has a "perfectly uniform" face (24) with eyes "perfectly honest, perfectly straightforward, perfectly stupid," running "perfectly" level with his eyelids; and casts a gaze "perfectly direct and perfectly level and perfectly unchanging" (26–27). And Leonora's referring to strangers as "nice people" is "an extraordinary thing to say. Quite extraordinary" (28).

29. On Dowell's Oedipal issues and infantilism, see Bruce Bassoff, "Oedipal Fantasy and Arrested Development in *The Good Soldier*," *Twentieth Century Literature: A Scholarly and Critical Journal* 34 (1) (Spring 1988): 40–47.

30. Dowell notes: "And he [Edward] loved, with a sentimental yearning, all children, puppies, and the feeble generally" (27).

31. On Dowell's would-be English identity, see Sarah Henstra, "Ford and the Costs of Englishness: 'Good Soldiering' as Performative Practice," *Studies in the Novel* 39 (2) (Summer 2007): 177–195.

32. Dowell says on page 87, "I am in love with Nancy Rufford . . . in my American sort of way."

33. Sigmund Freud (Smith [1990]), "Family Romances."

34. Freud, "Creative Writers," 152.

35. Dowell too is often kind and generous. He goes to Ceylon at Colonel Rufford's request to see if Nancy can recover from her madness (when Leonora refuses to go) and brings her home to England with him; he comes at a moment's notice to Branshaw at Edward's request to talk; he handles Old Hurlbird's charitable bequests with great care because he "didn't like the idea of their not being properly handled" (121); and he resolves (perhaps with the foolish impetuosity of Edward, as when he gives his home away) to leave all his money to young Carter, a distant relative "honest, industrious, high-spirited, friendly and ready to do anyone a good turn"—and whose "friendly image" he likes (155).

And yet, an irony shadows all of Dowell's acts of apparent generosity. His strenuous travels to help Nancy, his willingness to come to Edward at his summons, and his magnanimity toward Old Hurlbird and young Carter owe much to a plain fact: Dowell has nothing much else to do. The priorities of others fill up his life; he has time on his hands.

36. Freud, *The Interpretation of Dreams*, 490–491; Smith 930.

37. Schorer, introduction to Ford, *The Good Soldier*, xi.

38. Freud, *The Interpretation of Dreams*, 490–491; Smith 930.

39. This is in contrast to fully successful secondary revisions, which result in dreams that seem "logical and reasonable," arrive at conclusions "causing no surprise," and possess "an appearance of rationality" that veils a meaning "as far removed as possible from their true significance." Ibid.

40. Ibid.

41. This dream composition is composed mainly of "thought" (in contrast to the sensory images found in night-dreams) and represents an entity over which the dreamer has greater control. Comprehensive, fully successful secondary revisions are less likely with daydreams, which benefit from a "relaxation of censorship." Freud, *The Interpretation of Dreams*, 490–491; Smith 931–932.

42. Ibid., 670–688.

43. I am indebted for some of my observations to Patricia McFate and Bruce Golden, "*The Good Soldier*: A Tragedy of Self-Deception," *Modern Fiction Studies* 9 (1963): 50–60. But for opposing views, see R. W. Lid, "On the Time Scheme of *The Good Soldier*," *English Fiction in Transition* 4 (2) (1961): 9–10. Also see Richard Cassell, *Ford Madox Ford: A Study of His Novels* (Baltimore: Johns Hopkins University Press, 1961); and Patrick A. McCarthy, "In Search of Lost Time: Chronology and Narration in *The Good Soldier*," *English Literature in Transition (1880–1920)* 40 (2) (1997): 133–149.

44. This may not be entirely true. As Martin Stannard notes, "Trying to untangle the chronology has become a favourite party game for [the] Ford scholar" because the chronology *would* cohere "by altering one or two of the dates"—yet then "the book would

lose its power of self-deconstruction." Stannard allows that Ford himself may have made a few "mistakes," but he concludes that it's ultimately impossible to distinguish Ford's "intended errors" (to expose Dowell as an unreliable narrator) and the author's inadvertent inaccuracies. See "*The Good Soldier*: Editorial Problems," in *Ford Madox Ford's Modernity*, ed. Robert Hampson (Amsterdam: Rodop, 2003), 139.

45. No French translation survives in Ford's papers. Some scholars have cast doubt that he translated the full novel.

46. Dowell also meets Florence for the first time on Fourteenth Street (59). He may provide the would-be ages of Florence and Edward at the time of his writing to stress that their coterie was a "forty-ish" affair.

47. Sigmund Freud, *The Question of Lay Analysis*, 147; Smith, 4339.

48. Hanna Segal, *An Introduction to the Work of Melanie Klein* (New York: Basic Books, 1964), 70.

49. Melanie Klein, *The Psychoanalysis of Children* (London: Delacourt Press, 1975), 260.

50. Freud, *The Psychopathology of Everyday Life*, in *The Basic Writings of Sigmund Freud*, trans. and ed. A. A. Brill (New York: Modern Library, 1936), 247; Smith, 1317.

51. Ibid., 155.

52. Freud, "Libido Theory and Narcissim," 418; Smith, 3462.

53. According to folklorist numerology, to which Freud sometimes referred in his analyses of dream symbols and numbers, four represents the law of justice without mercy or tolerance. Its typical symbol is the square, whose four perfectly equal sides and angles symbolize divine justice. The number nine represents immutable truth, because it has the unique property of regenerating infinitely (e.g., $2 \times 9 = 18$, $1 + 8 = 9$; $3 \times 9 = 27$, $2 + 7 = 9$, $4 \times 9 = 36$, $3 + 6 = 9$). Nine is identified with Heaven and Hell. And in Dante's *Inferno*, the fourth circle contained all those who had abused the world's goods, particularly misers and spendthrifts. They carry dead weights in opposite directions when they meet and torment one another. Dante's ninth circle, the frozen waters of Cocytus, is where Satan is found and to which all the rivers of hell flow. Those who have done violence or betrayed their kin are punished here. For a good overview of the meaning of these two numbers in folklore and myth, see *Dictionary of Mythology, Folklore and Symbols*, ed. Gertrude Jobes (Lanham, MD: The Scarecrow Press, 1961), 605, 1171.

54. Sigmund Freud, "Introduction to Psycho-analysis and the War Neuroses"; Smith, 3667.

55. As we saw in Chapter Three, the concept has been formulated by René Girard, who posits that we usually desire love objects not for themselves, but rather because *others* possess them. See René Girard, *Violence and the Sacred* (Baltimore: Johns Hopkins University Press, 1981).

56. Sigmund Freud, "Psychoanalytic Notes on an Autobiographical Account of a Case of Paranoia," Standard Edition, vol. 12, 63.

57. Freud, "Creative Writers," 62; Smith, 140.

58. Ibid., 105; Smith, 139.

59. On these issues, see also Hoffman (note 8).

60. Hoffman, "Narrating Masculinity," 37.

61. Freud, "Creative Writers," 61; Smith, 130.

62. Ibid, 59; Smith, 128.

63. Freud, *Moses and Monotheism*; Smith, 4930.

64. Freud, *Future of an Illusion*; Smith, 4336.

65. Freud, "Creative Writers," 59; Smith, 126.

66. Ibid., 100; Smith, 137.

67. Freud, *Civilization and Its Discontents*, 54–55, 61.

68. Freud, *Beyond the Pleasure Principle*, 54–55.

69. Herbert Marcuse, *Eros and Civilization* (New York: Vintage Books, 1955), 137.

CHAPTER FIVE

1. Alistair Davies, "*Tarr*: A Nietzschean Novel," in *Wyndham Lewis: A Revaluation: New Essays*, ed. Jeffrey Meyers (London: The Athlone Press, 1980), 108 and *passim*. Coined by Alistair Davies, the term "Nietzschean novella" is usually applied to works such as Mann's *Death in Venice* that feature a hero who transcends the degenerate conditions of an ill or decaying social order and either succumbs to or triumphs over them. Of course, Lewis's *Tarr*, like the works of Mann, is a novel marked by numerous literary influences and philosophical currents. (Mann owes as much to Schopenhauer as Nietzsche, for example.)

What distinguishes Lewis's novel, however, and also makes the contention of a Nietzsche connection provocative and compelling, is that *Tarr*—unlike so much British fiction—bears strong affinities with a Continental European stream of fiction that is both open to stylistic experimentation and traffics in philosophical abstraction and essay-like reflection as part of the very plot and characterization. *Tarr* is not only a novel of ideas, but also an unprecedented literary experiment in British fiction with virtually no identifiable successors.

Critics such as Susan Sontag have written extensively about the differences in emphasis between British and Continental European fiction, finding the English-language novel much more conventional. Lewis is more "European" in this sense.

See, for instance, Susan Sontag: "A Report on the Journey," in *New York Times Book Review*, February 20, 2005, 16–18.

2. See, for instance, Eric P. Levy, "*Good Art Must Have No Inside*: The Mimesis of Cynicism in Wyndham Lewis's *Tarr*," *Wyndham Lewis Annual* 9-10 (2002–2003): 6–56; and Michael Nath, "Wyndham Lewis: A Review of the Thersitean Mode," *Wyndham Lewis Annual* (1994): 10–14.

3. Davies, "*Tarr*: A Nietzschean Novel," 109.

4. Wyndham Lewis, *The Art of Being Ruled* (London: Chatto and Windus, 1926), 113.

5. Ibid., 116.

6. See Alan Starr, "*Tarr* and Wyndham Lewis," ELH 49 (1) (Spring 1982): 179–189.

7. Davies, "*Tarr*: A Nietzschean Novel," 118.

8. On this point, see Starr, "*Tarr* and Wyndham Lewis."

9. "Art and Artist," in Otto Rank, *The Myth of the Birth of the Hero and Other Writings*, ed. Philip Freund (New York: Vintage Books, 1959), 149. Completed in 1932 under the title *Kunst und Künstler: Studien zur Genese und Entwicklung des Schaffensdranges*, Rank's study of the psychology of artistic living appeared first in English translation as *Art and Artist: Creative Urge and Personality Development* (New York: Tudor, 1932).

Written in German, yet not published until Rank had settled in New York City, *Art and Artist* is Rank's *chef d'oeuvre*. It warrants emphasis, however, that it has its origins in his first book, *Der Künstler* (Vienna: Hugo Heller, 1907). Written in 1905 when Rank was twenty-one, the fifty-six-page *Der Künstler* shows Rank's extraordinary precocity. Owing much to Freud and Wilhelm Stekel, and with a debt above all to Nietzsche, it represented the first psychoanalytic study published by a member of Freud's inner circle (besides Freud himself), and was the first book-length application of psychoanalysis to cultural history. Already we see Rank in this densely written essay groping toward his mature distinctions between the "creative" man and the neurotic, and indeed toward his brilliant conception of the neurotic as an *artiste manqué*. In a March 1909 letter, Freud praised *Der Künstler* as "the first introduction of psychology into historical studies." (Thus it preceded Freud's own initial foray, *Totem and Taboo* [1913], by several years.)

Der Künstler went through three subsequent, revised editions (two in 1918, and a much-expanded version in 1925) before the appearance of *Art and Artist*. Although *Der Künstler* was translated into English in 1923, Rank could not find a publisher for it. It was not published in English until 1980, under the sponsorship of the Otto Rank Association in its official journal. See *The Artist*, 4th ed., trans. Eva Salomon and E. James Lieberman, *Journal of the Otto Rank Association*, 15 (1) (1980). For information on the biographical aspects and publishing history of *Der Künstler*, see E. James Lieberman, *Acts of Will: The Life and Work of Otto Rank* (New York: Free Press, 1984), especially pages 42–43, 70, 80–82, 89, 98, 110, 111, 162, 163, and 204.

Inexplicably and with far greater injustice, *Art and Artist* suffered a similar fate in German to that of *Der Künstler* in English. Rank's masterwork went through five subsequent editions in English (1943, 1948, 1968, 1975, and 1989) before its publication under Rank's German title as *Kunst und Künstler: Studien zur Genese und Entwicklung des Schaffensdranges* (Giessen: Psychosozial-Verlag, 2000). Unless otherwise indicated, throughout this chapter I have used the original 1932 English-language edition of *Art and Artist*.

10. Nonetheless, even though Rank ultimately advanced a powerful critique of Nietzsche's psychology as he formulated his own conception of "will therapy," Nietzsche remained a revered figure and a lifelong intellectual presence for the mature Rank, as his goodbye meeting with Freud evinces. On 12 April 1926, Rank—now estranged from his erstwhile mentor and benefactor—paid his farewell call on Freud. His parting gift was an edition of the complete works of Nietzsche, recently published in twenty-three volumes bound in white leather. According to Rank's biographer, E. James Lieberman, "Rank's gift said, in effect: Here is the mentor of us both! Probably it also expressed Rank's undying wish to be understood better by the most important man in his life." E. James Lieberman, *Acts of Will: The Life and Work of Otto Rank* (New York: Free Press, 1985), 259–260. It is also worth noting that, although the Nazis permitted Freud to take only a small portion of his personal library with him when he emigrated to London

in 1938, he included the full set of Nietzsche volumes given to him by Rank. Although Rank and Freud never spoke or wrote to each other after this final meeting, Rank evidently did achieve some measure of his intention by means of his parting gift to Freud.

11. Although he or she is often a creative or performing artist, Rank's Artist is not restricted to being a painter, musician, writer, etc. He or she is a "creative person" who puts his will in the service of his personality and productive work. Also, the categories are only models, rarely found in their clinical forms. Virtually everyone possesses characteristics identifiable in at least two of the stages.

12. Unlike Freud, Jung, and Adler, Rank was not a medical doctor. His education was in literature and philosophy, and this fact doubtless explains much of the difference in subject matter and approach between Rank and the others.

13. Rank elaborates: "The creative impulse which leads to the liberation and forming of the individual personality—and likewise determines its artistic creativeness—has something positively anti-sexual in [it]. Correspondingly, my conception of repression differed from Freud's; for him it is the result of *outward* frustration, while I trace it to an *inward* necessity, which is no less inherent in the dualistic individual than the satisfying of the impulse itself." Rank, *Art and Artist* (New York: Agathon Press, 1968), xxiii.

14. Laura Langman, "The Estrangement of Being: An Existential Analysis of Otto Rank's Psychology," *Journal of Existential Psychiatry* 1 (1960–1961): 463. See also Otto Rank, *Beyond Psychology* (New York: Dover Books, 1958), 273: "How presumptive, and at the same time, naive, is this idea of simply removing human guilt by explaining it casually as 'neurotic.'" For an extended analysis of how Rank's views of self-renunciation, artistic productivity, and creative will bear on his view of neurosis, see R. G. Kainer, "Art and the Canvas of the Self: Otto Rank and Creative Transcendence," *American Imago* 41 (4) (Winter 1984): 359–372. Whereas Freud conceptualized neurosis within his theory of instinctual drives, Rank approached it as a failure of separation and individuation.

15. See Lewis's chapter on Nietzsche in *The Art of Being Ruled*, "Nietzsche as Vulgarizer," 113–118. For his views on Freud, see *Paleface: The Philosophy of the Melting Pot* (London: Chatto and Windus, 1929), where psychoanalysis is "a psychology foreign to the average European and his individualistic life" (208); "Freud and his assistants . . . have helped in short to build up the full Idiot, as he is emerging today" (238). Lewis considered Freud one of the chief villains advancing the "time-mind" philosophy of Bergson.

16. Young Rank on Nietzsche: "I bathed, as it were, in Nietzsche's spirit, and got charmed, weatherproof skin." See *Psychoanalytic Pioneers*, ed. Franz Alexander and Samuel Eisenstein (New York: Basic Books, 1966), 37. Late in life, in *Rude Assignment*, Lewis recalled that Nietzsche "was among my favorite reading" during his student days on the continent. See also E. W. F. Tomlin, "The Philosophical Influences," in *Wyndham Lewis: A Revaluation*, 29–46.

17. Tomlin called Lewis "the least provincial of modern English writers" in *Wyndham Lewis* (New York: The British Council, 1955), 7. Lewis's and Rank's writings both show a deep interest in the aesthetics of Wilhelm Worringer and Alois Riegl. Lewis was fluent in German and Rank thoroughly familiar with English literature of all periods. In a sense, Lewis was the practicing painter and writer that Rank wished he could have been. Some historians believe that Rank's failure to pursue a vocation in the lit-

erary or fine arts may account for his deep anxieties about both psychoanalysis and his break with Freud. As Philip Freund has observed, "Rank, feeling himself destined to be an artist, [was] diverted into the realm of psychology instead. . . . As a result, he had guilt feelings and a sense of inner conflict all his life. He attempted, therefore, to make psychoanalysis a new art form." Introduction to *Myth of the Birth of the Hero and Other Writings*, x.

18. Of Lewis's undeserved neglect, Fredric Jameson has written: "Lewis, unread, is customarily lumped together for convenience with the great moderns who were his sometime friends. . . . This honor . . . only serves to obscure the nature of his originality." Fredric Jameson, *Fables of Aggression: Wyndham Lewis, the Modernist as Fascist* (Berkeley: University of California Press, 1979), 87. Several of Rank's admirers have also sought to resurrect him. Jack Jones believes Rank "will probably turn out to have been the best mind psychoanalysis contributed to intellectual history" (*Commentary* 30 [1960]: 229). Jones elaborates on this view in "Five Types of Psychological Man: A Critical Analysis," *Salmagundi* 10 (1972): 86–114. Perhaps the greatest tribute to Rank, delivered on the publication of Rank's heterodox *The Trauma of Birth* (1923), was Freud's: "I don't know whether 66 or 33 percent of it is true, but in any case it is the most important progress since the discovery of psychoanalysis." Quoted in Ernest Jones, *The Life and Work of Sigmund Freud* (New York: Basic Books, 1957), 59. For details about Rank's life in general and his relationship to Freud in particular, see E. James Lieberman, *Acts of Will: The Life and Work of Otto Rank* (New York: Free Press, 1985).

19. Rank's theories have also been applied to two other great European modernist novels, Joyce's *Ulysses* and Proust's *À la recherche*. See Levy (note 2); and Stephen G. Brown, "The Curse of the 'Little Phrase': Swann and the Sorrows of the Sapphic Sublime," *College Literature* 30 (4) (Fall 2003): 89–113. See also Michael L. Shuman, "'A Woman's Face, or Worse': Otto Rank and the Modernist Identity," *Dissertation Abstracts International* 68 (4) (Oct 2007): 1455.

20. Otto Rank, *Will Therapy and Truth and Reality* (New York: Knopf, 1945), 209–210. Also quoted in Patrick Mullahy's classic on psychoanalysis (with a good summary of Rank's positions), *Oedipus: Myth and Complex: A Review of Psychoanalytic Theory* (New York: Hermitage House, 1948), 177.

21. Otto Rank, *The Trauma of Birth* (New York: Brunner, 1952), 190.

22. Rank's concept of the birth trauma is applied in related yet distinctive ways to my approach to *Tarr* by Stephen Watt in his chapter "[Eugene] O'Neill and Otto Rank: Doubles, 'Death Instincts,' and the Trauma of Birth," in *Critical Approaches to O'Neill*, ed. John H. Stroupe (New York: AMS, 1988). See also Maureen Frances Voigt, "Rank, Ibsen, and O'Neill: Birth Trauma and Creative Will in Selected Dramas," *Dissertation Abstracts International* 53 (2) (Aug 1992): 352A.

23. Rank, *Trauma*, 192.

24. Rank, *Art and Artist*, 19.

25. Mullahy, *Oedipus*, 182.

26. Rank, *Art and Artist*, 9.

27. Otto Rank, *Beyond Psychology* (New York: Dover Books, 1958), 50.

28. W. K. Rose, ed., *The Letters of Wyndham Lewis* (London: Methuen, 1963), 76.

29. "I make *Tarr* too much of my mouthpiece in his analysis of Humour, etc." Ibid.

30. Rank, *Art and Artist*, xii.

31. Wyndham Lewis, *Time and Western Man* (London: Chatto and Windus, 1927), 299–300.

32. Rank, *Art and Artist*, 288.

33. Ibid., 293.

34. "Cape" because his father "was a wealthy merchant at the Cape" (of Good Hope); "Cantabian" because Lewis has added an unusual suffix to "Cantab.," itself short for *Cantabrigiensis*, meaning (in Latin) "of Cambridge [University]," where Hobson matriculated.

35. Otto Rank, *Truth and Reality: A Life History of the Human Will* (New York: Knopf, 1936), 117.

36. Ibid., 119.

37. Ibid., 120.

38. Lewis, *Art of Being Ruled*, 118.

39. Ibid.

40. At least, this seems to be his protagonist's (if not Lewis's) intention. Rank and Hanns Sachs note in *Psychoanalysis as an Art and a Science*: "The artist can experience more in a very small event than the average man in the gayest adventures, because this is the only way for him to become acquainted with his inner Kingdom." (1913; Detroit: Wayne State University Press, 1968), 112.

41. Rank, *Truth and Reality*, 119.

42. Rank, *Art and Artist*, 59.

43. Ibid., 37.

44. Ibid., 39.

45. Ibid., 288. Rank posited that the urge for immortality was the human being's most powerful drive. In *Psychology of the Soul* and other works, he elaborated this view in such a way as to move beyond psychology and embrace an essentially religious view of history and human nature. On these points, see Marvin Goldwert, "Otto Rank and Man's Urge to Immortality," *Journal of the History of the Behavioural Sciences* 21 (2) (April 1985): 169–177.

46. Rank, *Truth and Reality*, 60.

47. Rank, *Art and Artist*, 428.

48. Ibid., 180.

49. Ibid., 149.

50. On the relation to these themes of Vorticism, see Michael Wutz, "The Energetics of *Tarr*: the Vortex-Machine Kreisler," *Modern Fiction Studies* 38 (1992): 845–869. See also Michael Nath (note 2); and Walter Michel, "On the Genesis of *Tarr*," *Enemy News: Journal of the Wyndham Lewis Society* 22 (Spring 1986): 22, 38–41.

51. Rank, *Myth*, 169.

52. Lewis often trafficks in *Tarr* in stereotypes such as "the Pole," "the German," "the French," etc. For an analysis of their significance in the novel, see Paul Peppis, "Anti-Individualism and the Fictions of National Character in Wyndham Lewis's *Tarr*," *Twentieth Century Literature: A Scholarly and Critical Journal* 40 (1994): 226–255. See

also Andreas Kramer, "Nationality and Avant-Garde: Anglo-German Affairs in Wyndham Lewis's *Tarr*," in Susanne Stark, *The Novel in Anglo-German Context: Cultural Cross-Currents and Affinities* (Amsterdam: Rodopi, 2000), 253–262.

53. Rank, *Art and Artist*, 27.

54. Sigmund Freud, "Inhibitions, Symptoms and Anxiety," in *The Complete Psychological Works of Sigmund Freud*, ed. James Strachey (London: The Hogarth Press, 1961), 106.

55. Sigmund Freud, "Libido Theory and Narcissism"; Smith, 3468.

56. Freud, "Inhibitions, Symptoms and Anxiety," 105.

57. A valuable comparative psychoanalytic study that comes to conclusions about Rank that differ somewhat from my own is Peter L. Rudnytsky, *Reading Psychoanalysis: Freud, Rank, Ferenczi, Groddeck* (Ithaca, NY: Cornell University Press, 2002).

58. See Rank's suggestive analysis of Shakespeare's and Michelangelo's sonnets. *Myth*, 158–162.

59. Rank, *Art and Artist*, 391.

60. Ibid.

61. Ibid., 152.

62. Ibid., 271.

63. "Dithyrambos" refers to Dionysus, meaning "double-doored." Dionysus entered life by the womb of his mother and the thigh of his father.

64. "Kreis" also means "top," and Kreisler "waltzes" at the dance like a whizzing top.

65. Rank, *Art and Artist*, 337.

66. Ibid., 372.

67. Ibid., 288.

68. Ibid., 289.

69. Ibid., 288.

70. Ibid.

71. Robert Chapman has called Tarr "one of the most self-aware characters in literature." See *Wyndham Lewis: Fictions and Satires* (London: Vision Press, 1973), 75. I agree, but Tarr's relationship to Anastasya exposes his fatal blind spot: the place of an intelligent woman in his aesthetic. On this point, see Ina Verstl, "*Tarr*—A Joke Too Deep for Laughter? The Comic, the Body and Gender," *Enemy News: Journal of the Wyndham Lewis Society* 33 (Winter 1991): 4–9.

72. Rank, *Art and Artist*, 288.

73. Ibid., 39.

74. Lewis's introduction to the London edition of *Time and Western Man* sounds like a Rankian "nomination": "For our only terra firma in a boiling and shifting world is, after all, our 'self.' That must cohere. . . . I will side and identify myself with the powerfullest Me, and in its interests I will work." *Time and Western Man*, 5, 6.

75. Rank, *Art and Artist*, 144.

76. Ibid., 169–170. Also see Rank, *Myth*, 169: "The artist is . . . primarily an individual . . . who is unable or unwilling to accept the dominant immortality-ideology of his age—whether religious, social or other . . . because it is collective, whereas he aspires to an individual immortality."

77. Rank, *Art and Artist*, 171–172.

78. For a discussion of Tarr's illusions as they relate to convictions about art, see Levy (note 2).

79. "No one could have a coarser, more foolish, slovenly taste than I have in women. . . . All the delicate psychology another man naturally seeks in a woman, the curiosity of form, windows on other lives, love and passion, I seek in my work and not elsewhere" (26).

80. Rank, *Art and Artist*, 288.

81. Ibid., 160.

82. Ibid., 159.

83. For an extended Rankian analysis of rivalry patterns in folk narratives, see Melville Herskovits and Frances Herskovits, "Sibling Rivalry, the Oedipus Complex, and Myth," *Psychology and Myth*, ed. Robert A. Segal (New York: Garland, 1996), 181–195.

84. On the topic of role substitution and doubling, see Watt (note 22).

85. Rank, *Art and Artist*, 191.

86. Ibid., 232.

87. Lewis echoes this in *The Wild Body*: "We are not constructed to be absolute observers." *The Wild Body* (New York: Harcourt, Brace and Co., 1921), 246–247.

88. Lewis's misogynistic personal views again suggest that he speaks in the novel through his protagonist Tarr: "Eventually, I believe, a considerable segregation of men and women must occur, just as segregation of those who decide for the active, the intelligent life, and those who decide (without any stigma attached to the choice) for the 'lower' or animal life, is likely to happen, and is very much to be desired." Lewis, *Art of Being Ruled*, 179.

89. Rank, *Art and Artist*, 245–246.

90. Rank, *Art and Artist*, 246. "Rose Fawcett," suggesting sentimental flux, and "Prism Dirkes," suggesting brilliance and self-reflection, imply a sad perpetuation and intensification of Tarr's conflict.

91. Ibid., 378–379.

92. Ibid., 72.

93. Ibid., 241.

94. Rank considered the Apollonian a "higher" type, with the Romantic closer to the "neurotic."

95. Ibid., 293.

96. Rank believed that the full expression of the creative will would unleash the best potentialities within human nature. Such expression is manifested in self-affirming, responsible choice, which forms the basis of the art of living. Esther Menaker provides an insightful discussion of these aspects of Rankian psychology in "Creativity as the Central Concept in the Psychology of Otto Rank," *Journal of the Otto Rank Association* 11 (2) (Winter 1976–1977): 1–17. See also William Rickel, "Concepts of Power in Personality as seen by Otto Rank and Reinhold Niebuhr," *Journal of Psychotherapy as a Religious Process* 3 (1956): 77–91.

CHAPTER SIX

1. Harrison contends:

> There is a tendency to assume a consequential relationship between metaphysical ideas and imaginative writing. Lawrence, however, in his foreword to *Fantasia of the Unconscious*, claimed the reverse, that his "pseudo-philosophy," as he ironically called it, was "deduced" from his imaginative writings. These [writings] are "pure passionate experience," whereas the philosophy consists of "inferences made afterwards, from the experience" (11). It was his "absolute need" (10) for some sort of satisfactory mental attitude towards himself and to the external world that made him abstract definite conclusions from his experiences as a man and a writer, although this metaphysic must always subserve the artistic purpose beyond the artist's conscious aim. Whether such a claim is justified, or simply an imaginative writer's attempt to assert the primacy of intuitive perceptions over rational analysis, is an important question regarding the relationship between his art and his metaphysic, and the nature of his creative processes. . . . Where commentators have examined the ways in which Lawrence's intellectual themes are incorporated into his fiction, they have tended to do so by adopting the consequential view that his ideas pre-existed their imaginative expression.

See John R. Harrison, "The Flesh and the Word: The Evolution of a Metaphysic in the Early Work of D. H. Lawrence," *Studies in the Novel* 32 (Spring 2000): 36. On these points, see also Daniel Dervin, "D. H. Lawrence and Freud," *American Imago* 36 (1979): 95-117.

2. Nonetheless, studies such as Daniel Weiss's *Oedipus in Nottingham* treat Lawrence's novels as little more than fictional illustrations of Freudian psychoanalysis. Similarly, Alan Friedman begins an essay on Lawrence with the assertion, "D. H. Lawrence was a virtual textbook embodiment of Freud's theories about the pleasure principle and the death instinct."

My own view is, however, much closer to that of Eugene Goodheart, who opened a pioneering article devoted to Lawrence's metaphysics as follows:

> No modern writer presents such formidable problems to the Freudian critic as does Lawrence. Unlike the work of other "psychological" writers, Lawrence's work defies the Freudian categories. Indeed, Lawrence's psychology has its own laws which are irreducible to the laws of Freudian psychology . . . Lawrence, like Freud, looks beneath the surface of literary works to find unspoken psychological motives. But even in the criticism the resemblance is external. Where Freudian criticism tends to reduce a work to a meaning that seems to compromise its original value for us, Lawrence's criticism (*Studies in Classic American Literature* is a beautiful instance) recreates the work, releasing its most vital tendencies.

See Alan Friedman, "D. H. Lawrence: Pleasure and Death," *Studies in the Novel* 32 (Summer 2000): 207; and Eugene Goodheart, "Freud and Lawrence," *Psychoanalytic Review* 47 (1960): 56.

3. John Worthen, *D. H. Lawrence, The Early Years, 1885–1912* (Cambridge: Cambridge University Press, 1991), 210.

4. Worthen, *D. H. Lawrence*, 211–212.

5. Ibid., 211.

6. Ibid.

7. Ibid.

8. Ibid., 549.

9. H. M. Daleski, *The Forked Flame* (London: Faber and Faber, 1965), 136.

10. F. R. Leavis, *D. H. Lawrence: Novelist* (London: Faber & Faber, 1955), 181.

11. Daleski, *Forked Flame*, 136.

12. Ibid.

13. Ibid.

14. As Daleski observes, the beetle image also surfaces in Lawrence's correspondence during the early stages of *Women in Love*'s composition. Lawrence writes: "We have had another influx of visitors: David Garnett and Francis Birrell turned up the other day—Saturday. I like David, but Birrell I have come to detest. These horrible little frowsy people, men lovers of men, they give me such a sense of corruption, almost putrescence, that I dream of beetles. It is abominable. . . ." Letter to S. S. Koteliansky (April 1915). See D. H. Lawrence, *Collected Letters* (New York: Viking Press, 1962), vol. I, 333.

15. Robert Chamberlain, "Pussum, Minette, and the Afro-Nordic Symbol in Lawrence's Women in Love," PMLA 78 (1963): 407.

16. Lawrence's satirical target is London Bloomsbury. For instance, Hermione Roddice is based on Lady Ottoline Morrell. Minette's lover, the languid, spineless Julius Halliday, is Lytton Strachey. Gudrun Brangwen and her lover Gerald Crich are drawn (with considerable exaggeration of their negative attributes) from the (subsequently married) couple Katherine Mansfield and John Middleton Murry. (Lawrence wrote these scenes while he was residing with Katherine and Murry in 1916.) As I discuss at greater length, the artist Loerke is a vicious and thinly veiled portrait of Mark Gertler, Dora Carrington's first lover. Loerke is also partly based on the sculptor Gaudier-Brzeska, which partly explains both Loerke's artistic profession and clarifies some of his personal proclivities.

17. See Lawrence, *Collected Letters*. Lawrence explicitly satirizes this work of Gertler in his portrait of Loerke, mentioning Loerke's "roundabouts." This is a transparent allusion to Gertler's *Merry-Go-Round* (later *Roundabout*), an anti-war sculpture in which the horses (and figures depicted on them) are mechanized as a protest against the manufacture of human cannon fodder by the war machine state.

18. Gretchen Gerzina, *Carrington: A Life of Dora Carrington, 1893–1932* (London: John Murray, 1989).

19. Letter to Julia Strachey, quoted in Gerzina, *Carrington*, xviii.

20. On "my daydream character," see Jan Marsh, *Bloomsbury Women: Distinct Figures*

in Life and Art (New York: Henry Holt and Company, 1995), 97. See also Jeffrey Meyers, *Painting and the Novel* (Manchester: Manchester University Press, 1975), 69; Gerzina, *Carrington*; Jane Hill, *The Art of Dora Carrington* (London: Thames and Hudson, 1994); Virginia Nicholson, *Among the Bohemians: Experiments in Living, 1900–1939* (London: Viking, 2002).

21. However inflated Carrington's reputation may have become in recent decades, it is undeniably true that Lawrence undervalued her and completely omitted reference to her talents in *Women in Love*. Her reputation began to ascend in 1976 when Sir John Rothenstein, formerly director of the Tate Gallery in London, declared that Carrington was "the most neglected serious painter of her time." Quoted in Gerzina, *Carrington*, xv.

22. Meyers, *Painting*, 69.

23. Quoted in Michael Holroyd, *Lytton Strachey, A Critical Biography: The Years of Achievement, 1910–1932* (New York: Holt, Rinehart, and Winston, 1968), 187.

24. Letter of 4 March 1924, Dora Carrington, *Letters*, ed. David Garnett (London, 1970), 283. Quoted in Meyers, *Painting*, 69.

25. For other, different resonances implied by the name change, see Lucas Carpenter, "The Name 'Minette' in *Women in Love*," *English Language Notes* 32.1 (September 1994): 70–73.

26. See, for example, D. H. Lawrence, *Studies in Classic American Literature* (New York: Penguin, 1977), 57–58. For an insightful discussion of these issues, see Leo Hamalian, "D. H. Lawrence and Black Writers," *Journal of Modern Literature* 16.4 (Spring 1990): 579–596.

27. Lawrence's views on race and gender have generated much controversy and critical commentary. Recent critics have argued that Lawrence's embattled psyche led him to devise a grandiose racial philosophy determined by—and displacing—his deep misogyny. For instance, as Granofsky notes:

> Races seem to be polarized for Lawrence by their degree of feminization. Races which he disapproves of—English and Jewish primarily—are either female in cultural predilection or produce men who are cowed to the point of impotence. Women become "cocksure," men "hensure," in Lawrence's terms. Those of whom he approves—Italians for a time, American natives, Aztecs—put women in their place. . . . Race becomes a displaced battleground for Lawrence's fight with women, a fight he would like to give the aura of political significance but which in reality stems from his childhood dependence upon his mother. . . . In Lawrence's case, the hidden roots of anti-Semitism appear to lie in an equally irrational but more understandable (because traceable) misogyny. His work retains its fascination, among other things, as the creation of a tremendously conflicted man whose struggles can teach us something about race hatred.

Ronald Granofsky, "'Jews of the Wrong Sort': D. H. Lawrence and Race," *Journal of Modern Literature* 23.2 (Winter 1999–2000): 222–223. See also Booth's essay on Lawrence's attitudes to race within the twin contexts of psychoanalysis and of post-colonial theories about the construction of subjectivity: Howard J. Booth, "'Give me *differences*': Lawrence, Psychoanalysis, and Race," *D. H. Lawrence Review* 27 (1997–1998): 190.

28. J. B. Bullen, "D. H. Lawrence and Sculpture in 'Women in Love,'" *The Burlington Magazine* 145.1209 (December 2003): 841–846. As we have noted, the character of Hermione Roddice is also based on a Bloomsbury acquaintance of Lawrence, Lady Ottoline Morrell. In the view of many critics and readers, she is also ill-treated by Lawrence's portrait in *Women in Love*.

29. For an insightful discussion of Lawrence's treatment of primitivism in *Women in Love*, see Brett Neilson, "D. H. Lawrence's 'Dark Page': Narrative Primitivism in *Women in Love* and *The Plumed Serpent*," *Twentieth Century Literature* 43.3 (Fall 1997): 310–326. Neilson observes: "The 'unspiritual knowledge' of primitivism suggests to him a mode of sexual activity that is free from the normative constraints of heterosexuality. . . . The fetish offers Birkin precisely the flexibility he is denied by the novel's plot, an 'other way' that would leave him free to marry Ursula and to pursue an intimate relationship with Gerald."

30. Analogously, whereas Gudrun creates diminutive figures in a modern "primitive" style, Halliday collects primitive or African carvings.

31. For a probing inquiry into Gudrun's mentality and the novel's epistemology, see Jack F. Stewart, "Dialectics of Knowing in *Women in Love*," *Twentieth Century Literature* 37.1 (Spring 1991): 59–76.

32. Jack F. Stewart makes this connection in "Dialectics of Knowing in *Women in Love*."

33. See Ronald Granofsky, "'Jews of the Wrong Sort': D. H. Lawrence and Race," 218.

34. D. H. Lawrence, *Fantasia of the Unconscious: Psychoanalysis and the Unconscious* (New York: Penguin, 1960), 126–127.

35. On these points, see John B. Humma, in "Lawrence in Another Light: *Women in Love* and Existentialism," *Studies in the Novel* 24.4 (Winter 1992): 391–410.

36. Bullen, "Lawrence and Sculpture," 842.

37. Ibid., 841.

38. On the relation between "diabolic reducing down," touching "rock bottom," and the dynamics of sexual attraction in the novel, see Gerald Doherty, "A Question of Gravity: The Erotics of Identification in *Women in Love*," *D. H. Lawrence Review* 29.2 (2000): 25–41.

39. As Andrew Howe observes, Gerald "is most definitely a sadist in every sense of the word, with the other three characters at various times exhibiting both masochistic and sadistic qualities." Howe argues that Lawrence "sidesteps" bringing the sadomasochism issue from the "private to the public by having the sadistic acts carried out against animals instead of humans":

> In *Women in Love*, the struggles inherent in human relationships, ones based on dominance and ownership, are projected onto animal proxies. . . . Gerald Crich is abusive and cruel to both mare and rabbit, slashing the former with spurs and

> nearly killing the latter with a blow to the head. As Gudrun doubles these two animals, Gerald is exacting this dominant behavior on her. He owns her and can do with her as he wishes. The sadistic and masochistic needs for violence between the two human characters can only be fully explored through the use of animal doubles.

See Andrew Howe, "Beastly Desire: Human/Animal Interactions in Lawrence's *Women in Love*," *Papers on Language & Literature* 38.4 (Fall 2002): 430–431.

Selected Bibliography

Alter, Robert. *Rogue's Progress*. Cambridge: Harvard University Press, 1964.

Beasley, Jerry C. "Amiable Apparitions: Smollett's Fictional Heroines." In *Augustan Subjects: Essays in Honor of Martin C. Battestin*, 229–248. Ed. Albert J. Rivero. Newark, DE: University of Delaware Press, 1997.

Boucé, Paul-Gabriel. *The Novels of Tobias Smollett*. New York: Longman, 1976.

Brown, Ford K. *The Life of William Godwin*. New York: E. P. Dutton, 1926.

Brown, Norman O. *Life Against Death*. New York: Anchor Books, 1962.

Bruce, Donald. *Radical Doctor Smollett*. London: Victor Gollancz, 1964.

Bruhm, Steven. "Roderick Random's Closet." *English Studies in Canada* 19.4 (1993): 401–415.

Bullen, J. B. "D. H. Lawrence and Sculpture in 'Women in Love.'" *The Burlington Magazine* 145.1209 (December 2003): 841–846.

Carpenter, Lucas. "The Name 'Minette' in *Women in Love*." *English Language Notes* 32 (1994): 70–73.

Chamberlain, Robert. "Pussum, Minette, and the Afro-Nordic Symbol in Lawrence's *Women in Love*." PMLA 78 (1963): 407–416.

Clemit, Pamela. *The Godwinian Novel: The Rational Fictions of Godwin, Brockden Brown, Mary Shelley*. Oxford: Oxford University Press, 1993.

Daleski, H. M. "Figures in the Carpet." *Victorian Literature and Culture* 19 (1991): 257–275.

———. *The Forked Flame*. London: Faber and Faber, 1965.

Davies, Alistair. "*Tarr*: A Nietzschean Novel." In *Wyndham Lewis: A Revaluation—New Essays*. Ed. Jeffrey Meyers. London: Athlone Press, 1980.

Dike, D. A. "A Modern *Oedipus*: *The Mayor of Casterbridge*." *Essays in Criticism* 2 (1952): 169–179.

Doherty, Gerald. "A Question of Gravity: The Erotics of Identification in *Women in Love*." *D. H. Lawrence Review* 29 (2000): 25–41.

Edwards, Duane. "*The Mayor of Casterbridge* as Aeschylean Tragedy." *Studies in the Novel* 4 (1972): 608–618.

Ermarth, Elizabeth. *Realism and Consensus in the English Novel*. Princeton: Princeton University Press, 1983.

Fodor, Nancy, ed. *Dictionary of Psychoanalysis*. New York: Philosophical Library, 1950.

Ford, Ford Madox. *The Good Soldier*. Second edition. Ed. Martin Stannard. New York: W. W. Norton, 2012.

Freud, Sigmund. *Civilization and Its Discontents*. London: Hogarth Press, 1946.

———. *The Standard Edition of the Complete Psychological Works of Sigmund Freud*. Ed. James Strachey. London: The Hogarth Press, 1961.

———. *Freud—Complete Works*. Electronic edition of *The Standard Edition of the Complete Psychological Works of Sigmund Freud* (ed. James Strachey). Published by Ivan Smith, 2000.

———. *An Outline of Psychoanalysis*. New York: W. W. Norton, 1969.

———. *The Question of Lay Analysis*. Ed. James Strachey. New York: W. W. Norton, 1978, 1950.

Furbank, P. N. "Godwin's Novels." *Essays in Criticism* 5 (1955): 214–228.

Girard, René. *Deceit, Desire, and the Novel*. Baltimore: Johns Hopkins University Press, 1965.

———. "Myth and Ritual in Shakespeare: *A Midsummer Night's Dream*." In *Textual Strategies*. Ed. Josue Harari. Ithaca: Cornell University Press, 1977.

———. *To Double Business Bound*. Baltimore: Johns Hopkins University Press, 1978.

———. *Violence and the Sacred*. Baltimore: Johns Hopkins University Press, 1977.

Godwin, William. *Enquiry Concerning Political Justice and its Influence on Morals and Happiness*. Ed. F. E. L. Priestly. Toronto: University of Toronto Press, 1946.

———. "Of Human Innocence," "Of the Rebelliousness of Man," and "Of Self-Love and Benevolence." In *Thoughts on Man*. London: Effingham Wilson, 1831.

———. *Things As They Are, or The Adventures of Caleb Williams*. New York: Rinehart Press, 1960.

Gold, Alex. "It's Only Love: The Politics of Passion in Godwin's *Caleb Williams*." *Texas Studies in Language and Literature* 19 (1977): 135–160.

Goldberg, M. A. *Smollett and the Scottish School*. Albuquerque: University of New Mexico Press, 1959.

Graham, Kenneth W. *The Politics of Narrative: Ideology and Social Change in William Godwin's Caleb Williams*. New York: AMS Press, 1990.

Granofsky, Ronald. "'Jews of the Wrong Sort': D. H. Lawrence and Race." *Journal of Modern Literature* 23.2 (Winter 1999–2000): 209–223.

Grant, Damian. *Tobias Smollett: A Study in Style*. Manchester: Manchester University Press, 1977.

Gregor, Ian. *The Great Web: The Form of Hardy's Major Fiction*. London: Faber and Faber, 1974.

Hamalian, Leo. "D. H. Lawrence and Black Writers." *Journal of Modern Literature* 16.4 (Spring 1990): 579–596.

Handwerk, Gary, ed. *Caleb Williams/William Godwin*. Peterborough, Ontario: Broadview, 2000.

Hardy, Florence. *The Early Life of Thomas Hardy*. New York: Macmillan, 1928.

———. *The Later Years of Thomas Hardy*. London: Macmillan, 1930.
Hardy, Thomas. *Jude the Obscure*. London: Harper and Brothers, 1895.
———. *The Life and Death of the Mayor of Casterbridge, A Story of a Man of Character*. New York: New American Library, 1962.
———. *The Return of the Native*. New York: Signet, 1999.
———. *Tess of the D'Urbervilles*. 1891. Ed. Juliet Grindle and Simon Gatrell. Oxford: Clarendon, 1983.
Highsmith, James. "Smollett's Nancy Williams: A Mirror for Maggie." *English Miscellany* 23 (1972): 113–123.
Holroyd, Michael. *Lytton Strachey, A Critical Biography: The Years of Achievement, 1910–1932*. New York: Holt, Rinehart, and Winston, 1968.
Howe, Andrew. "Beastly Desire: Human/Animal Interactions in Lawrence's *Women in Love*." *Papers on Language & Literature* 38.4 (Fall 2002): 430–431.
Humma, John B. "Lawrence in Another Light: *Women in Love* and Existentialism." *Studies in the Novel* 24.4 (Winter 1992): 392–410.
Hunter, J. Paul. *Before Novels: The Cultural Contexts of Eighteenth-Century English Fiction*. New York: Norton, 1990.
Hunter, Richard, and Ida Macalpine. "Smollett's Reading in Psychiatry." *Modern Language Review* 51 (1966): 409–411.
Hynes, Samuel. "The Epistemology of *The Good Soldier*." *Sewanee Review* (1961): 225–235.
Ingersoll, Earl. "Staging the Gaze in D. H. Lawrence's *Women in Love*." *Studies in the Novel* 26.3 (Fall 1994): 268–281.
Kietzman, Mary Jo. *Mary Carleton: The Self-Fashioning of an Early Modern Englishwoman*. Burlington, VT: Ashgate, 2004.
Klein, Melanie. "Contribution to the Psychogenesis of Manic-Depressive States." In *Contributions to Psychoanalysis*, 262–289. London: The Hogarth Press and the Institute of Psychoanalysis, 1948.
———. "Mourning and Its Relation to the Manic-Depressive States." In *Contributions to Psychoanalysis*, 347–360. London: The Hogarth Press and the Institute of Psychoanalysis, 1948.
———. "Notes on Some Schizoid Positions." In *Developments in Psychoanalysis*, 207–219. London: The Hogarth Press and the Institute of Psychoanalysis, 1952.
———. *The Psychoanalysis of Children*. London: Delacorte Press, 1975.
Lawrence, D. H. *Fantasia of the Unconscious and Psychoanalysis and the Unconscious*. New York: Penguin, 1960.
———. *Studies in Classic American Literature*. New York: Penguin, 1990.
———. *Women in Love*. 1922. New York: Viking Press, 1996.
Leavis, F. R. *D. H. Lawrence: Novelist*. London: Faber and Faber, 1955.
Levenson, Michael. "D. H. Lawrence's 'Dark Page': Narrative Primitivism in *Women in Love* and *The Plumed Serpent*." *Twentieth Century Literature* 43.3 (Fall 1997): 310–326.
Levy, Eric. "'Good Art Must Have No Inside': The Mimesis of Cynicism in Wyndham Lewis's *Tarr*." *Wyndham Lewis Annual* 9–10 (2002–2003): 6–56.
Lewis, Wyndham. *The Art of Being Ruled*. London: Chatto and Windus, 1926.
———. *Collected Letters*. Ed. W. K. Rose. London: Methuen, 1963.

———. *Paleface: The Philosophy of the Melting Pot*. New York: Gordon Press, 1972.
———. *Tarr*. Ed. Paul O'Keefe. Santa Rosa, CA: Black Sparrow Press, 1990.
———. *Time and Western Man*. London: Chatto and Windus, 1927.
Lieberman, E. James. *Acts of Will: The Life and Work of Otto Rank*. New York: Free Press, 1984.
Linebaugh, Peter. *The London Hanged: Criminal and Civil Society in the Eighteenth Century*. Cambridge: Cambridge University Press, 1992.
Mancing, Howard. "The Protean Picaresque." In *The Picaresque: Tradition and Displacement*, 273–291. Ed. Giancarlo Maiorino. Minneapolis: University of Minnesota Press, 1996.
Marcuse, Herbert. *Eros and Civilization*. New York: Vintage Books, 1955.
McFate, Patricia, and Bruce Golden. "*The Good Soldier*: A Tragedy of Self-Deception." *Modern Fiction Studies* 9 (1963): 50–60.
Miller, J. Hillis. *Thomas Hardy: Distance and Desire*. Cambridge: Harvard University Press, 1970.
Monro, D. H. *Godwin's Moral Philosophy*. London: Oxford University Press, 1953.
Nath, Michael. "Wyndham Lewis: A Review of the Thersitean Mode." *Wyndham Lewis Annual* (1994): 10–14.
Pinion, F. B. *A Hardy Companion*. London: Macmillan, 1976.
Rank, Otto. *Art and Artist: Creative Urge and Personality Development*. New York: Tudor, 1932.
———. *The Artist*. Fourth edition. Trans. Eva Salomon and E. James Lieberman. *Journal of the Otto Rank Assocation* 15 (1), 1980.
———. *Beyond Psychology*. New York: Dover Books, 1958.
———. *The Myth of the Birth of the Hero and Other Writings*. Ed. Philip Freund. New York: Vintage Books, 1959.
———. *The Trauma of Birth*. New York: Brunner, 1952.
———. *Truth and Reality: A Life History of the Human Will*. New York: Knopf, 1936.
Rosenblum, Michael. "Smollett as Conservative Satirist." *Journal of English Literary History* 42 (1975): 556–579.
Ross, Ian Campbell. "Language, Structure, and Vision in Smollett's *Roderick Random*." *Etudes Anglaises* 31 (1978): 52–63.
Sander, Fred M. "Psychoanalysis, Drama, and the Family: The Ever-Widening Scope." *Annual of Psychoanalysis* 29 (2001): 279–300.
Sartre, Jean-Paul. *Search for a Method*. New York: Vintage, 1963.
Schweik, Robert. "Character and Fate in Hardy's *Mayor of Casterbridge*." *Nineteenth-Century Fiction* 21 (December 1966): 249–262.
Segal, Hanna. *An Introduction to the Work of Melanie Klein*. New York: Basic Books, 1964.
Sena, John. "Smollett's Portrait of Narcissa's Aunt: The Genesis of an Original." *English Language Notes* 14 (1977): 270–275.
Sherman, G. W. *The Pessimism of Thomas Hardy*. Madison, NJ: Farleigh Dickinson, 1976.
Smith, Ivan. *Freud—Complete Works*. Electronic edition of *The Standard Edition of the Complete Psychological Works of Sigmund Freud* (ed. James Strachey). 2000.

Smollett, Tobias. *The Adventures of Roderick Random*. New York: Oxford University Press, 1999.

Stannard, Martin. "*The Good Soldier*: Editorial Problems." In *Ford Madox Ford's Modernity*. Ed. Robert Hampson and Max Saunders. Amsterdam: Rodopi, 2003.

Starzyk, L. "Hardy's *Mayor*: The Antitraditional Basis of Tragedy." *Studies in the Novel* 4 (1972): 592–607.

Stewart, J. F. "Dialectics of Knowing in *Women in Love*." *Twentieth Century Literature* 37.1 (Spring 1991): 59–76.

Storch, Rudolf. "Metaphors of Private Guilt and Social Rebellion in Godwin's *Caleb Williams*." *English Literary History* 34 (1967).

Tanner, Tony. "Colour and Movement in Hardy's *Tess of the D'Urbervilles*." *Critical Quarterly* 10 (1968): 219–239.

Tilghman, Carolyn. "Unruly Desire, Domestic Authority, and Odd Coupling in D.H. Lawrence's *Women in Love*." *Women's Studies* 37.2 (March 2008): 89–109.

Watt, Ian. *The Rise of the Novel: Studies in Defoe, Richardson and Fielding*. Berkeley: University of California Press, 1957.

———. "Serious Reflections on the Rise of the Novel." *Novel* 1 (1968).

White, Hayden. "Ethnological 'Lie' and Mystical 'Truth.'" *Diacritics: A Review of Contemporary Criticism* 8 (10) (Spring 1978): 2–9.

Wicks, Ulrich. *Picaresque Narrative, Picaresque Fictions: A Theory and Research Guide*. New York: Greenwood Press, 1989.

Woodcock, George. *William Godwin*. London: Porcupine Press, 1946.

Worthen, John. *D. H. Lawrence: The Early Years, 1885–1912*. Cambridge: Cambridge University Press, 1991.

Index

Acts of Will: The Life and Work of Otto Rank (E. James Lieberman), 210n9, 210n10, 212n18
Adler, Alfred, 119, 132, 211n12
Alter, Robert, 9, 189n2, 190n6
Aristotle, 59, 60
Auerbach, Erich, 60
Austen, Jane, 11

Banville, John, 187n7
Beck, Aaron, 4
Becker, Ernest, 4, 6
Bergson, Henri, 90, 136, 203n84, 211n15
Blake, William, 45
Boucé, Paul-Gabriel, 9, 10, 189n1, 190nn5–10, 193n26
Brenan, Gerald, 170
Brett, Dorothy, 169
Bullen, J. B., 181, 219n28, 219nn36–37

Carleton, Mary, 191n12
Carrington (Christopher Hampton), 169
Carrington, Dora, 168–171, 217nn16–17, 217n20, 218n21, 218n23
— Fictional portrayals:
Blyth, Betty (*The Apes of God*, Wyndham Lewis), 170
Bracegirdle, Mary (*Crome Yellow*, Aldous Huxley), 170
Brooke, Eleanor (*Life Class* and *Toby's Room*, Pat Barker), 170
Lehmann, Rosamond (*The Weather in the Streets*, Anna Cory), 170
"Carringtonianism," 170
Chambers, Jessie, 165
Characters and characterization, 1–6; "inner worlds and outer limits," 1, 4; psychodynamics of "between," 1, 4, 5, 185n1
Comte, Auguste, 90, 203n84
Coney, Christopher, 89
Coriolanus, 79
Corke, Helen, 162
Crome Yellow (Aldous Huxley), 170

Daleski, H. M., 165, 167, 199n19, 200n42, 217nn9–10, 217n14
Darwin, Charles, 90, 203n84
De Boland, Chanson, 90
De Maistre, Joseph, 90
Descartes, René, 137
D. H. Lawrence: Novelist (F. R. Leavis), 167, 217n10
Don Giovanni (Mozart), 99
Don Quixote (Cervantes), 69, 203n86

Dostoyevsky, Fyodor, 61
Durkheim, Emile, 59, 90

Eliot, George, 2
Ellis, Albert, 4
Eminent Victorians (Lytton Strachey), 6
eros, 2, 3, 5, 27, 45–48, 97, 126, 161
Eros and Civilization (Herbert Marcuse), 49, 127, 209n69

Flaubert, Gustave, 61
Ford, Ford Madox, 2, 5, 95–128, 186, 204n3, 204nn8–9, 205n10, 207n37, 207n44; and *Blast*, 113; marital hardships and nervous breakdown of, 205n10
— Works:
"Dedicatory Letter to Stella Ford," 96, 100, 113, 205n10
Good Soldier, The, 2, 95–128, 204nn1–3, 205n10, 205n21, 207, 208
— Characters:
Ashburnham, Edward, 96–101, 103, 106–110, 112–114, 116–117, 119–124, 126–128, 206n28, 207n35, 208n46
Ashburnham, Leonora, 97–98, 101, 103, 106–110, 112–114, 116–117, 119–124, 126–127, 206n28, 207n35
Dowell, Florence, 97, 99, 101, 103, 106, 107, 109, 111–114, 116–117, 119–127, 205n20, 206n28, 208n46
Dowell, John, 95–101, 103–117, 119–124, 126–128, 204n7, 205n10, 205n21, 206n28, 207n35, 207n44, 208n46
Jimmy, 103, 109, 114, 119, 121, 124
Maidan, Maisie, 97, 100, 103, 109, 112–113, 120–121, 125
Mother Superior, 126
Old Hurlbird, 109, 114, 120–121, 126, 206n28, 207n35
Rufford, Nancy, 96–98, 101, 103, 107, 109, 111, 113–114, 116, 119–123, 126–128, 205n21, 207n35
— Themes and topics:
"August 4," 96, 112–114, 117, 119, 121
Catholicism, Roman, 101, 108, 123, 124, 126, 205n10
coincidence, 96, 106, 112, 114, 116, 120, 121
Dowell's use of superlatives, 112, 206n28
impressionism, 95, 117
M—— (trip), 112–114, 123
madness, 95, 97–99, 109, 113, 120, 122, 207n35
minuet de la cour, 96, 99–101, 103, 105, 108, 114, 123, 124, 127
narrative technique, 96, 98, 107, 111, 206n28
passion, 96–98, 103, 106, 108, 120, 121, 126, 128
"Saddest Story," 99, 107, 127, 204n3
"shock-proof world," 98, 103, 105, 106, 123, 124
Ford, Stella, 96, 100, 113, 205n10
Forked Flame, The, 217n11
Fraiberg, Louis, 189n10
Frazer, James, 59, 197n12, 198n15; *The Golden Bough*, 197n12, 198n15
Freud, Sigmund, 3–7, 10, 11, 18, 25, 27–28, 30, 34–35, 38, 40–42, 44–51, 54, 56, 59, 61, 62–63, 65, 88–89, 96–98, 104–106, 108, 111, 116, 119–120, 122–124, 126–127, 132–134, 147–148, 158, 161–163, 185, 186n2, 188n9, 190n8, 190n11, 192n13, 194n8, 196n46, 200n38, 200n47, 205n21, 207n41, 208n53, 210n9, 211n12, 211nn14–15, 211n17, 212n18, 214n57, 216n2
— Themes and topics:
archaic heritage, 43–44, 124
castration anxiety, 38, 122, 147
dream composition, 18, 25, 27, 34–37, 42, 46, 96, 98, 104, 105, 108, 111, 112, 116, 119, 120, 124, 190n8, 205n21, 207n41
folklorist numerology, 208n53
homosexuality, 25, 34, 37–38, 40–41, 65,

88, 96, 117, 120–122, 147–149, 169–170, 192n21, 201n50, 202n70
homosexual object-choice, 40
libidinal development, 10–11, 25, 27, 30, 42, 96, 97, 98, 120, 132, 144
libido (concept), 30, 40, 49, 97–98, 105, 120, 127
Little Hans, 38–39, 65, 122, 147–148
manic defenses, 16, 19
narcissism, 11, 22, 27, 30, 40, 50, 97–98, 120; dream world, 10, 18, 22, 25, 96, 108, 111, 139; primary, 11, 27, 40, 97
neurosis, 3, 13, 28, 44, 45, 99, 105, 124, 126, 131, 132, 134–135, 142–143, 145–146, 148–152, 210n9, 211n14, 215n94
Nirvana and Nirvana Principle, 27, 47–48, 99, 113, 126–127
Oedipus complex, 41, 65
parricide, 41–43, 124, 195
persecution complex, 88, 147
phylogenesis, 25, 42, 97, 150
pleasure principle, 42, 46–48, 50, 124, 216n2
primal fear, 134, 145
reality principle, 27, 42, 46, 48–49, 97, 124, 127
secondary revision, 25, 35, 37, 96, 111, 116, 119, 207n39, 207n41
Thanatos, 45–48, 126
triangles, patterning; Oedipal, 54, 56, 65
— Works:
Beyond the Pleasure Principle, 47–48, 126, 196n45, 209n68
Civilization and Its Discontents, 25, 41, 45, 50, 97, 123, 126–127, 192n14, 195n36, 205n12, 209n67
"Creative Writers and Daydreaming," 98, 108, 205n18; daydream, 96–98, 104, 106–108, 111–112, 124, 207n41, 217n20; family romance, 28–30, 33, 41, 96, 105–109, 111–112, 120, 124, 127
Ego and the Id, The, 62
Future of an Illusion, 42, 124, 209n64
Group Psychology and the Analysis of the Ego, 62
Interpretation of Dreams, The, 162, 195n21, 205n21, 207n36, 207n38, 207n41
"Libido Theory and Narcissism," 40, 97, 98, 195n31, 195n35, 205n14, 208n52, 214n55
Moses and Monotheism, 25, 42, 124, 195n39, 209n63
Fry, Robert, 169
Furbank, P. N., 25, 194n7

Garnett, David, 169, 217n14, 218n23
Gertler, Mark, 169–171, 217n17; *Merry-Go-Round*, 169, 217n17
Gifford, Emma, 54
Girard, René, 4–6, 56, 58–63, 65–67, 69, 74, 77–79, 81, 85–91, 93, 197n13, 198n15, 199n22, 199nn24–26, 199n28, 199n35, 200n38, 200n42, 201n50, 201n59, 201n69, 202n70, 202n72, 203n81, 203nn85–86, 204nn87–88, 208n55
— Themes and topics:
desire, 56, 58–63, 65–67, 69–71, 73, 76–77, 80, 83, 87–88, 91–93, 107, 121–122, 128, 199n35, 200n38, 200n42, 202n70, 203n86, 209n55; imitative/mimetic, 55–56, 58, 59–63, 66, 73, 121, 200n38, 200n42, 202n70; mediated, 65, 200n42, 203n86; triangular, 59, 91
doubling, 121, 215n84
envy, 55, 59, 201n59
Freud, 5, 56, 59, 61, 63, 65, 88, 89
generative violence, 59, 61, 63, 77
model, 3, 11, 56, 61–63, 65, 69–71, 75, 78, 83, 88, 202n70, 204n87
pharmakos, 89, 202n72
ritual, 56, 59–62, 79, 86, 89–90, 198n14
sacrifice, 65, 68, 81, 89, 90, 92, 198n15, 203n86
scapegoat, 60, 61, 63, 81, 85
triangles, patterning, 55–56; confronta-

tional, 57, 59, 73, 77, 83; love, 54–55, 197n13, 203n86; mimetic, 65, 66, 85, 88, 91, 92, 200n42
victimage, 59, 61–63, 66, 81, 85, 89, 91; surrogate, 61, 63, 81, 89–91
violence, 56, 59, 61–63, 74, 76–77, 79, 81, 85, 89–91, 93, 203n80, 203n86, 204n87; reciprocal, 61–63, 74, 77
— Works:
Deceit, Desire and the Novel, 59, 199n24
To Double Business Bound, 59, 199n26
Violence and the Sacred, 59, 90, 199n25, 208n55
Godwin, William, 1–2, 6, 23–52, 193n6, 194n8, 195n29, 195n40, 196n52
— Works:
Caleb Williams, 1–2, 6, 23–52, 193n1, 193n4, 194n8, 195n25
— Characters:
Brightwel, 44, 49–50
Collins, 25, 30–31, 33–39, 46, 195n20
Cuxom, Mother, 89
Denison, Farmer, 29
Emily, 35, 37–39, 44–45
Falkland, Lord, 25, 27, 29–42, 44–47, 195n25, 196n40
Forester, 30–32, 34, 36–37, 46–47
Gines, 32, 36–38, 40
Grimes, 35, 37–38, 45
Hawkins, 33, 35–38, 44, 47
Laura, 25, 29–30, 33–37, 41–42, 50, 195n25
Malvesi, Count, 45
Marney, Mrs., 33, 36
Melville, Emily, 35, 44
Raymond, Captain, 25, 30, 33, 44–45, 49
Spurrel, 30–32, 37–38
Tyrrel, 33–35, 37–38, 44–48
Williams, Caleb, 24–25, 27–42, 44–50, 193, 195n20, 195n40
Williams, Farmer, 29–30
— Themes and Topics:
chivalry, 40
coincidence, 28, 35, 36
innocence and guilt, 23, 27, 31, 33–34, 37–38, 42–46
"mangled tale," 23–26, 38
miraculous accident, 35–36
narrative structure, 9, 26
omnipotence, 23, 25, 26, 30, 38, 42
omniscience, 27, 35–37, 40, 45
political philosophy, 23–26, 33, 41–42, 45, 194n9
psychology, 1–7, 25–27, 34, 38, 41–42, 44–48, 54, 193n6, 194n8
religious meanings, 33, 42, 49, 195n40
revenge, 38, 46–48
Of Self Love and Benevolence, 44
Political Justice, 23–25, 27
Thoughts on Man, 23, 25, 196n52
Gold, Alex, 40, 194n9, 195n26
Goodheart, Eugene, 216n2
Granofsky, Ronald, 179, 218n27, 219n33
Grant, Damian, 10, 18, 190n7, 193n25
Great Web, The (Ian Gregor), 59, 64, 199n23, 200n43
Gregor, Ian, 59, 64, 199n23, 200n43
Gross, Adolf, 162

Hardy, Emma, 54
Hardy, Florence, 53, 196n2, 204n89; *Early Life of Thomas Hardy, The*, 53, 204n89; *Later Years of Thomas Hardy, The*, 196n2
Hardy, Thomas, 1, 5, 6, 53–94, 196nn1–2, 197n12, 198n15, 198n18, 199n19, 199n21, 200n42, 200n45, 203n84; and architecture, 53–94, 198n16, 201n53; Casterbridge, 53, 64, 66, 68, 70, 73–74, 78–81, 83, 86–89, 93, 202n70; classical tragedy, 53, 57, 59, 62, 66, 74, 78, 85, 88, 93, 196n1, 196n3, 198n18; coincidence, 90, 91, 96, 199n21; *Gemeinschaft*, 1, 64, 80; *Gesellschaft*, 1, 64, 86; Greek drama, 53–54, 61–62, 66; "modern" Oedi-

pus, 53–54, 56, 59, 63, 88, 93, 196n1; and "Oedipus Rex," 53, 56, 59, 62–63, 68, 85, 196n1, 196n3; stylistic faults, 199n21; triangles (patterning), 55–56, 57, 58, 59, 63, 65, 69, 73, 74, 81, 83, 84, 89, 91, 93; triangles, confrontational, 57, 59, 73, 77, 83; triangles, family, 57, 58, 64, 66, 67, 73, 77, 83, 84, 89, 91, 92, 196n1, 196n3, 198n18, 199n18; love, 55, 57, 91, 92, 197n13, 199n19, 200n42, 203n86; triangles, mimetic, 65, 66, 85, 88, 91, 92, 200n42; triangles, Oedipal, 54, 56, 65
— Works:
Far from the Madding Crowd, 91
Jude the Obscure, 53–54, 92, 196n1, 200n45
Mayor of Casterbridge, The, 1, 5, 53–94, 196–202; as "modern Oedipus," 53–54, 56, 59, 63, 88, 93, 196n1; as war story, 55, 59, 70
— Characters:
Elizabeth-Jane, 54–55, 57–58, 64, 66–69, 71, 73–81, 83–87, 89, 91–93, 202n70
Farfrae, Donald, 54, 55, 57–59, 64, 67–71, 73–81, 83–90, 201n66, 202n70
Henchard, Michael, 54–55, 57–59, 64–71, 73–81, 83–90, 93, 197n3, 201n49, 202n70
Jopp, 76, 78, 81, 87
Newson, 54–55, 57–58, 66–67, 74–75, 80–81, 83–86, 89, 202n70
Templeman, Lucetta, 54–55, 57–58, 64–65, 68, 71, 74–77, 79–81, 83, 86–87, 89, 202n70
Pair of Blue Eyes, A, 54
Return of the Native, The, 91, 200n42, 203n86
Tess of the D'Urbervilles, 55, 92, 197n12, 199n19, 201n51
Hegel, Georg, 61
Herrick, Robert, 205n21
Hesse, Hermann, 188n9, 189n9
Hiles, Barbara, 169
Hogarth, William, 20, 185
Holroyd, Michael, 170, 218n23
Hynes, Samuel, 95, 97, 204n5, 205n13

James, Henry, 2
Jones, Jack, 212n18
Joyce, James, 129, 212n19
Jung, Carl, 3, 132, 188n9, 204n9, 211n12

King Lear (Shakespeare), 56
Klein, Melanie, 4, 6, 10–11, 13, 16, 19, 25, 27, 37, 96, 105, 117, 190n11, 192n15, 192n17, 193n6, 193n29, 194n8, 195n23, 206n24, 208n48; anxiety, 13, 27, 37, 105, 117, 122; bad part-objects, 13, 19, 28, 30, 105; good part-objects, 13, 19, 28, 105; inner world, 13, 16, 22, 27, 30, 105; Kleinian theory, 13, 16, 18, 19, 30, 37, 105, 116, 192n15, 194n8; and narcissism, 10, 11, 13, 16, 18–19, 22, 25, 27–30, 96, 105; paranoid position, 11, 13, 19, 27, 37, 105, 109, 116, 120, 192; schizoid personality, 18; schizoid position, 11, 13, 18, 22, 27, 37, 105, 116, 122, 192n17; splitting, 13, 27, 104–105, 158
— Works:
"Contribution to the psycho-genesis of manic-depressive states, A," 192n17
"Mourning and its relation to manic-depressive states," 193n29
"On Narcissism," 97
Psycho-Analysis of Children, The, 37, 117, 194n12, 195n24, 208n49

Lawrence, D. H., 1–3, 5–6, 161–185, 186nn2–3, 187n4, 216nn1–2, 217n14, 217nn16–17, 218n21, 218n27, 219nn28–29, 219n39
— Themes and topics:
"Arctic," 161, 171, 174, 179, 181, 187n4
blood consciousness, 3, 161

Bloomsbury as satirical target, 217n16
Blutbruderschaft, 165, 173–174
Dora Carrington, 168–171, 218n21
Jews and Jewishness, 3, 179, 187n4, 218n27
"Lawrentian psychology," 3, 7, 161, 165–167, 174–175, 179, 181
mind (concept), 3, 5, 163, 165–166, 168, 171–174, 179, 187n4
"phosphorescent consciousness," 162, 165
primitivism, 154, 161, 179, 219n29
racial ideology, 3, 172, 174, 179, 218n27
— Works, fiction:
"Coal Dust," 171
"Continental," 178
"Modern Lover, A," 162
"New Heaven and Earth," 162
"None of That," 170
Plumed Serpent, The, 160, 219
"Saga of Sigmund, The," 162
"Shades of Spring, The," 165
Trespasser, The, 162
Woman Who Rode Away and Other Stories, The, 170
Women in Love, 1, 3, 161–185, 217n14, 218n21, 218n25, 219n28, 219n31, 219nn38–39; Bohemia chapters, 167, 171, 173, 175; Café Pompadour, 167, 172
— Characters:
Birkin, Rupert, 161, 165–166, 170, 173–177, 179, 182, 184, 219n29
Brangwen, Gudrun, 166–167, 174–179, 181–182, 184, 217n16, 219nn30–31, 219n39
Brangwen, Ursula, 175, 178, 182, 184, 219n29
Crich, Gerald, 161, 163, 165, 167–168, 170–179, 181–182, 184, 187n4, 217n16, 219n29, 219n39
Darrington, Minette, 3, 161, 165–176, 178, 181–182, 184, 217n16, 218n25
Halliday, Julius, 166–168, 171–172, 174, 181–182, 184, 217n16, 219n30
Libidnikov, Maxim, 167, 172
Loerke, 3, 167, 169–171, 175–176, 178–179, 181–182, 184, 187n4, 217nn16–17
miners, 167–168, 171, 175, 181
— Works, prose:
Fantasia of the Unconscious, 3, 161–162, 165, 216n1, 219n34
Psychoanalysis and the Unconscious, 3, 161, 179, 187n4, 219n34
Studies in Classic American Literature, 2, 186n2, 216n2, 218n26; function of the critic, 186; "trust the tale," 2, 186
Leavis, F. R., 167, 217n10
Lévi-Strauss, Claude, 59, 186n2
Lévy-Bruhl, Lucien, 59
Lewis, Wyndham, 2, 5, 113, 129–160, 170, 186n3, 209n1, 211n15, 211n17, 212n18, 213n40, 213n52, 214n74, 215n88; and "Dionysian," 142, 158–159, 214n63; and time-mind, 129, 211n15; and Vorticism, 204n3, 213n50
— Works:
Apes of God, The, 170
Art of Being Ruled, The, 138, 209n4, 211n15, 213n38, 215n88
Blast, 113, 141
Decay of Lying, The, 153
Paleface, 211n15
Rude Assignment, 211n16
Tarr, 2, 129–160, 209n1, 209n8, 212n22, 213n39, 213n50, 213n52, 214n71
— Characters:
Bertha, 131, 140, 142, 144, 149, 151, 154–158
Dirkes, Prism, 151, 215n90
Fawcett, Rose, 151, 215n90
Hobson, Alan, 131, 135–140, 142, 154–155, 213n34
Kreisler, Otto, 131–132, 142–150, 151, 153, 155–159
Kreisler Sr., 145–148, 150
Lipmann, 145, 156
Lowndes, 131, 135–140, 142, 145, 154

Lunken, Bertha, 131, 135, 140, 142, 144, 149, 151, 154–158
Soltyk, Louis, 144–150, 156
Tarr, 129–132, 135, 137–140, 142, 150–159, 214n71, 215n78, 215n88
Thornton, 139
Vasek, Anastasya, 144–147, 149–151, 153, 155–158, 214n71
Volker, 145–147, 152
— Themes and topics:
collectivism, 130–132, 134–138, 140, 142, 143, 153, 155, 159
"das Weib," 144–146, 148–149
"mechanical," 136–137, 154
as Nietzschean novella, 129–132, 153, 159, 209n1, 209n17
"Overture," 135, 140, 142, 151, 154, 156–158
womb, 132–134, 136, 137, 145, 149–151, 214n63
Time and Western Man, 129, 136, 213n31, 214n74
Wild Body, The, 215n87
Life Class (Pat Barker), 170
Lodge, David, 186n2

Malinowski, Bronislaw, 59
Mann, Thomas, 129, 209n1
Marcuse, Herbert, 48–50, 127, 196n46, 209n69
Menacker, Esther, 215n96
Meyers, Jeffrey, 170, 209n1, 217n20
Miller, J. Hillis, 54, 56, 67, 197nn7–8, 198n14, 198n17, 200n42, 201n54
Morrison, Greta, 170
Munro, D. H., 23, 193n3

narrative, 1, 4–5, 7, 9–11, 13, 17, 19, 24–27, 29, 34, 36, 37, 55, 56, 58, 59, 64, 73, 88, 90, 96–98, 108, 111, 114, 116–117, 119–120, 123, 135, 141–142, 151, 190n3, 195n20, 198n14, 205n11, 215n83
narrative mode and structure, 2, 6, 9–10, 25–26, 96, 111, 190, 191n12, 192n13, 198n16
narrator, 2–3, 9–11, 13, 17–18, 22, 25, 28–30, 34–37, 41–42, 64, 66, 68–70, 74, 85, 95–96, 105, 107, 109, 111–112, 116–117, 122, 124, 152, 154, 168, 191n12, 204n9, 207n44
New Age, 162
New Criticism, 6
Nietzsche, Friedrich, 130–133, 134, 138–139, 153, 162–163, 165, 186n2, 209n1, 209nn9–10, 211n16; *Thus Spake Zarathustra*, 163
Nietzsche in Outline and Aphorism (A. E. Orage), 162

Pinion, F. B., 55, 197n11, 200n45
Plato, 59, 61
psychoanalytic theory, 2–4, 10–11, 18, 25–26, 42, 48, 77, 96–97, 124, 132–133, 147, 158, 185, 189n10, 192n13, 193n6, 200n44, 205n21, 210n9, 214n57

Rank, Otto, 4, 6, 131–137, 142–143, 148–153, 155–159, 188n9, 210n9, 211nn11–15, 211n17, 212nn18–20, 213n40, 213n51, 214n57, 215n83, 215n96
— Themes and topics:
art-ideology, 154–155
"Artist," 130–132, 135–136, 138, 140, 143, 151–154, 158, 211n11
artiste-manqué, 143, 150, 210n9
"average man," 135–139, 143, 213n40
birth trauma, 133–134, 142, 149–150, 154, 158, 212n18
"creative man," 130–132, 136, 138, 143, 152–153, 157, 210n9
fear of death, 132, 134, 142, 153, 157, 159
fear of life, 132, 134, 142, 148–150
Freud-Rank relationship, 210n9
hero, 152, 158

immortality, 143, 153, 213n45, 213n51, 214n76
individuation, 134, 137, 156, 211n14
neurotic personality, 105, 124, 126, 131, 132, 134–135, 142–143, 145–146, 148–150
nomination, 152–155, 158, 214n74
pseudo-artist, 132, 138, 139, 140, 142
Will and counter-will, 135, 140, 142–143, 150, 152
Will and creation of personality, 130–135, 137–138, 140, 142–143, 145, 149, 152–154, 156, 211n11
Will Psychology, 133–135, 150, 159, 191n11, 210n10, 215n96
— Works:
Art and Artist, 131, 133, 136, 148, 210n9, 211n13
Beyond Psychology, 211n14, 212n27
Der Künstler (The Artist), 133, 210n9
Myth of the Birth of the Hero, 210n9, 211n17
Psychoanalysis and the Unconscious, 3, 161, 179, 187n4, 219n34
Psychology of the Will, 132
Trauma of Birth, The, 133, 212n18
Truth and Reality, 212n20
Will Therapy, 212n20
Rilke, Rainer Maria, 129, 188n9
Rise of the Novel, The (Ian Watt), 6, 187n5
Rousseau, Jean-Jacques, 45, 153

Saint-Simon, Claude Henri, 90
Sartre, Jean-Paul, 64, 200n44
Schopenhauer, Arthur, 90, 132, 134, 203n84, 209n1
Schorer, Mark, 95, 111, 204n4, 207n37
Search for a Method (Jean-Paul Sartre), 64, 200n44
Segal, Hanna, 192n15, 193n27, 195n23, 208n48
Sennett, Ronald, 185n1, 186n1
Shakespeare, William, 61, 199n22, 214n58
Sherman, G. W., 203n84
Skinner, B. F., 4
Slade School of Fine Arts, 168–169
Smollett, Tobias, 2, 5, 6, 9–22, 189n2, 190n3, 190nn8–9, 190n11, 191n12, 192nn19–20, 193n26; studies medicine and surgery, 190n8
— Works:
Peregrine Pickle, 190n8, 192n20
Roderick Random, 2, 6, 9–22, 189n1, 190nn2–3, 191n12, 192n19, 193n26
— Characters:
Bagshawe, 114
Banter, 16
Bowling, Lieutenant Thomas, 15–16, 18–19
Crab, 19, 192n19
Crampley, 17
d'Estrapes, M., 15
Mackshane, 19
Melinda, 19
Morgan, 15, 19
Narcissa, 9–10, 13, 15–17, 19, 22, 190n8, 192n20
Oakum, Captain, 19
Potion, Mr., 19
Quiverwit, 16
Random, Roderick, 9–11, 13, 15–19, 22, 190n9, 191n12, 192n17, 192n19, 192n21, 193n24
Rodrigo, Don, 13, 15, 19, 192n21
Sagely, Mrs., 19
Straddle, Lord, 16
Strap, 15–16, 18–19
Strutwell, Earl, 16, 192n19
Thicket, Sir Timothy, 16
Thomson, 15, 18, 19
Thunder, 9, 16–17
Weazel, Captain, 16
Williams, Farmer, 29–30
Williams, Miss, 15, 18–19, 190n9
Williams, Mrs., 29
— Themes and topics:
coincidence, 9–10, 18

ending of, 22
narrative technique, 9, 10, 11, 13, 17
as picaresque novel, 9–11, 190n2, 191n12
"picaresque proletariat," 191n12
Treatise on Madness, 190n8
Socrates, 153
Sontag, Susan, 209n1
Sophocles, 62, 191n11
Spencer, Herbert, 90, 203n84
Stannard, Martin, 204n1, 207n44
Stendhal (Marie-Henri Beyle), 61
Storch, Rudolf, 3, 194n19
Strachey, Lytton, 6, 169–170, 217n16
Studies in Hysteria (Josef Breuer), 190n8
Swinburne, Algernon, 53, 196n2

Taine, Hippolyte, 90
Thomas Hardy: Distance and Desire, 197n7, 198n17, 201n54
Tiresias, 63, 81, 87
Toby's Room (Pat Barker), 170
Trilling, Lionel, 185n1
Turner, Victor, 59

Ulysses (James Joyce), 129, 212n19

Voltaire (François-Marie Arouet), 45

Warren, Robert Penn, 187n7
Watt, Ian, 6, 187n6, 187n8
Weber, Max, 59
Weekley, Frieda, 162, 164
White, Hayden, 90, 203n83, 203n85
Woodcock, George, 23, 193n2, 193n5
Worthen, John, 162–163, 165, 217nn3–4

Lightning Source UK Ltd.
Milton Keynes UK
UKOW02f1605301016
286429UK00002B/52/P

9 781477 312230